SHORTLIST

Amsterdam

WHAT'S NEW | WHAT'S ON | WHAT'S BEST

www.timeout.com/amsterdam

Contents

Amsterdam by Area

Essentials

Published by Time Out Guides Ltd
Universal House
251 Tottenham Court Road
London W1T 7AB
Tel: + 44 (0)20 7813 3000
Fax: + 44 (0)20 7813 6001
Email: guides@timeout.com
www.timeout.com

Managing Director Peter Fiennes
Editorial Director Ruth Jarvis
Business Manager Dan Allen
Editorial Manager Holly Pick
Assistant Management Accountant Ija Krasnikova

Time Out Guides is a wholly owned subsidiary of Time Out Group Ltd.

© Time Out Group Ltd
Chairman Tony Elliott
Chief Executive Officer David King
Group General Manager/Director Nichola Coulthard
Time Out Communications Ltd MD David Pepper
Time Out International Ltd MD Cathy Runciman
Time Out Magazine Ltd Publisher/Managing Director Mark Elliott
Production Director Mark Lamond
Group IT Director Simon Chappell
Marketing & Circulation Director Catherine Demajo

Time Out and the Time Out logo are trademarks of Time Out Group Ltd.

This edition first published in Great Britain in 2009 by Ebury Publishing
A Random House Group Company
Company information can be found on www.randomhouse.co.uk
Random House UK Limited Reg. No. 954009
10 9 8 7 6 5 4 3 2 1

Distributed in the US by Publishers Group West
Distributed in Canada by Publishers Group Canada

For further distribution details, see www.timeout.com

ISBN: 978-1-84670-134-4

A CIP catalogue record for this book is available from the British Library.

Printed and bound in Germany by Appl.

The Random House Group Limited supports The Forest Stewardship Council (FSC), the
leading international forest certification organisation. All our titles that are printed on
Greenpeace approved FSC certified paper carry the FSC logo. Our paper procurement
policy can be found on www.rbooks.co.uk/environment.

Time Out carbon-offsets all its flights with Trees for Cities (www.treesforcities.org).

Amsterdam Shortlist

The **Time Out Amsterdam Shortlist** is one of a new series of guides that draws on Time Out's background as a magazine publisher to keep you current with what's going on in town. As well as Amsterdam's key sights and the best of its eating, drinking and leisure options, the guide picks out the most exciting venues to have opened in the past year and gives a full calendar of annual events. It also includes features on the important news, trends and openings, all compiled by locally based editors and writers. Whether you're visiting for the first time, or you're a regular, you'll find the *Time Out Amsterdam Shortlist* contains all you need to know, in a portable and easy-to-use format.

The guide divides central Amsterdam into seven areas, each of which contains listings for Sights & Museums, Eating & Drinking, Shopping, Nightlife and Arts & Leisure, with maps pinpointing all their locations. At the front of the book are chapters rounding up these scenes city-wide, and giving a shortlist of our overall picks in a variety of categories. We include itineraries for days out, plus essentials such as transport information and hotels.

Our listings give phone numbers as dialled within the city. The international code for the Netherlands is 31. To call from outside the country, follow this number with the code for Amsterdam, 020, dropping the initial 0.

We have noted price categories by using one to four euros signs (€-€€€€), representing budget, moderate, expensive and luxury. Major credit cards are accepted unless otherwise stated. We have also indicated when a venue is NEW.

All our listings are double-checked, but places do sometimes close or change their hours or prices, so it's a good idea to call a venue before visiting. While every effort has been made to ensure accuracy, the publishers cannot accept responsibility for any errors that this guide may contain.

Venues are marked on the maps using symbols numbered according to their order within the chapter and colour-coded according to the type of venue they represent:

❶ Sights & Museums
❶ Eating & Drinking
❶ Shopping
❶ Nightlife
❶ Arts & Leisure

Map key	
Selected House Number	*463*
Major Sight or Landmark	
Hospital or College	
Pedestrianised Street	
Railway Station	
Metro Station	Ⓜ
Area Name	LEIDSEPLEIN

Time Out **Amsterdam** Shortlist

EDITORIAL
Editor Steve Korver
Deputy Editor Nicola Homer
Assistant Editor Steven McCarron
Proofreader Mandy Martinez

DESIGN
Art Director Scott Moore
Art Editor Pinelope Kourmouzoglou
Senior Designer Henry Elphick
Graphic Designers Kei Ishimaru,
  Nicola Wilson
Advertising Designer Jodi Sher

Picture Editor Jael Marschner
Deputy Picture Editor Lynn Chambers
Picture Researcher Gemma Walters
Picture Desk Assistant Marzena Zoladz
Picture Librarian Christina Theisen

ADVERTISING
Commercial Director Mark Phillips
International Advertising Manager
  Kasimir Berger
International Sales Executive Charlie Sokol
Advertising Sales (Amsterdam) Randy Abels,
  Maikel Bouricius, Ulrica Carlsson,
  Kate Hutchinson

MARKETING
Marketing Manager Yvonne Poon
Sales & Marketing Director, North America
  & Latin America Lisa Levinson
Senior Publishing Brand Manager Luthfa Begum
Art Director Anthony Huggins

PRODUCTION
Production Manager Brendan McKeown
Production Controller Damian Bennett
Production Co-ordinator Kelly Fenlon

CONTRIBUTORS
This guide was researched and written by Joost Baaij, Georgina Bean, Willem de Blaauw,
Dara Colwell, Shyama Daryanani, Monique Gruter, Karina Hof, Kate Holder, Luuk van Huêt,
Cecily Layzell, Steve Korver, Steven McCarron, Kim Renfrew, Marinus de Ruiter and Mark
Wedin. The editor would like to thank Karina Hof, Katie Holder, Russell Joyce, Klaas&Nel,
Steven McCarron and Kim Renfrew.
  A special thanks to all the staff at *Time Out Amsterdam*, who have collaborated in the
production of this book.

PHOTOGRAPHY
Photography Wilmar Dik, except: pages 7, 27, 32, 34, 40, 43, 59, 68, 76, 82, 85, 88,
89, 90, 92, 98, 99, 110, 114, 116, 117, 119, 120, 122, 123, 127, 128, 130, 136, 140,
147, 149, 154, 157, 159, 165, 169, 171, 177 Michelle Grant; page 9 INDG Amsterdam;
page 23 Abel Minnee; pages 26, 107 Carlos Silva Pinto; pages 17, 47, 55, 56, 79, 125,
139 Anne Binckebank; pages 52, 53, 62, 63, 66, 69, 72, 75, 86, 96, 109, 133, 143,
161, 162, 176 Olivia Rutherford; page 113 © Hans Van Heeswijk; page 153 Eric
Gevaert/Shutterstock.

The following images were provided by the featured establishments/artists: cover images,
and pages 12, 13, 45, 49, 50, 105, 143
Cover photograph: Red light district. Credit: © Tips Images.

MAPS
JS Graphics (john@jsgraphics.co.uk).

About **Time Out**

Founded in 1968, Time Out has expanded from humble London beginnings into
the leading resource for those wanting to know what's happening in the world's
greatest cities. As well as our influential what's-on weeklies in London, New York
and Chicago, we publish nearly 30 other listings magazines in cities as varied as
Beijing and Minmee. The magazines established Time Out's trademark style: sharp
writing, informed reviewing and bang up-to-date inside knowledge of every scene.
  Time Out made the natural leap into travel guides in the 1980s with the City Guide
series, which now extends to over 50 destinations around the world. Written and
researched by expert local writers and generously illustrated with original photography,
the full-size guides cover a larger area than our Shortlist guides and include many
more venue reviews, along with additional background features and a full set of maps.
  Throughout this rapid growth, the company has remained proudly independent,
still owned by Tony Elliott four decades after he started Time Out London as a single
fold-out sheet of A5 paper. This independence extends to the editorial content of all
our publications, this Shortlist included. No establishment has been featured because
it has advertised, and no payment has influenced any of our reviews. And, for our
critics, there's definitely no such thing as a free lunch: all restaurants and bars
are visited and reviewed anonymously, and Time Out always picks up the bill.
For more about the company, see www.timeout.com.

Don't Miss

"FASHION IS DEFINED BY WHAT LATER BECOMES OUT OF FASHION"
YVES SAINT LAURENT
DESIGNER, 1964

Rijksmuseum p134

WHAT'S BEST

Sights & Museums

There has recently been a serious drop in visitor levels. The number of Japanese tourists visiting Amsterdam in the first two months of 2009 plummeted by 42 per cent in comparison to 2008, and American tourist numbers fell by 35 per cent, according to city council figures. So why is this happening? Are pleasure-seekers being scared off by those stories of Amsterdam being 'cleaned up' (see box p79)? Has the prolonged renovation of the Rijksmuseum (p134) dissuaded art lovers from visiting the city? Visitors needn't worry; in fact, there is plenty to keep visitors amused, whether they're inclined towards experimenting with vices or more cerebral, nobler pursuits.

In the city centre lies the old port and the fast-developing waterfront, along with its medieval buildings, the Red Light District, the grand 17th-century merchants' houses,

the high spires of ancient religious institutions, the oldest and prettiest canals, as well as many of Amsterdam's most famous sights. Except to stroll to Vondelpark and Museumplein – where you can enjoy the sight of three major museums and the world-class concert hall Concertgebouw – many visitors rarely leave the *grachtengordel*, that tranquil concentric belt of Golden Age canals, which marks the fascinating and historic Old Centre. Make sure that you don't make the same mistake: venture to the newly gentrified, pretty residential areas of the Pijp and the Jordaan to discover the latest trends in cuisine and culture.

Most things lie within half an hour's walk from each other, and the excellent network of trams provides back-up for those low on energy. You can join the slipstream of locals by saddling up on a bike

Amsterdam ArenA World of Ajax Tours

Always fancied a `backstage' view of the Amsterdam ArenA and Ajax? Make your dream come true!

Enjoy a 1-hour guided tour through the stadium. After the tour you visit the Ajax Museum. Daily departure times between 11 AM and 4.30 PM. No reservation needed.

Rates Adults: € 10,50   (5 - 12 year): € 9,50

Opening hours and tour departure times are subject to change on and around event days.

www.amsterdamarena.nl/en
Telephone: + 31 (0)20-311 1336
E-mail: world.of.ajax@amsterdamarena.nl

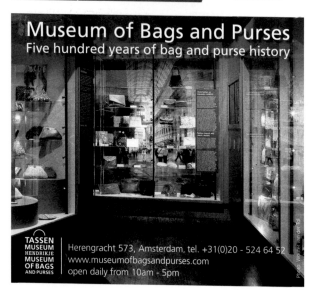

Museum of Bags and Purses
Five hundred years of bag and purse history

TASSEN MUSEUM HENDRIKJE MUSEUM OF BAGS AND PURSES
Herengracht 573, Amsterdam, tel. +31(0)20 - 524 64 52
www.museumofbagsandpurses.com
open daily from 10am - 5pm

(although beware of trams and cycle thieves); or better still, beg or borrow a boat to absorb the city on a cruise down the canals – surely the angle from which it was meant to be viewed. There's also a bewildering array of other modes of transport: horse and carriage, rickshaws, interactive guides for mobile phones and Segways. Hertz is even renting out electric scooters to tourists, to the annoyance of locals.

Another shock to the system has occurred: there are now cheerful 'Welcome Teams' dressed in red, waiting at Centraal Station and other busy central locations, to help tourists with directions, transport and tips for events. This is part of a larger campaign aimed at making Amsterdam more hospitable for visitors. It includes encouraging shop assistants and bar/restaurant staff to raise their levels of service, as they're often accused of being indifferent. Although many locals attribute this lack of interest to poor levels of pay, see for yourself the programme is coming along by visiting the old-school bruin cafés in Jordaan, or historic drinking holes Twee Zwaantjes (p98) and Wynand Fockink (p75).

Constant change

Unlike many nearby cities, Amsterdam was not devastated by bombing during World War II. So much of its charm lies in how little it has changed, even though modern schemes remain in flux – especially the Noord-Zuidlijn metro line (see box p66), and the developments around Centraal Station and directly across the IJ in Amsterdam Noord. Most of the more appealing sights have been around for many decades or, more usually, for centuries. However, you should be aware that two of the city's most prominent museums are undergoing major

SHORTLIST

Classic art
- Rijksmuseum (p134)

Best newcomer
- Hermitage aan de Amstel (p113)

Cutting-edge photography
- Foam (p100)
- Huis Marseille (p95)

Entering the past
- Amsterdams Historisch Museum (p83)
- City Archives (p102)
- Concertgebouw (p141)
- Ons Lieve Heer in de Zolder (p182)
- Verzetsmuseum (p115)

Back to the future
- Eastern docklands (p119)
- NEMO (p122)

For a religious experience
- Bibliotheca Philosophica Hermetica (p132)
- Joods Historisch Museum (p112)
- Nieuwe Kerk (p68)
- Oude Kerk (p68)
- Portuguese Synagogue (p112)

Cheerful Dutch cliché
- Bloemenmarkt (p105)

Sex & drugs
- Erotic Museum (p67)
- Red Light District (p62)

Most scenic canals
- Brouwersgracht (p92)
- Leliegracht (p92)
- Prinsengracht (p92)

Getaways
- Artis (p110)
- Hortus Botanicus (p110)
- Vondelpark (p133)

changes. The Stedelijk Museum of Modern Art (p134) is currently homeless, while its usual location on Museumplein is being transformed –but its collection is being exhibited in temporary locations, until it reopens in spring 2010. The renovation of the Rijksmuseum (p134 and box p142), which is home to Rembrandt's outstanding *Night Watch*, is also a blessing of sorts: their vast collection is so overwhelming that the present exhibition of 400 Golden Age masterpieces in the Philips Wing is more than enough to satisfy art lovers over the course of a single visit. While the Maritime Museum won't open until 2011, children can still board an East India Trading Company tall ship via NEMO (p122).

Also in the news, the Hermitage on the Amstel (see box p113), the first outpost of the famous Russian museum, opened to much fanfare in June 2009. The impressive Royal Palace (p67) is slated to reopen later in the year, and the recently unveiled City Archives (p102) have proven themselves to be among the best freebies in town with the pseudo-Egyptian tomb-like setting of its 'treasure room'. And if you like mysteries, delve into the newly restructured Bibliotheca Philosophica Hermetica (p132).

Museum hopping

There's good news for under 13s: from September 2009, they will be give free admission to most of the nation's museums. Even for older visitors, prices are still reasonable; despite the fact that most museums charge for admisision, prices are rarely more than €10. However, if you're thinking of taking in a few museums in one go, then the Museumkaart (Museum Card) is a steal, at €35 for adults and €17.50 for under-25s (plus a €4.95 administration fee for first-timers). The card offers users free or discounted admission to more than 400 attractions in the Netherlands, and is valid for a year from the date of purchase. The museums with discounted or free entry for card-holders are denoted in this guide's listings by the letters 'MK'. You

Nederlands Filmmuseum p141

Stedelijk Museum of Modern Art p134

can purchase the card at museums participating in the scheme.

The Amsterdam Tourist Board (p186) also sells a savings pass, the I amsterdam Card, which gives you free entry to major museums, free rides on public transport and a complimentary canal trip, along with a hefty 25 per cent discount at certain tourist attractions and restaurants. It costs €38 for 24 hours, €48 for 48 hours and €58 for 72 hours. For a list of all major museums across the city and their programmes, check out the website www.amsterdammuseums.nl.

Sights unseen

Much of Amsterdam's charm derives from what remains hidden to the untutored eye. For instance, there's an awful lot more to absorb than just sex and drugs in the Red Light District. A strange mix of prostitutes, clerics, schoolkids, junkies, carpenters and cops may offer you a peek at their strange brand of social cosiness. It's all pretty harmless, so long as you

remember that window girls do not like having their pictures taken and remain alert to drug dealers.

Then there are the local *hofjes* or almshouses, many of which are gorgeously peaceful, the most famous being the Begijnhof (p81). Most are concentrated in the Jordaan. The best known are the Venetiae (Elandsstraat 106-36), the Sint Andrieshofje (Egelantiersgracht 107-14), the Karthuizerhof (Karthuizerstraat 21-31), the Suyckerhofje (Lindengracht 149-63), the Claes Claesz Hofje (1e Egelantiersdwarsstraat 3), the Raepenhofje (Palmgracht 28-38), and oldest by far, the Lindenhofje (Lindengracht 94-112). The art of *hofje*-hopping is a gamble, because entrances are sometimes locked in deference to the residents. But take a chance and you may be surprised by the delights inside.

Meanwhile, the major canals and radial streets are where the real Amsterdam exists. What they lack in sights, they make up for as places for scenic coffee drinking, quirky shopping and aimless walks.

HOUSE OF 🛡 BOLS
1575
COCKTAIL & GENEVER EXPERIENCE

Complete your visit to the museum quarter
with a delicious cocktail at House of Bols,
where you can taste, smell, see, hear
and touch the exciting world of cocktails
and bartending.

Of course you can also learn to 'slurp' the
traditional Dutch white spirit: Genever.

TOUR INCLUDING A COCKTAIL

HOUSE OF BOLS, OPPOSITE VAN GOGH MUSEUM Paulus Potterstraat 14, Amsterdam
OPENING HOURS (min. age 18 years) 12:00 pm - 6:00 pm daily (Closed on Tuesdays)

WWW.HOUSEOFBOLS.COM

Neighbourhood hopping

Of course, Amsterdam's infamous ground zero of consumerism, vice, entertainment and history is the Old Centre, which is bounded by Prins Hendrikkade to the north, Oudeschans and Zwanenburgwal to the east, the Amstel to the south and Singel to the west.

Within these borders, the Old Centre is divided into the New Side (west of Damrak and Rokin) and the Old Side (east of Damrak and Rokin). The Old Side, roughly covering the triangle formed by Central Station, the Nieuwmarkt and the Dam, is notorious for hosting the Red Light District. However, the area is also home to the epic Oude Kerk (p68) and the menacing De Waag (p63). The New Side, on the other hand, is the Old Side's gentler sister, featuring a history entwined with the intelligentsia, thanks to its many bookshops, brown cafés and the various buildings of the University of Amsterdam.

The *grachtengordel* ('girdle of canals') that guards the Old Centre is pleasant, idyllic and uniquely Dutch, and now boasts two of the most fascinating arrivals on the local sightseeing scene: the Tassenmuseum (p102) and the City Archives (p102). It is also home to Anne Frank Huis (p95), the Westerkerk (p95) and two rather intriguing photography museums: Foam (p100) and Huis Marseille (p95). For ease of use, we have divided the areas covered by canals into two sections: Western Canal Belt denotes the stretch of canals to the west and north of Leidsegracht, whereas Southern Canal Belt covers the area that lies to the east, taking in Leidseplein and Rembrandtplein. This split is historically justified by the fact that the western girdle was complete before work on the eastern half began.

The area around Waterlooplein, just east of the Old Centre, was settled by Jews four centuries ago, and so took its name, Jodenbuurt, from this rich culture. Now the heritage of Russia stands nearby at the Hermitage on the Amstel (box p113) and oases of flora occupy the Plantage neighbourhood, east and south-east of Waterlooplein, among them the Hortus Botanicus and Artis (p110). Further east (Oost) lies the Tropenmuseum (p112).

Once the gateway to prosperity, Amsterdam's Waterfront is now emerging as the setting for some of Europe's most inspired architecture. Traditional sights may be few, but the eastern stretch in particular is attracting thousands of new residents and developing as a boulevard of contemporary arts and nightlife.

Over in the other direction, the Westelijke Eilanden links up nicely with the charming neighbourhood of the Jordaan, bordered by Brouwersgracht, Prinsengracht, Leidsegracht and Lijnbaansgracht. Working-class stalwarts here rub shoulders with affluent newcomers in an area that, while lacking the grandiose architecture of the canals, wants for nothing in terms of character.

Spotlighted by its world-class museums and some incredibly sophisticated emporia of high-class fashion, Amsterdam's Museum Quarter is a mix of culture, in the form of the Museumplein, and couture at the PC Hooftstraat. Against all the odds, the Pijp has remained a cultural melting pot, even though the area has been thoroughly gentrified for several years. It proves that the city is still full of charm, despite the continual development of recent years.

Westergas Terras p22

Eating, Drinking & Smoking

The hotel-restaurant-café business, or 'horeca', as it is often called here, is a crazy rollercoaster, with bars and eateries dropping like flies into the proverbial soup. They are quickly replaced by an almost endless stream of new – and, considering the times, often daring – ventures. Minibar (Prinsengracht 478, www.minibaronline.com), for example, has gotten rid of the barman altogether – hand over ID in exchange for a key to one of the 45 fridges and ask the concierge to order food. It might just work. But it remains to be seen if new 'mood food deli' My Dabba (Rokin 100, www.mydabba.eu) will prove popular. Time will tell.

One noteworthy enterprise which has recently opened to great success encompasses the community-spirited nature of the city. The brewing company De Prael (see box p70) and Freud restaurant (www. restaurantfreud.nl) are proudly run by people with mental health issues.

Rising Dutch

It used to be that the term 'Dutch cuisine' inspired only the mirth of serious foodies; these days it's been reduced to the occasional chuckle. Well-travelled native chefs have returned home to apply their skills to fresh local and often organic ingredients (source your own at Noordermarkt's Saturday organic market; p132). The land is most suited to growing spuds, cabbage and carrots, but the nation is now employing its greenhouses to grow a startling array of ingredients,

Jet Lounge p97

year-round. Things are looking so good that local restaurant critic Johannes van Dam gave the revered nine or above rating to 14 of the 44 restaurants he reviewed in 2008. He gave his first 10 to Le Restaurant (p146), which saw the return of Michelin starred chef Jan de Wit. And it's not without good reason – things on the food front in the city are getting better and better.

In medieval days it was fish, gruel and beer that formed the holy diet. During the Golden Age, the rich indulged in hogs and pheasants. Then with Napoleonic rule at the dawn of the 19th century, the middle classes were seduced by the Mediterranean flavours of herb and spices.

Only in the last century has Amsterdam taken to international cuisine. After World War II, the rich spicy food from Indonesia re-eroticised the Dutch palate (see box p103). Indonesian *rijsttafel* ('rice table'), along with the fondue – a 'national' dish shamelessly stolen from the Swiss because its shared pot appealed to the Dutch sense of democracy – are both foods of choice for any celebratory meals. Other waves of immigrants helped create today's vortex of culinary diversity. But there's still nothing quite like the hotchpotch of mashed potato, crispy bacon and crunchy greens, holding a well of gravy and loads of smoked sausage, to prove that traditional Dutch food can still hit the spot.

The most feverish buzz remains around places that combine straight and honest cookery with eccentric locations. Besides the watery ones (see box p123), there's Open (p124) atop an old railway bridge, De Kas (www.restaurantdekas.nl) in an old greenhouse, Dauphine (www.caferestaurantdauphine.nl) in a former car showroom, As (www.restaurantas.nl) in a remodelled modernist church and Polder (www.cafe-restaurant polder.nl) in a corrugated shack in the heart of the 'Science Park'. And, Ctaste (p102) also has a special location – but since its concept is 'dining in the dark' it's hard to tell.

Other news is the development of two 'culinary-boulevards'. One is located on a stretch of connected streets in the Jordaan that is home to the Spanish La Oliva (p128). It's known as 'Little Italy' for having such highly regarded restaurants as La Trattoria Di Donna Sofia (Anjeliersstraat 300), Hostaria (Tweede Egelantiers dwarsstraat 9) and La Perla (Tweede Tuindwarsstraat 1). A few blocks away there's also a Japanese Pancake World (Tweede Egelantiersdwarsstraat 24), a great Thai Kinnaree (Eerste Anjeliersdwarsstraat 14) and an excellent Afghani Mantoe (Tweede Leliedwarsstraat 13).

The other culinary strip is Amstelveenseweg that borders the south end of Vondelpark. There's the Indonesian Blauw (p137), fairtrade foodies' Umoja (No. 154) and dessert restaurant Sucre (No. 152), along with many cheaper options.

And if you do prefer to stroll, here are a few additional tips: go to the Pijp or Amsterdam East if you crave economic ethnic; cruise the eateries of Haarlemmerstraat, Utrechtsestraat, Nieuwmarkt, the 'Nine Streets' area and Reguliersdwarsstraat if you want something more upmarket; and only surrender to Leidseplein if you don't mind being gravely overcharged for a cardboard steak and day-old sushi.

Check the web for local culinary knowledge at www.iens.nl and www.specialbite.nl, the latter reliably offers the scoop on all the latest restaurant openings. And don't forget that a snack in Amsterdam can go a long way (see box p72).

Drinking

As the local barfly-cum-columnist Simon Carmiggelt once observed; 'going for one drink is like jumping off a roof with the plan of falling only one floor'. So knowing some

S H O R T L I S T

Best newcomers
- Flo Amsterdam (p104)
- Le Restaurant (p146)

Sybaritic sipping
- Bubbles and Wines (p71)
- Harry's Bar (p85)
- La Oliva (p128)

Outdoor drinking
- 't Blauwe Theehuis (p137)
- Brouwerij 't IJ (p115)
- 't Smalle (p130)

Made for music lovers
- Bitterzoet (p91)
- Struik (p130)

Best cocktails
- Getto (p71)
- Jet Lounge (p97)

A taste of the old school
- Café Chris (p128)
- Café 't Mandje (p71)
- Twee Zwaantjes (p98)
- Wynand Fockink (p75)

Beers of distinction
- 't Arendsnest (p97)
- Brouwerij 't IJ (p115)

Lush lunches
- De Bakkerswinkel (p69)
- Latei (p73)
- Small World Catering (p128)

Cheap vegetarian delights
- De Peper (p137)

Cheap traditional eating
- Hap Hmm (p104)

Posh and proud
- NEVY (p124)
- La Rive (p104)

Dining on a ship's deck
- Pont 13 (p123)

WHEREVER CRIMES AGAINST HUMANITY ARE PERPETRATED.

Across borders and above politics.
Against the most heinous abuses
and the most dangerous oppressors.
From conduct in wartime
to economic, social, and cultural rights.
Everywhere we go,
we build an unimpeachable case
for change and advocate action
at the highest levels.

HUMAN RIGHTS WATCH TYRANNY HAS A WITNESS

WWW.HRW.ORG

HUMAN
RIGHTS
WATCH

basic rules is a plus. For instance: buy rounds when in a group, do not use German when ordering rounds, and expect a long and drawn out answer if you ask the bartender 'How are you?'

Perhaps the most fundamental rule for Brits is not to whine about the 'two fingers' of head that comes with a glass of draft pils ('lager'). You are not being ripped off; it's the 'crown' and the reasoning behind it is sound: by letting a head form during tapping, the beer's hoppy aroma – and hence full flavour – is released, and the drinker's gas intake is minimised (leaving more room for more beer of course).

Another handy tip is to avoid getting completely legless by acquiring a sound knowledge of *borrel hapjes* (booze bites). These tasty bar snacks are formulated to line the stomach during drinking sessions. Inevitably, such menus begin with the strongest of stereotype reinforcers: *kaas* (cheese), which can be ingested either via *tostis* (grilled cheese sandwiches), or pure with dipping mustard. But the most universal and tastiest of *hapjes* are definitely *bitterballen* ('bitter balls'), which are essentially just cocktail versions of the *kroket* (see box p72).

A barfly can also score some major points by giving the Dutch their rightful credit for inventing gin. In around 1650 a doctor in Leiden came up with the process that allowed juniper berries to be infused into distilled spirits and gin was born – or rather *jenever*, as the local version is called. A few decades later, the Dutch were exporting 10 million gallons of the stuff, as a supposedly innocuous cure for stomach and kidney ailments. They graded the gin by age – *jong*, *oud* and *zeer oud* (young, old and very old) – but also by adding various herbs,

spices and flavours. Such liquid elixirs can still be found at *proeflokalen* (tasting houses) like Wynand Fonkink (p75).

If many bars in town look as if they've been around forever, that's because they have; Wynand Fockink and Café Chris (p128) both vie for the title of Amsterdam's longest-serving. Meanwhile the original 'lesbian biker bar' 't Mandje (p71) finally reopened in all its original glory after decades of closure.

The café (or bar – the line between the two is suitably blurred) is central to Dutch social life, serving both as a home-from-home and after dark hub at all hours of the day and night (most cafés open in the morning and don't shut until one in the morning; some stay open as late as three or four at weekends). Whatever the hour, you're as likely to find punters sipping a coffee or coke as the foaming head of a pils – or a shot of local gin.

Le Restaurant p146

For the last couple of years, Korte Leidsedwarsstraat is where the glamorous drinkers have headed for their *appletinis*. More dressed-down (but just as cool), are the crowd who frequent the nearby area around Kamer 401 (p104). A short hop in the other direction is Reguliersdwarsstraat, the centre of the gay scene. And Amsterdam's newest and best gay bar, Prik (p86), which serves everyone's favourite bubbly – prosecco – on tap, is but a ten-minute walk away.

Away from the neon, the Jordaan is awash with *bruin* cafés, so called because they've been stained brown by decades of smoking and spilt coffee. Befitting the area's gentrified status, many, like Café Thijssen (Brouwersgracht 107, 623 8994), are teeming with wealthy nouveau residents; nearby bars, though, are still filled with the last vestiges of the local working-class population. Not far away stands the Westergasfabriek (p132) which has several appealing drinking spots, including the WestergasTerras. A similar scene to the Jordaan is to be found in the Pijp, a great place to wander between trendy drinking spots and more salt-of-the-earth watering holes.

Wine buffs will find themselves justly underwhelmed in Amsterdam's cafés and bars. If you are aghast at the prospect of a beaker of unspecified red or white, head to NEVY (p124) or La Oliva (p128), both a new breed of establishment which specialise in pairing posh food with fine wine.

Cocktails, of course, remain ever popular; be they a do-it-yourself 'craftini' thrown together on a craft night at Nieuwe Anita or the ultra-posh secret concoctions made behind closed doors at Door74 (www.door74.nl). There's also a middle way; new friendly neighbourhood cocktail bar Jet Lounge (p97) mixes a decent elixir, and all with a DJ soundtrack.

Beer, though, is resoundingly the local drink of choice: in most places the pils is Heineken or Amstel, but every bar offers a range of Belgian brews and there are several specialist beer bars like In de Wildeman (Kolksteeg 3, 638 2348/www.indewildeman.nl). For a real taste of all the low countries' native brews, 't Arendsnest (p97) has a huge range to choose from.

Smoking

In the name of keeping the peace with the EU, some politicians have suggested making coffeeshops into private clubs, solely for local use – essentially sending tourists onto the street to score. But as things stand, that won't be happening anytime soon. So for the time being, Amsterdam's unique selling point remains that you can walk into a café and buy drugs. You can also get coffee and snacks to feed the munchies, but, since the first of April 2007 you may no longer have a beer with your spliff; booze was banned from the city's coffeeshops as part of the creeping resistance movement against lax marijuana laws. And from July 2008 smoking tobacco is not officially allowed in coffeeshops (most provide herbal mixes as tobacco-substitutes). The power of the anti-coffeeshop movement means that there have been no new openings for years, but trends still develop: you won't get very far without stumbling across organic (bio) highs, which don't pack quite the same punch as genetically modified (and often terrifyingly potent) hydroponic skunk. Dutch weed is known the world over for its unprecedented quality and strength, so if you're a beginner, or used to less powerful dope (Brits, take note), go easy.

Patta Exclusive Sneakers p89

WHAT'S BEST
Shopping

The global financial crisis was slow to affect the Netherlands. Of course, there were plenty of banks that needed bailing out, but the general populace seemed to continue to spend. It was even announced that the chichi Tiffany's was going to open a shop in 2009 at PC Hooftstraat 86-88. Hadn't anyone heard of the 'Tulip mania' of the 17th-century Golden Age, when single bulbs were traded for cash, castles and mountains of cheese, before it all climaxed in an orgy of bankruptcies and suicides?

The buoyancy of the retail sector could be explained by the fact that the Netherlands is a wealthy country (it was listed seventh in the EU's rich list). Indeed, the Port of Amsterdam was founded on the principles of exchange. Yet the population is perhaps less obsessed with shopping than residents of other countries. The influence of Calvinism, that most pared-down of lifestyle choices, is still etched deep into the national psyche and most people are happy to pack a cheese sandwich for lunch rather than eat out at a stylish café. Contradictions abound, but whatever your outlook, you shouldn't feel guilty for spending a little here.

Off to Market

Tulips are perhaps what Amsterdam is best known for exporting, and you can certainly pick up bargains at the floating flower market Bloemenmarkt (p105). At such traditional general markets, you'll find people truly enjoying shopping; they bounce between vendors while sniffing out special offers. With food as the great modifier, the market is among the few places at which the multi-ethnic diversity of the city is visible.

Get the local experience

Over 50 of the world's top destinations available.

Ah yes, food is a great unifier. It brings together all walks of Dutch life at the Albert Cuypmarkt (p148), which claims to be Europe's longest street market, and snakes all the way through the heart of the Pijp. The daily market offers plenty of snacks, ranging from raw herrings to Surinamese sherbets, along with all manner of household goods. It lies in close proximity to many pretty cafés, in which you can recharge yourself over a cool drink.

Other neighbourhoods in the city tend to have their own markets: the Ten Katemarkt in Oud West, the Dappermarkt in Oost and the Lindenmarkt in Jordaan are all worth a trip for their authentic shopping experience. Also located in the Jordaan, Saturday's Noordermarkt (p132) is the place to buy organic farmers' produce among more well-heeled shoppers; the same crowd is back on Monday morning to pick through bric-a-brac and antiques, at a much smaller (yet infinitely superior) variation in Waterlooplein's tourist trap.

Fashion does exist

It's true. The average burgher doesn't always think through their attire every time they rush out of their front door. Nevertheless, a fair few designers have achieved success against the odds in Amsterdam, and the country can hold its head high in the catwalk stakes – after all, it's the home city of avant-garde darlings Viktor & Rolf, whose headquarters lie in Museumplein. Marlies Dekkers (p138) continues to scintillate the world with her feminine lingerie. Street fashion king Daryl van Wouw (p105) now has his own boutique, and the locally produced gentleman's style journal *Fantastic Man* is considered to be one of the hottest new fashion magazines on

SHORTLIST

Best newcomers
- 240 Square Meters (p117)
- Marqt (p138)

Fancy pants
- Marlies Dekkers (p138)
- Paars (p89)

Local fashion
- Blue Blood (p98)
- Daryl van Wouw (p105)
- SPRMRKT (p132)

Spoil yourself
- Rituals (p106)
- Skins Cosmetics (p99)

Kiddy winkels
- Joe's Vliegerwinkel (p77)
- 't Klompenhuisje (p77)

Grown-up pleasures
- Absolute Danny (p75)
- Dampkring (p88)

Gifts for granny
- Geels & Co (p77)

Unmissable markets
- Albert Cuypmarkt (p148)
- Bloemenmarkt (p105)

Blocks of chocs
- Puccini Bomboni (p78)
- Unlimited Delicious (p132)

Cheesy pleasers
- Boerenmarkt (p130)
- De Kaaskamer (p99)

Pre-owned treasures
- Brilmuseum/Brillenwinkel (p99)
- Nic Nic (p99)
- Noordermarkt Monday Morning (p132)
- Waterlooplein flea Market (p118)

Blue Blood p98

the planet. It could be said that the biannual Amsterdam Fashion Week is having a rather trendsetting effect.

A couple of Dutch brands have brought street style home: Gsus and G-Star Raw. The latter even has its own branded ferry, which you might see cruising around town. The former, which works alongside the Fair Wear Foundation to protest against sweatshop production, is available at De Bijenkorf (p87).

The fashion map of Amsterdam is divided along clear lines: head to PC Hooftstraat, as star footballers do, for top-end designer clothes; visit the Kalverstraat for high-street stalwarts such as H&M, HEMA – which has countless branches in Amsterdam – and Zara (p91), for catwalk fashion at cut-down prices. Even though Amsterdam has long lacked an abundance of good boutiques,

a wander around the Jordaan, the Nine Streets and Damstraat areas affords the fresh discovery of outlets selling quirkier and home-grown labels.

For something hip, try SPRMRKT (p132) or such 'concept stores' as 290 Square Meters (p117) and Sid Lee (p148). There's also the new 'secret boutique', Destination Shop (Weteringschans 146, 06 1920 0480, www.destinationshop.nl), which perceives itself as a 3-D magazine of sorts, frequently changes its selection of out-there fashion, along with exhibitions of graphic design and video art.

Even though sartorial fashion sense can slip by the populace, in terms of interior design and architecture, the Dutch lead the world (see itinerary p49). To assault your eyes with designs of all kinds, from seriously high-end homeware to truly swanky jewellery, check out

Utrechtsestraat. Overtoom and Rozengracht are also much-coveted furnishing destinations.

Open books

The Dutch are bookish. They enjoy reading, collecting book ends, participating in book weeks – and even book months. Amsterdam proudly held the title of UN World Book Capital in 2008. So if you're a bookworm, you'll be in good company. Head straight to Spui, bounded at one end by the mighty Waterstone's (p91) and at the other by the American Book Center (p87), both of which are multistorey giants of English literature. Smaller scale reading pleasures can be found on the shelves of multilingual Atheneum (p87), a veritable treasure trove of journals in all languages. Another singular browsing experience awaits if you cross the Rokin to reach Oudemanhuispoort, a covered passageway belonging to the University of Amsterdam – which has been selling books and prints since the 18th century.

Incredible edibles

If you're hoping to pick up edible souvenirs, you'll be truly spoiled for choice in Amsterdam; head to De Kaaskamer (p99) and you'll see a mountain of cheese – there are more than 200 types, including plenty of local specialities such as the popular Reypenaer. For fishy dishes, you can pick up smoked eel, raw herring or tiny North Sea shrimps from any number of fish stalls dotted around town. Head to Holtkamp (see box p72) for an array of cakes displayed in a beautiful interior, in which you can see how this gourmet shop cooks the humble *kroket*. If you fancy locally

produced, organic food, visit Marqt (p138); if they happen to have lamb from the North Sea island of Texel, or white asparagus when it's in season, make sure you try some.

Talking shop

In general, local shops are open from 1pm to 6pm on Mondays (if they open at all on this quiet day); 10am to 6pm from Tuesday to Friday (with many open until 9pm on Thursday); and 9am to 5pm on Saturday. Amsterdam boasts regular Sunday shopping, especially along Kalverstraat and PC Hooftstraat, with stores usually open between noon and 5pm. Smaller shops tend to have more erratic opening hours. Credit card payment is not quite universally accepted, so as a rule of thumb, make sure that you take enough cash with you when you go out shopping.

Noordermarkt p132

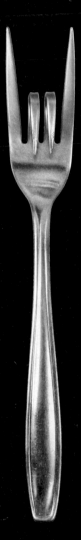

WE WILL
WE WILL
FEED YOU

Come and join us to eat or drink in the restaurant or by our waterside bar. Visit the Rock Shop and purchase one of our limited edition city tee's. We are situated in the heart of the city centre.

AMSTERDAM

De Nieuwe Anita p33

Nightlife

Amsterdam's nightlife is many things but it's most definitely diverse – you can find everything from minimalist grooves to maximum noise. There are scuzzy venues for students and rockers, meat markets for stags and stalkers and cutting-edge clubs for hipsters. And when it comes to live music, there has most definitely been a renaissance of late.

But one thing Amsterdam is not, is a 24-hour city. You might occasionally get lucky with a decent after-party, but in general the only option post four or five (on weekends – more like two or three on weekdays) is home; from where you can contact the beer taxi (www.biertaxiamsterdam.nl/06 223 100 66) to get a late-night delivery. Locals attribute this to the general trend towards conservatism of society under the Christian Democrat-led national coalition.

Some feel as if the city is becoming the victim of over-zealous legislation: smoking has been banned; mushrooms are banned; what next? Beer? This begs the question, is anything actually allowed any more? In short: yes. The people are rebelling the only way they know how: by partying harder.

It's all live

Ever cruised down the road humming Shocking Blue's *Venus,* or the now classic bass line to Golden Earring's *Radar Love*? Or danced a night away to Armin van Buuren or Junkie XL? No? Perhaps you've settled down for an evening in, with Mahler performed by the Royal Concertgebouw Orchestra? Whatever your musical bent, these are just a handful of the Netherlands's diverse musical exports. And on any given night

DON'T MISS

in Amsterdam you can be sure to find something to suit your aural taste, from the classy jazz of improv drummer Han Bennink and saxophonist hero Benjamin Herman of the New Cool Collective, to the ex-squatpunks The Ex who jam with Ethiopian roots musicians. Alternatively, drink and dance to the Eastern European party sounds of the Amsterdam Klezmer Band or Caspian Hat Dance; or marvel at local underground brass band fanfare De Kift; and get goose bumps from the violin-fuelled pop songs of alternative rockers Hospital Bombers. The more musical genres you throw into the mix (think heavy metal, art rock, hip hop and Frisian fado), the longer the list of Dutch musical innovators gets.

Alongside the homegrown talent are a plethora of international acts. With Amsterdam firmly established as one of the world's most important ports of call on the international touring circuit, thanks to such iconic venues as Paradiso (p106) and Melkweg (p106), whatever you're seeking, it'll be readily available within close proximity of the canal ring. Paradiso will be particularly busy over the next couple of years as they start programming for two new venues in Amsterdam North and Amsterdam Southeast. The Tropenmuseum (p112) is also getting a new venue, which is great news – while they have always booked world-class roots bands, there's never been enough room to dance. Fans of alternative music should follow the good work of Subbacultcha (www.subbacultcha. nl) who are booking all the up-and-coming underground guitar bands.

It's always worth keeping your eyes peeled; you might discover a performance by your favourite band or DJ is but a train ride away.

SHORTLIST

Best newcomer
- Trouw (p117)

Full-on cultural experiences
- Studio K (p118)
- Sugar Factory (p108)

Superclubs to the rescue
- Melkweg (p106)
- Panama (p126)
- Paradiso (p106)

Cosy clubbing
- Bitterzoet (p91)
- Flex (p132)
- Studio 80 (p106)

Live music on tap
- Melkweg (p106)
- Paradiso (p106)

Big bands on a budget
- Club 3voor12 (p118)

Weird and wild venues
- Skek (p74)
- Winston Kingdom (p78)

Jazz hands clapping
- Badcuyp (p148)
- Bimhuis (p126)

Bustling neighbourhoods
- Leidseplein (p100)
- Nieuwezijds Voorburgwal (p81)
- Rembrandtplein (p100)

Where life's a beach party
- Blijburg (p123)

Gays of glory
- Getto (p71)
- Prik (p86)

Best one-off parties
- NDSM (p123)
- Westergasfabriek (p132)

Bimhuis p126

Clubland Amsterdam

The club scene definitely felt a void when Club 11 closed in 2008. But its founders were quick to follow up with Trouw (p117) which seems set to continue the legacy of progressive programming, all in an odd post-industrial setting. And it's just this kind of grassroots operation, run by a group of like-minded friends, that has taken on the mega-clubs of yesteryear. At the cosiest end of the scale are intimate nooks such as De Nieuwe Anita (www.denieuweanita.nl), Bitterzoet (p91), and most recently, ClubUp (http://clubup.nl) that go for funky quality over capacity. Similar vibes can be found further afield at Studio K (p118) and Canvas (see box p117) in the east, or Club 8 (www.club-8.nl) in up-and-coming De Baarsjes neighbourhood.

Even the larger operations such as Flex (p132), Sugar Factory (p108) and Studio 80 (p106) keep things homely and unpretentious. And don't forget the city's decent clutch of smaller, DJ-friendly bars along Nieuwezijds Voorburgwal between the Dam and Spui square, and on the Marnixstraat just west of Leidseplein. There's also the hang-out for the Dance Valley festival crowd TWSTED (www.twstd.nl), and friendly cocktail bar Jet Lounge (p97).

Fans of dubstep will be particularly well-served as the scene here is huge – and growing – with parties that are known to set up in temporary locations. And if you're after the more commercial dance scene, there are always the highly acclaimed Panama (p126) and Supperclub (p86).

In general, clubbing in the capital is really no different from clubbing in any large international city. All venues have bouncers, so show up on time and with a mixed crowd to increase your chances of getting in. Storing your coat in the cloakroom might set you back, as might using the toilets (typically between €0.50 and €1), but in many clubs outside the city centre they're free. As a rule, the Dutch aren't great tippers at the bar; if you are feeling generous, however, a 15 per cent tip is considered very generous. Almost no one will actually be inside a club before midnight: people are either at home or in a bar loosening up.

As for drugs, weed and hash are still fine in the smoking areas, but it's always unwise to solicit for anything stronger – undercover cops have started to appear at the larger techno parties. Plus, what you might think you're buying is not likely to be what you will get.

Gay capital

After a couple of years of serious hand-wringing about whether or not Amsterdam still deserved the Gay Capital title – the doubt largely inspired by a sad spate of incidents, many involving Moroccan youths, – the city seems to be getting back on track. Local political parties have made a real effort to make Amsterdam gay-friendly. And politician Ahmed Marcouch has taken the fight to his district of Slotervaart, where many Moroccans live, by suggesting that a gay café is established and that it should become a starting point for the Pride canal parade. Amsterdam Pride (see box p96) has gone the way of many others by embracing corporate sponsorship – some major companies and banks now even have their own floats to make sure the spectators get the message (the main message being that they're keen to emphasise their employee diversity).

Pink Point (www.pinkpoint.org), in a stall just opposite the Homomonument (p95), serves as a good first port of call for gay or lesbian visitors. Despite both enjoying a range of venues, the scenes for gay men women are still quite separate. Each group tends to keep to its own favourite places, only getting together on occasions such as Queen's Day, Pride, or one-off parties like the mighty Love Dance. There's also a shared archive Homodok (www.ihliq.nl) in the new library Openbare Bibliotheek Amsterdam (p122)

Also on the up, gay clubbing has been reinvigorated by a wealth of young talent and plenty of fresh faces: cruising club Church (see box p107) and bars such as Prik (p86) have opened, and several new one-off parties are popping up. A word of warning, though: free condoms aren't universal on the scene, and a range of STDs – including HIV – are on the up, with barebacking as popular and controversial here as in any other big city.

Finger on the pulse

The capital's main ticket retailer is the Amsterdam Uitburo (AUB), which operates an elaborate online sales point for events at www.aub.nl, as well as a personal service at the AUB Ticketshop at Leidseplein 26 (open 10am to 7.30pm Monday to Saturday; noon to 7.30pm Sunday).

Before you buy, it helps to know what's on when. Pick up the English-language *Time Out Amsterdam* monthly listings magazine at newsagents and selected book shops, or the AUB's free monthly magazine *Uitkrant* (pronounced 'out-krant'), both available in theatres, bars, bookshops and the AUB Ticketshop, which is also a great place to collect flyers and other listings leaflets. They are also home to the Last Minute Ticket Shop (www.lastminuteticketshop.nl), which shifts tickets at half their face value from noon (every day of the week), for musical and theatrical events showing that night.

Sugar Factory p108

Stadsschouwburg p108

Arts & Leisure

Welcome to a city that likes to situate itself at the centre of the cultural universe. The locals give standing ovations to Mahler symphonies; they lap up the latest operas from Robert Wilson or Peter Sellars; some even know their NoMeansNo. And come Queen's Day – or any day the Dutch national side are kicking off – it's everyone's duty to dress in orange and get more than a little merry.

For a tiny town, Amsterdam packs a cultural punch, with more than its share of world-class venues for every form of cultural endeavour. Add to this an active underground scene, and visitors are spoilt for choice. The breadth and quality of the Amsterdam arts experience is also due to enlightened funding from government and city alike, resulting in a wealth of arts festivals, along with new buildings such as the Muziekgebouw (p126).

Recently however, the Kunstraad, responsible for city-wide arts funding, has been accused of being misguided and out of touch. But it might just be a case of change being unpopular – even the detractors can't fail to appreciate the talents of some of the recent beneficiaries of the scheme, amongst them street dance troupe ISH (www.ish-events.com) and the mutant new media/theatre/DJ collective PIPS:lab (www.pipslab.nl), who have been given the golden opportunity to develop their art whilst making a living.

Integration and diversity are key words when it comes to the city's cultural scene. In the case of Leidseplein, this has been interpreted literally; a brand new building now connects pop venue Melkweg (p106) to old municipal theatre the Stadsschouwburg (p108). Completed in 2009, the complex features a new flat stage that will be programmed by both institutions, as well as being home to residents Toneelgroep Amsterdam (see below). They will also be co-organising indoor festivals, with capacities of 5000. The venture looks like being good news all round; Stadsschouwburg scores points for hipness, while Melkweg gets more opportunity to spread its love to a wider audience. The theatre also opened their excellent café/restaurant, Stanislavski.

Rembrandtplein is also getting a facelift, but it's Leidseplein again that will benefit when the new €60 million Nieuwe de La Mar theatre, with two venues, opens in 2010 on Marnixstraat.

The art scene

While old fashioned picture painting does still have its place, the art scene is now more about the blur between street art, design, photography and new media. And there's one major industry that is doing very well from the crossover between art and commerce: the local gaming development industry is one of the few that didn't seem to get hit when the credit crunch came along.

It has often been said that Amsterdam, with its soggy climate and bleak winters was designed to look as good in black and white as it does in colour, making it especially appealing to amateur photographers. And, as home to Ed van Elsken (1925-1990) and Rineke Dijkstra, the city is a strong supporter of the photographic arts, with Foam (p100) providing solid institutional backing. Also, the studio of Erwin Olaf – who's moving away from the weird towards the emotionally charged – functions as a graduate school of sorts for young photographers.

The currently in-limbo alternative publication *Amsterdam Weekly* has long provided a home to many of the city's up-and-coming photographers, designers and illustrators, picking up many international awards in the process. Meanwhile one can check out local style magazine Blend; the international fashion periodical Fantastic Man; the various paper products coming from alternative music platform Subbacultcha and even the supplements of some of the daily newspapers, to locate the pulse of the local scene.

Amsterdam has embraced new media like few other cities. The pioneering Waag Society (www.waag.org) and the happily subversive Mediamatic (p108) both arose from the 'tactical media' scene that perhaps accounts for the city's strong activist streak – which was strengthened after the emergence of the populist politician and failed film-maker Geert Wilders. Mediamatic have been particularly acclaimed since their 'El HEMA' project remixed iconic Dutch department store HEMA into an outlet for Muslim-inspired design.

The Pakhuis de Zwijger (p126) acts as a hub for a gamut of cutting-edge outfits, complete with a programme of events, conferences and exhibitions. An annual congress in September, the 'cross-media week' PICNIC (www.picnicnetwork.org), was also an immediate success with talks and seminars on the latest developments in media, technology, art, science and entertainment.

A whole slew of advertising firms such as 180 and Wynand Kennedy, provide the city's creatives with their bread and butter. Other communication firms such as Kesselskramer and Submarine combine working for big brand clients with more quirky and uncommercial projects. Meanwhile the front line in the fight between art and commerce can be found at the former shipyards of NDSM (p123), where an 'art city' of studios butts heads with the European headquarters of MTV.

Fuelling Amsterdam's reputation as an international creative melting pot are its art schools; the Rietveld Academy and the Sandberg Institute bring in students from across the globe. This, along with generous state funding, helps explain why Amsterdam's galleries are more adventurous and welcoming to young artists and curators than those of other art hubs. The Jordaan (see box p131) remains the top spot to wander for art, but De Pijp, De Baarsjes and the Eastern Docklands are quickly attracting new galleries. And in Amsterdam-West, the new arts complex Smart Project Space (p142) is proving to be an invaluable addition to the scene.

Still, the art scene remains relatively down-to-earth; witness any event at the Volkskrantgebouw (see box p117), any opening at the Chiellerie (www.chiellerie.nl), or one of the monthly previews at W139 (p81), which could be anything from video installation to performance art. Similarly eclectic, new initiative Art Market (www.artmarketamsterdam.nl) finds places to display everything from crafting to conceptual art.

The silver screen

While not strictly a Dutch production, *Hunger* by local resident Steve McQueen was naturally celebrated as such in 2008. And native actress Carice van Houten continued to develop her international career by playing alongside Tom Cruise in *Valkyrie*, after her starring role in *Black Book* (2006), the film that marked the over-the-top homecoming of Paul Verhoeven from his Hollywood hideout. As the most expensive film

SHORTLIST

Total sporting experience
- Ajax (p39)

Interdisciplinary agendas
- De Balie (p108)
- NDSM (p123)

Singular screening experiences
- Nederlands Filmmuseum (p141)
- Pathí Tuschinski (p108)

World-class jazz acts
- Bimhuis (p126)

Best classical
- Concertgebouw (p141)
- Muziekgebouw (p126)

Cutting-edge contemporary
- NDSM (see box p125)
- Westergasfabriek (p132)

Underground vibes
- W139 (p81)
- NDSM (p123)
- Westergasfabriek (p132)

Regular gallery openings
- W139 (p81)

Big bands on a small scale
- Melkweg (p106)
- Paradiso (p106)

International belly laughs
- Boom Chicago (p108)
- Comedy Theatre (p80)

World music
- Badcuyp (p148)
- KIT Tropentheater (p118)
- Melkweg (p106)

Best creative festivals
- Over het IJ (p42)
- De Parade (p44)
- Robodock (p44)

ever to be shot in the Netherlands, it was also the country's most commercially successful. Currently Verhoeven's working on an English-language version of the Russian *Azazel*, based on Boris Akunin's 1998 novel, the *Winter Queen'*.

Meanwhile, Verhoeven's old friend Rutger Hauer is also back in the country, teaching acting master classes, and lending his skills to smaller independent productions. Also in town of late is Peter Greenaway, who released his personal documentary *Rembrandt's J'Accuse*. An essayistic exploration of 17th-century Amsterdam, it explores the different characters depicted in Rembrandt's famous painting *Nightwatch*.

Perhaps the most relevant Dutch director working today, Eddy Terstall has just completed *Vox Populi*, his final film in a trinity about sex, death and politics. His films, including 2004's *Simon,* often use his own home neighbourhood of the Jordaan as a backdrop.

There is also a new 'town' in town. Cineville (www.cineville.nl) has brought together 13 local art-house and repertory cinemas, which together screen around 100 films daily. There's also a healthy underground film screening scene focused around Cavia (www.filmhuiscavia.nl), De Nieuwe Anita (www.denieuweanita.nl) and OT301 (p141), plus local initiatives such as Future Shorts (www.future shorts.nl) and the Klik! Amsterdam Animation Festival are keeping the scene fresh.

The City Theater on Leidseplein, with its seven screens, will finally reopen in 2010. This 1935 classic of Dutch functionalism will come with trendy Little Buddha restaurant and an adjoining gambling hall.

Meanwhile around the corner, the cinema Uitkijk (Prinsengracht 452, 623 7460, www.uitkijk.nl) –

so purist that they refuse even to serve popcorn – have announced that they will expand their screenings to include special programmes for autistic people.

Theatre & dance

Amsterdam is home to a truly outstanding theatre scene. Ivo van der Hove's Toneelgroep Amsterdam at Stadsschouwburg is just one of many, but their abilities were recently noted by none other than playwright Tony Kushner, who came to see their Dutch-language version of his play *Angels in America*. He was so impressed that he agreed to write a piece specifically for them.

If language is a barrier, then the multi-purpose, multimedia De Balie (p108) is worth checking out. Alternatively, NDSM (p123) mounts regular site-specific pieces that transcend linguistic limitations. The Over het IJ (p42) and De Parade (p44) fests are worthy of attention, or pack a picnic and head for the Vondelpark's Openluchttheater (p142). Alternatively, if apocalyptic grandeur appeals, try the Robodock festival which will hopefully set up on new turf after being ejected from NDSM (p123) in 2008.

The Amsterdam Fringe Festival (p44), sees underground companies performing on the main stages of more established theatres and rewriting the rules as they go. It's also worth checking on the whereabouts of the English Theatre of Amsterdam (www.tetoa.nl), which has recently put on successful productions of *Hysteria* and *A Streetcar Named Desire*.

Comedy and cabaret are also becoming more popular. *Boom Chicago* (p108) is still going strong after 10 years, and Comedy Theater (p80) mix both English and Dutch acts. Dutch cabaret star Hans Teeuwen has crossed over to English but only in the UK – in Holland he now only performs as a very convincing Frank Sinatra-inspired crooner.

Amsterdam plays home to countless choreographers and companies, a relatively recent phenomenon, again thanks to enlightened funding. The Muziektheater (p109) is home to the internationally renowned company De Nederlandse Ballet and often hosts the equally acclaimed Nederlands Dans Theater. Smaller companies who've made a name on the world stage (and who perform regularly inside the capital) include Dansgroep Krisztina de Châtel, Het Internationaal Danstheater and most recently ISH (www.ish-events.com).

Classical music

Many of the greatest international orchestras perform in Amsterdam – typically for little more than the price of the biggest rock or pop concerts, and frequently for considerably less.

The city is also home to world renowned orchestras and soloists, and renditions of the classics are not limited only to the grand concert venues, but can be heard alongside canals, in parks, on the streets or in the halls of the new building of the Conservatory of Amsterdam (p126) – whose composers-in-training are being brought to the fore thanks to the likes if the Asko Ensemble and Schönberg Ensemble.

The Royal Concertgebouw Orchestra, led by chief conductor Mariss Jansons, is one of the world's most famous. They play at home most weeks during the cultural season – if you get the chance, even just for a lunch concert, don't pass it up.

Meanwhile, famed German conductor Marc Albrecht has just signed to the post of chief conductor of the Netherlands Opera and Netherlands Philharmonic Orchestra and Chamber Orchestra, and contemporary composer Louis Andriessen is still vying for immortality status; most recently he teamed up with film-maker Hal Hartley for *La Commedia*, an opera based on Dante's Divine Comedy.

The sporting life

Football remains the city's main game, with fans still pining for Johan Cruijff's and Marco van Basten's '70s and '80s glory days. While plenty of young stars, such as Arjen Robben and Robin van Persie, have made their names and riches internationally, the magic spark is still missing from the national side. The same goes for local team Ajax, who have never really hit their stride since occupying the Amsterdam ArenA (Arena Boulevard 1, Amsterdam Zuidoost, 311 1333, www.amsterdamarena.nl) over a decade ago – even after taking on Van Basten as head coach. Fans complain that while the squad is a great training ground, the good players get sold to the big international teams once they've hit their peak. Klaas Jan Huntelaar, Rafael van der Vaart and Wesley Schneider, who have all recently found lucrative homes playing for Real Madrid, rather prove the point.

The desire to be the best has, however, payed off elsewhere, and in field hockey, ice skating, swimming, darts and cycling, Dutch stars manage to bag medals on a regular basis. Recently there have been murmurings about Amsterdam hosting the 2028 Olympics. But no-one should book a hotel room quite yet.

Calendar

Queen's Day

Dates in **bold** are public holidays.

January

1 Nieuwjaarsdag (New Year's Day)

Mid Jan **Amsterdam International Fashion Week**
Various locations
www.aifw.nl
Putting the city on the fashion map.

Late Jan/early Feb **Chinese New Year**
Nieuwmarkt (Map p55 E3)
Celebrations and fireworks.

Late Jan/early Feb
International Film Festival Rotterdam
Various locations in Rotterdam
www.filmfestivalrotterdam.nl

March

Early Mar **Unheard Film Festival**
Various locations
Listen up: it's about cinematic sound.

Early Mar **Amsterdam Restaurant Week**
Various locations
www.restaurantweek.nl
Special deals on dining out in selected restaurants across the capital.

Mid Mar **Stille Omgang**
Spui, Red Light District
www.stille-omgang.nl
Silent procession commemorating the 14th-century Miracle of Amsterdam.

Mid Mar **Boekenweek**
www.boekenweek.nl
Week of events promoting literature and reading throughout the city.

Mid Mar **Keukenhof**
Lisse
www.keukenhof.nl
Millions of bulbs bloom until late May.

Mar/Apr **Goede Vrijdag (Good Friday)**

Mar/Apr **Eerste Paasdag (Easter Sunday)**

Mar/Apr **Tweede Paasdag (Easter Monday)**

Mar/Apr **Motel Mozaïque**
Rotterdam
www.motelmozaique.nl
Three-day music, theatre and arts fest.

April

Early Apr **Movies that Matter**
www.amnestyfilmfestival.nl
Screenings of films on the subject of human rights, which used to be called the Amnesty International Film Festival.

Early/mid Apr **CinemAsia**
Various locations
www.cinemasia.nl
Screenings of pan-Asian features and cutting-edge documentaries.

Early Apr **National Museum Weekend**
Various locations
www.museumweekend.nl
Free or cheap entry to the city's many museums, plus special events.

Mid Apr **Imagine Film Festival**
Various locations
www.imaginefilmfestival.nl
Formerly the Amsterdam Fantastic Film Festival, this event delivers more than a week of silver screen schlock, horror, splatter and trash.

29 **Queen's Night**
All over Amsterdam
The start of Queen's Day (see below); paint the town orange.

30 **Queen's Day**
All over Amsterdam
This epic celebration is a giant open air disco-cum-flea-market enjoyed by all, republicans included. See box p43.

Late Apr **London Calling**
New rock and pop from the UK (and elsewhere, since they stopped checking passports).

Late Apr **Roze Wester Festival**
Homomonument (p95)
www.gala-amsterdam.nl
Lesbian and gay open-air party.

Late Apr-late June
World Press Photo
Oude Kerk (p68)
www.worldpressphoto.com
Exhibits the best of press photography.

May

4 **Dodenherdenkingsdag (Memorial Day)**
Dam Square
7.30pm ceremony, remembering those who lost their lives in World War II.

5 **Bevrijdingsdag (Liberation Day)**
Various locations
www.amsterdamsbevrijdingsfestival.nl
Marking national liberation from Nazi occupation with many concerts.

Mid May **Art Amsterdam**
Amsterdam RAI Congress Centre
www.artamsterdam.nl
Huge, commercial, five-day exhibition.

Mid May **National Windmill Day**
Around the Netherlands
www.molens.nl
Windmills spin sails and open to the public in this quaintest of celebrations.

Mid May **Kunstvlaai**
Westergasfabriek (p132)
www.kunstvlaai.nl
Hip art for the discerning masses.

May **Hemelvaartsdag (Ascension Day)**

Late May **Open Studios**
Westelijke Eilanden
www.oawe.nl
Artists open their doors to the public.

June

May/June **Eerste and Tweede Pinksterdag (first and second Pentecost)**
The Dutch celebration lasts two days; Sunday and the subsequent Monday.

Early June **Hindustaans Film**
Nederlands Filmmuseum (p141)
www.hindustaansfilmfestival.nl
Screenings of the best of the previous year's Bollywood offerings.

Early June **Arab Film Festival**
Various locations
www.arabfilmfestival.nl

Three days of shorts, documentaries and features by Arabic film-makers.

Early June **Beeld voor Beeld**
Tropenmuseum (p112)
www.beeldvoorbeeld.nl
Cultural and anthropological documentary film festival.

Early June-mid Aug
Openluchttheater
Vondelpark
www.openluchttheater.nl
Open-air stage featuring performances from classical to urban to kids' stuff.

Mid June **Amsterdam Roots Festival**
Various locations
www.amsterdamroots.nl
World music festival, whose highlight is the free outdoor Roots Open Air in Oosterpark.

Early June **Holland Festival**
Various locations
www.holndfstvl.nl
Huge, popular and varied arts and contemporary music festival.

Mid June **Oerol Terschelling**
www.oerol.nl
For a fortnight, the Frisian island of Terschelling, which lies 120 km north of town, stages 200 theatre acts.

Mid June **Open Garden Days**
Various locations
www.opentuinendagen.nl

July

Ongoing Openluchttheater
(see June)

July **Julidans**
Various locations
www.julidans.nl
A month-long international dance festival that draws big names and crowds.

Early July **Cinedans International Dance Film**
Various locations
www.cinedans.nl

Eclectic dance and choreography film screenings for stage enthusiasts.

Early July **5 Days Off**
Various locations
www.5daysoff.nl
Techno, drum 'n' bass, house and mad electro mash up.

Early July **Over het IJ**
NDSM (p123)
www.overhetij.nl
International festival of large-scale, avant-garde theatrical projects.

Mid July **North Sea Jazz**
Rotterdam
www.northseajazz.nl
Internationally renowned jazz festival.

Mid July **Amsterdam International Fashion Week**
(see January)

Late July **Amsterdam Tournament**
ArenA Stadium
www.amsterdamarena.nl
International footie friendlies.

Late July-mid Aug **Kwakoe**
Bijlmerpark
www.kwakoeamsterdam.nl
Free festie in the multicultural suburbs.

Mid to late July **Dance Valley**
Spaarnwoude
www.dancevalley.nl
Mega dance music festival

Late July **Raw Rhythm Festival**
Westergasterrein
www.rawrhythmfestival.com
Cutting-edge, progressive dance music.

August

Ongoing Openluchttheater
(see June); Kwakoe (see July)

Early Aug **Amsterdam Gay Pride**
Various locations
www.amsterdamgaypride.nl
See box p96. Also look out for the boat parade on Prinsengracht.

The Queen of all parties

First-time visitors to Amsterdam arriving on 30 April often get confused and exclaim, 'I heard Amsterdam was a happening town, but this is crazy!' And it's lucky for everyone that this chaotic day only occurs once a year. Party lovers, rubbish collectors and students of the surreal should, however, make sure that their visit coincides with this date, when up to a million extra people pour into the city, rendering every single street and canal dense with jubilant crowds.

Queen's Day, or *Koninginnedag*, to the locals, is (in theory) a celebration of Beatrix's birthday. As it happens, her birthday falls in the winter, so the ever-pragmatic Dutch choose to celebrate it on her mother's birthday, when the climate tends to be more clement.

However, Her Highness is soon forgotten amid the revelry. You're as likely to happen upon a leather-boy disco party on one side street, or an old-school crooner on the other, as you are to witness a boat bellowing out heavy metal,

only to have its amps short-circuited at the next bridge, by a gang of boys – dressed head-to-toe in orange – urinating on them. If nothing else, you'll come away with a few stories of debauchery to tell the grandchildren. (If you have your own offspring in tow, head to Vondelpark, which is dedicated to children.)

Dam Square becomes a fairground; prepare for a mind-boggling overdose of sensations – and for your pockets to empty themselves, as you get tricked into buying just what you always (read: never) wanted. How are you going to explain that pair of orange clogs when you get back home?

Meanwhile, the gay and lesbian festivities spread out like ripples from the Homomonument (p95) and the Reguliersdwaarsstraat.

What with all the performances, the markets, the crowds and, of course, the readily flowing alcohol, the streets of Amsterdam offer all anyone could dream of – at least for a day.

Early Aug **De Parade**
Martin Luther Kingpark
www.deparade.nl
Travelling circus-style theatre festival.

Mid Aug **Grachtenfestival**
Various locations
www.grachtenfestival.nl
Canalside classical music concerts.

Mid Aug **Appelsap**
Oosterpark
www.appelsap.net
Free outdoor hip hop festival.

Mid Aug **Hartjesdag**
Zeedijk
www.hartjesdagen.nl
An ancient celebration re-invented:
cross-dressing, jazz and fireworks.

Mid Aug **Open Haven Podium**
Java-eiland
www.openhavenpodium.nl
Art, music, theatre and kids' activities
out on one of Amsterdam's islands.

Mid Aug **Lowlands**
Walibi World
www.lowlands.nl
Dutch Glastonbury: the latest bands,
comedy, global food and fashion.

19-23 Aug 2010 **SAIL Waterfront**
www.sail-amsterdam.nl
Every five years millions stroll the
harbour front to admire dozens of
tall ships and thousands of modern
boats.

Late Aug **Uitmarkt**
Various locations
www.uitmarkt.nl
Open-air preview of the coming cultural season: theatre, opera and dance.

Late Aug **Amsterdam Restaurant
Week**
See Mar

September

Early Sept **Sweelinck Festival**
Oude Kerk (p56)
www.sweelinckorgancompetition.com

This biannual, popular organ music
festival returns in 2010.

Early Sept **Nederlands Theater
Festival**
All over Amsterdam
www.tf-1.nl
Showcase for Dutch and Belgian the-
atre, plus Amsterdam Fringe Festival.

Early Sept **Gaudeamus
Music Week**
Muziekgebouw (p116)
www.muziekcentrumnederland.nl
Contemporary classical music.

Early Sept **Africa in the Picture**
Various locations
www.africainthepicture.nl
Features, docs and shorts from Africa.

Mid Sept
Open Monumentendag
Various locations
www.openmonumentendag.nl
Free or cheap entry to historic sites.

Mid Sept **Experimenta Design**
Various locations
www.experimentadesign.nl
Six week design biennial that began in
2008, which brings design to the streets.

Mid Sept **Dam tot Damloop**
Amsterdam to Zaandam
www.damloop.nl
Long-running mini-marathon.

Mid Sept **Jordaanfestival**
Marnixstraat/Elandsgracht
www.jordaanfestival.nl
Tears in your beers singalongs.

Late Sept **Picnic '08**
Westergasfabriek (p122)
www.picnicnetwork.org
Gathering for new media industries
from across the world.

Sept **Robodock**
www.robodock.org
Spectacular theatre festival with robots
and mechanical installations. Forced to
leave NDSM location in 2008 but is planning to return in some form elsewhere.

A year in film festivals

Whether you want to submerge yourself or just take a dip in the celluloid pool, Amsterdam's cornucopia of film festivals are all worth checking out. The following are only the tip of the iceberg.

The year of film festivals begins an hour's train ride from Amsterdam, with the **International Film Festival Rotterdam** (p40; www.filmfestival rotterdam.com), the largest film festival, as well as one of the largest cultural events, in the country. In 2009, it ran for 12 days and attracted 340,000 visitors. Expect arthouse cinema from all over the world, and large numbers of directors showing up for talks. Befriend a volunteer for access to the best after-parties.

Movies that Matter (p41; www. amnestyfilmfestival.nl) takes place at several venues in mid March, screening quality films that focus on global inequality and the quest to make the world a fairer place.

Late April brings the **Imagine Film Festival** (p41; www.imagine filmfestival.nl) for gore-fiends and kiddos alike. Re-branded in 2009 after spending 20 years as the Fantastic Film Festival, it still offers up intriguing flicks and maintains a cosy atmosphere.

Even Amsterdam can get sultry on August evenings, and open-air screens litter the city, with a highlight being **Pluk de Nacht** (www.plukdenacht.nl). On the programme are screenings of unreleased gems of the year, and excellent food and drink.

The biggest documentary film festival in the world touches down in Amsterdam at the end of November in the form of the **IDFA** (p46; www.idfa.nl), which also spawned the appropriately named **Shadow Festival** (p46; www.shadow festival.nl). Whereas the former's massive quantity of titles is geared towards neophyte and diehard alike, Shadow is more experimental – with mixed results.

Over in Utrecht, the same month brings the **Holland Animation Film Festival** (www.haff.nl), five days of pixelated pleasure. Meanwhile, Amsterdam has its own cutting-edge animation festival in September, in the form of **Klik Festival** (www.klikamsterdam.nl), whose organisers also hold other film events throughout the year.

Finally, the cinematic year is capped off with the lesbigay film festival **Roze Filmdagen** (p46; www. rozefilmdagen.nl) in December.

October

Early Oct **International Buddhist Film Festival Europe**
Nederlands Filmmuseum (p132)
www.ibff-europe.eu
Movies inspired by the Buddhist faith.

Mid Oct **Rocket Cinema Festival**
Various locations
www.rocketcinema.nl
Old movies re-scored.

Mid Oct **ING Amsterdam Marathon**
Various locations
www.amsterdammarathon.nl

Mid/late Oct **Cinekid Festival**
Various locations
www.cinekid.nl
Child-centred film and media festival.

Mid/late Oct **Amsterdam Dance Event**
Various locations
www.amsterdam-dance-event.nl
Dance music festival and conference.

End Oct **Bock Beer Festival**
Beurs van Berlage (p63)
www.pint.nl
Festival of seasonal beer.

End Oct **Gay Leather Pride**
Various locations
www.amsterdamleatherpride.eu
Leather boys and their hangers-on and strap-ons.

November

Early Nov **Museum Night**
Various locations
www.n8.nl
Late-night opening and special events.

Early Nov **Jewish Film Festival**
Het Ketelhuis
www.joodsfilmfestival.nl
Four days of Jewish movies.

Mid Nov **London Calling**
Various locations
www.londoncalling.nl (see Apr).

Mid Nov **Sinterklaas Intocht**
Prins Hendrikkade, Dam to Leidseplein
www.sintinamsterdam.nl
Children's Christmas parade.

Mid Nov **Crossing Border**
The Hague
www.crossingborder.nl
International literature and music fest.

Mid/late Nov **International Documentary Film Festival (IDFA)**
Various locations
www.idfa.nl
The mother of all international documentary festivals.

Late Nov **High Times Cannabis Cup**
Various locations
www.cannabiscup.com
Contest promoting cannabis.

Late Nov **Shadow Festival**
Various locations
www.shadowfestival.nl
Documentary fringe festival.

December

1 **Lovedance**
Paradiso (p106)
www.lovedance.nl
World AIDS Day charity gala.

5-6 **Sinterklaas (St Nicolas)**
Various locations
Traditional gift-giving parties, which are popular with children.

Mid Dec **Roze Filmdagen**
Various locations
www.rozefilmdagen.nl
International queer film festival.

25 **Eerste Kerstdag (Christmas)**

26 **Tweede Kerstdag (Boxing Day)**

31 **Oudejaarsavond (New Year's Eve)**
All over Amsterdam, including Dam and Nieuwmarkt
This brings plenty of excitement and fireworks.

Itineraries

Airline flights are one of the biggest producers of the global warming gas CO_2. But with **The CarbonNeutral Company** you can make your travel a little greener.

Go to **www.carbonneutral.com** to calculate your flight emissions then 'neutralise' them through international projects which save exactly the same amount of carbon dioxide.

Contact us at **shop@carbonneutral.com** or call into the office on **0870 199 99 88** for more details.

CarbonNeutral®flights

Living by Design

The Dutch love of design comes into view as you descend towards **Schiphol Airport** and glide over a Mondrian-like grid pattern of landscape. A dedication to arrangement is apparent in the ballet-like elegance of Dutch football players, who open space to score and close lines to defend. And an eye for detail underpins a multitude of creative spheres, from art to architecture, whether on paper, canvas or computer.

The history of Dutch design has been influenced by the orderliness of Calvinism and the 20th-century modernist movement De Stijl. Drawing upon that part of the Dutch psyche that craves order, abstraction artists such as Theo van Doesburg, Piet Mondrian and Gerrit Rietveld sought rules of equilibrium, which can be applied to everyday design as much as art. Just surf the web, leaf through *Wallpaper** magazine or buy a White Stripes album to see the legacy of the style today. And yet a counterpoint has always existed in the Dutch people's strong desire for personal expression (perhaps an echo of the stubbornness required to battle the sea).

This eclectic mix of functionality and wit has resulted in worldwide acclaim – just consider the playful, lego-like residential building Silodam by MVRDV Architects in the western Docklands area – so much that even the tourist board has jumped on the bandwagon by sponsoring www.coolcapitals.com.

Furthermore, there's an active sense of 'city design' at work: urban planners carefully read the work of sociologist Richard Florida, who argues that the 'creative class' can play a beneficial role in urban development. Creative types are starting work in deprived neighbourhoods, ranging from the Red Light District to De Baarsjes district west of the Jordaan, and the former shipyards **NDSM** (p123).

Droog Design

Start this local design tour in the **Red Light District** (p79). As you begin to wander around, you may notice yourself endlessly looping in towards its geographical centre; there's poetry in this: Albert Camus in *The Fall* described the radiating canal girdle as resembling the circles of hell. But it can also be interpreted as a form of social control: it has traditionally kept visiting sailors (and later packs of stag-celebrating Brits) centralised, while leaving the rest of the city for residents to live their daily lives.

To witness how design has infiltrated every level of Dutch life, cross the Damrak from the Red Light District to visit a major outlet of the ubiquitous department store **HEMA** (Nieuwendijk 174-76/www.hema.nl). A quarter of the Dutch population wakes to the ring of a HEMA alarm clock, one in three men wear HEMA underwear, and one in four women a HEMA bra. The department store sells 506,000 kilograms of liquorice every year, 14 million units of *tompouce* (a pink-glazed custard cake) annually, and one smoked sausage per second. New smaller outlets are now appearing at train stations and a larger outlet recently opened in the *banlieues* of Paris. Even though HEMA remains the economical place to shop for basics, it's made a name for itself as a source of affordable design objects – even their sales flyers are graphics classics. They have featured products designed by big names such as Piet Hein Eek, Gijs Bakker and Hella Jongerius, and had a hit with their Le Lapin whistle kettle, selling more than 250,000 units. If you like to shop, you'll enjoy HEMA, and you might also want to check out **Marqt** (p138), which has taken branding to the next level.

For a stroll deep into the heart of local design, visit that most higgledy-piggledy neighbourhood, the Jordaan. From Nieuwendijk, take the Mandenmakerssteeg, Dirk van Hasseltssteeg, Lijnbaansteeg, Herenstraat and Prinsenstraat (all in a straight line), to a former school at Westerstraat 187, now the studio of design star and inventor of the Knotted Chair, **Marcel Wanders** (www.marcelwanders.com). On the ground floor, step into his stylish store, **Moooi** (www.moooi.com), the showroom for his work and the portfolios of other creatives such as Studio Job, Piet Boon and Jurgen Bey. But don't come here expecting to shop for bargains. Another disciple of Richard Florida, Wanders is now actively 'designing' other creative hubs elsewhere in the city.

T-shirt fanatics should then visit **SML.X** (Donker Curtiusstraat 11, Westerpark (681 2837, www.sml-x. com, noon-6pm Fri; noon-5pm Sat), a shop/gallery that exclusively stocks the silkscreen-printed shirts of leading Dutch graphic designers and graffiti artists.

Since the 1980s, there has been a backlash against Conceptual art's anti-functional rhetoric, which would have pleased adherents of De Stijl, who hoped the future would bring a frenzy of cross-disciplinary activity. Photographers (Anton Corbijn, Rineke Dijkstra), cartoonists (Joost Swarte) and architects (Rem Koolhaas) are considered to be 'artists'. The Eindhoven-based, free-thinking artist and architect John Körmeling will design the Dutch pavilion, Happy Street, at the World Expo 2010 in Shanghai while the whimsical and bright inventions of the Atelier van Lieshout in Rotterdam are to be found in museum collections across the world. The nation's colleges have been a catalyst for this process by encouraging artists and designers to study together while welcoming a large number of foreign students, who have forged universal visual languages. 2008 saw the première of biennale ExperimentaDesign, which brought culture to the city's streets.

After taking in the bustling design scene, backtrack into town via Rozengracht, which hosts a whole range of different design and furniture stores, including the upmarket but funky **SPRMRKT** (p132). Then take a right down the north side of Prinsengracht to one of the city's most-famed Valhalla,

Frozen Fountain (p89). This is a paradise for lovers of contemporary furniture and homeware. While staying abreast of innovative young Dutch designers, such as furniture maestro Piet Hein Eek, the 'Froz' exhibits and sells international ranges of products, by the likes of Marc Newson, modern classics and even photography.

The surrounding **Nine Streets** area (p88) is a great place in which to wander at leisure. On reaching Spui square, browse in the **Athenaeum Nieuwscentrum** (p105), a great place to buy Amsterdam-centric design books and magazines, before continuing further north-east, down Lange Brugsteeg and Grimburgwal, to take a left into Oudezijds Achterburgwal. At the corner of Rusland, stop at **WonderWood** (p96), which sells wonderfully sculpted original woodworks, re-editions of global classics and plywood items from the '40s and '50s.

At the end of Rusland, take a right down Kloveniersburgwal and a left down the picturesque Staalstraat, where you'll reach the shop of Amsterdam's famed design collective: **Droog Design** (p95). This can rightfully lay claim to having the wittiest selection of products around, thanks to the likes of Marcel Wanders, Hella Jongerius, Richard Hutten and Jurgen Bey. Droog's clout remains apparent: in the depths of the current economic downturn, it heightened its international profile by opening a shop in New York City, which has a vast floor area to showcase the larger objects from its inspired collection. But, if the prices seem a little expensive, visit the HEMA around the corner, at Kalverstraat 212, to hunt for some more friendly-priced Dutch products. There's design for every budget in this creative city.

Docklands

Down by the Water

Amsterdam's eastern dockland area is the city's up-and-coming eating and entertainment hotspot. But, perhaps more interestingly, it's also a fantastic showcase for the Netherlands' rather daring experiments in residential living. If you want to explore the future of Amsterdam, hop on a bike, pick up a map and get moving.

First, head north-west of Centraal Station to the **Westelijke Eilanden** (Western Islands) near the Jordaan, to get a taste of life during the Golden Age, when Amsterdam was the richest port in the world. These artificial islands were originally created in the 17th century to sustain maritime activity. Although there are trendy warehouse flats and a yacht basin on Realeneiland, Prinseneiland and Bickerseiland – where one-time shipyards, tar distillers and salters and smokers of fish were based – the area still remains the city's best

setting for a scenic stroll evoking seafaring times, a fact aided in no small measure by the sizeable community of local artists.

Since 1876, the route to the open sea has been the North Sea Canal. Because the working docks also lie to the west, there's little activity on the IJ behind Centraal Station, aside from a handful of passenger ships and free ferries sailing across the water to Amsterdam Noord – one of which will take you to the vibrant cultural breeding ground that is the former shipping yard **NDSM** (p123). Here, vivid apocalyptic splendour, artistic endeavours and old-school squat aesthetics can be found alongside funky student container housing and the state-of-the-art MTV headquarters – the epitome of old-meets-new.

If you keep to the south side, follow the water eastwards from Centraal Station before joining up with and following Oostelijke

NDSM

Handelskade and its parallel boardwalk. Initially, you pass the **Muziekgebouw** (p126), an epicentre of new music, which is also home to the **Bimhuis** (p126), and incorporates studios, rehearsal spaces, exhibition galleries, and a grand café and restaurant, complete with a terrace overlooking the scenic waters of the IJ. Its close neighbour is the spectacular, wave-shaped, glass passenger terminal for luxury cruise ships. Visit the website www.pta.nl for lists of all docking times, should you wish to admire the ships in situ.

Before proceeding to clubs **Café Pakhuis Wilhelmina** (p126) and **Panama** (p126), restaurant **Odessa** (p124), former shipping canteen **Koffiehuis** KHL (p124) and the youth prison-turned-designer accommodation **Lloyd Hotel** (p175), take a walk down the airy Jan Schaeferbrug to the left – starting off by going through the Pakhuis de Zwijger (p126), an old cocoa storage warehouse that has been reinvented as a new media centre. If you are

more culturally curious, pop in for a drink at its charming café.

The bridge will take you to the tip of Java-eiland, which at first glance, may look like a dense, designer confinement, but it's not hard to be charmed by the island's dividing pedestrian street, which will have you crossing canals on funky bridges and walking passing a startling variety of architecture. At **Azartplein**, the island suddenly changes its name to KNSM-eiland, in honour of the Royal Dutch Steam Company (KNSM), once based here. Here you can opt to visit **De Kompaszaal** (KNSM-laan 311, 419 9596, www.kompaszaal.nl), a café and restaurant in the former hall of arrivals and departures of KNSM, which has the feel of a 1950s cruise ship, complete with watery views from the terrace. Otherwise, veer north and follow **Surinamekade**, with houseboats on one side and the visible interiors of artist studios on the other. Pass 'Black Widow' tower and loop around the island's tip and back along KNSM-laan, turning left into **Barcelonaplein**, and then right when you pass through the abstract sculpted steel archway. You may also want to make some time for refreshment at one of the waterside bars and restaurants, or invest in an art coffin at the alternative burial store **De Ode**; either way, linger and look at the imposing residential Piraeus building by German architect **Hans Kollhoff**, if only for its eye-twisting inner court.

The two peninsulas to the south are **Borneo** and **Sporenburg**, the work of urban planning and landscape architecture firm West 8. The plots are all differently sized, to encourage the many architects involved – a veritable Who's Who of international stars – to come up with creative low-rise living. Cross over to Sporenburg via the Verbindingsdam to the building that has probably already caught your eye: the mighty silver **Whale** residential complex, designed by architect Frits van Dongen, over on Baron GA Tindalplein. In folky contrast, a floating Styrofoam park produced by erstwhile Provo Robert Jasper Grootveld has been set in front of it on Panamakade.

From here, cross over to Borneo on the swooping red bridge. Turn left up **Stuurmankade** – past a still more violently undulating pedestrian bridge – and pause to enjoy the view at the end (and imagine an even better one, enjoyed by the residents of the blue and green glass cubes that jut out of the buildings). Then return west along **Scheepstimmermanstraat**, easily Amsterdam's most eccentric architectural street, where every single façade on show – from twisting steel to haphazard plywood – manages to be more bizarre than the next.

Where Panamalaan meets Piet Heinkade, you may opt to take the IJtram from CS to IJburg (the stop is right by the huge public artwork **Folly for the Bees**, the stack of giant tables with beehives below), or return to **Oostelijk Handelskade** and to the singular Lloyd Hotel and its neighbouring café **De Kantine** (Rietlandpark 375, 419 4433). Another option is to head up Czar Peterstraat, a once dangerous street, but now pleasant area, with quirky shops and cafés, and go for a home-brewed beer at **Brouwerij 't IJ** (p115).

More energetic types might prefer to take a 20-minute bike ride to **IJburg**, heading south via C van Eesterenlaan and Veelaan, then left down Zeeburgerdijk. This in turn connects up with **Zuiderzeeweg**, which then merges into a bridge that ends at a set of traffic lights. Here, follow the cycle path to the right, which takes you to IJburg.

When finally completed in 2012, the six islands here will be home to 45,000 people inhabiting more than 18,000 units, many of which will float on the water. It will also be a showcase for Dutch landscape and residential architecture, with houses that combine thrilling aesthetic forms with cutting-edge, environmentally friendly mod-cons. That said, there's already plenty to look at with two islands already complete, housing 10,000 residents, and the funky beach **Blijburg** (p123) a clear highlight.

On the way back to town, make sure that you stop at the chip stand, **Eiburgh Snacks** (Zuiderzeeweg, beside #2), which you may have already spotted on the corner between the two bridges. The snack store serves some of the best fries in town, along with a hearty, homemade pea soup.

For more detailed information on architectural tours of all these areas and more, contact ARCAM (www.arcam.nl).

Red Light District

Walk on the Wild Side

Amsterdam has been embroiled in a city re-building and re-branding frenzy over the last few years. Coffeeshops are closing, smart shops are no longer allowed to sell mushrooms and the Red Light District is cleaning up its act (see box p79) to attract the hip, moneyed masses. With all this gentrification taking place, it can be hard to find some of the good old-fashioned sex, drugs and rock 'n' roll, that has won over generations of hippies since the flower power era.

Many love children from the 1970s seeking a place to rediscover their lost youth and salve their consciences invested in the city during the booming 1990s, and now come here to relax a few times a year. Follow their creative lead with our alternative tour of the city, taking in the favourite haunts of hippies of the '70s, artistic squatters of the '80s and hedonistic clubbers of the '90s.

Start in front of the **Athenaeum Nieuwscentrum** (p87) on Spui square, which is home to the University of Amsterdam, whose students tend to like studying their sub-cultures. Many freethinkers have congregated here since the '60s. The **Lieverdje** ('Little Darling') statue, a spindly and pigeon dropping-covered statue of a boy wearing knee socks, was the site for Provo 'happenings'. Alternately called the flashiest of street scene-makers or proto-Yippies, the **Provos** played absurdist mind games with the unsuspecting powers of their day. They took on tobacco companies by chain smoking; they testified to the benefits of trepanation – the act of drilling a hole in one's head to release pressure, open the third eye and induce a pleasant high; they promoted the 'White Constable Plan', which envisaged cops dressed in white, distributing sparks for joints, chickens to the hungry and oranges to the thirsty; and they even disrupted the wedding of Queen Beatrix of

Red Light District

Orange with rumours of LSD in the water supply and horse feed, to craze the animals that drew the Royal Carriage. To cut a long story short, it was classy hippy fun. The provo's main jester was 'anti-smoke magician' Robert Jasper Grootveld, who went on to make Styrofoam garden arks that can be spotted docked or even motoring around town. He died in 2009, but his legacy lives on at www.drijvende tuinen.nl, which has a map of ark locations and workshop times.

After the movement ended, many ex-Provos squatted outside the city limits at Ruigoord (www.ruigoord. nl), which remains an artists' village of eco-hippies who hold solstice festivals on their grounds and concerts in their church. Although **Spui square** itself is less absurdist these days, the Friday book market still retains a certain contra vibe from the time of the Provos, thanks in part to the resident harpist.

Head north down **Spuistraat** to discover a squatting landmark. The city's first inhabitants, squatters all of them, settled what was to become Amsterdam in about 1000 AD. With the building of the first city walls in 1342, the impoverished founders had to squat outside the wall's perimeter, setting the trend for the poor to move increasingly outwards as the city expands, which continues to this day. Nevertheless, it was only in 1969 that the *Handbook for Squatters* became a national bestseller.

Today, many nostalgic residents weep for the salad days of the 1980s and '90s, when less political and more cultural squats such as **Silo** and **Vrieshuis Amerika** provided the coolest cheap studio space around and threw the best parties. Over the following years, the powers-that-be shut down these squats, until they realised that such cultural beehives would enhance the city's creative image under the brand name of Iamsterdam. So, in an effort to claw back some of their lost prestige and emigrating artists, they have created less affordable non-squat squats called *broedplaatsen* (breeding grounds).

The world of Amsterdam's squats is divided into umpteen categories. As well as *broedplaatsen*, there are proper squats, re-appropriated buildings that have been left empty for more than a year; 'anti-squats', with temporary residents paying little rent so squatters can't move in; and 'bought squats', sold cheaply by the city to their inhabitants to relieve themselves of a headache. Stop at **The Vrankrijk** (Spuistraat 216, www.vrankrijk.org) to see the most famous example of this latter type, mainly thanks to its colourful exterior. And across the street, you can enjoy a similarly greasy – and smoky – ambience at punk rock night bar The Minds (Spuistraat 245, www.theminds.nl).

Next, backtrack to Spui square and head eastwards, along the Singel canal to arrive opposite the floating flower market, the **Bloemenmarkt** (p105), where you can pay homage to the legendary nightclub **RoXY**, opened in 1987 at Singel 465 by, among others, the DJ Eddy de Clercq and the artist Peter Giele. Not all squatters partied constantly in those days. Some worked hard as artists in their studios, and were ready to reap the benefits by selling their work for inflated prices during the global art boom of the late 1980s. With money in pocket, they could then party continuously; and the RoXY came to represent that era. While de Clercq and DJ Joost van Bellen brought house music to the city, Peter Giele helped provide the club with different thematic decors, which happily embraced a certain

ITINERARIES

hedonistic attitude that filtered through to those that danced. Ecstasy not only helped them to have a good time, but played a part in building a sense of community. Ironically, the party ended on 21 June 1999, when, during Giele's wake, the club burned downed after fireworks were let off in tribute to his life's motto: 'from one flame comes many'.

From here, you can follow the Amstel river to Amstelstraat 24, where Manfred Langer opened another legendary nightclub, iT, in 1989. It was intended to be the ultimate gay disco, and indeed became a magnet for two-metre tall transvestites wearing acres of leather. Soon straights and international names were clamouring to get in, but the club started to fade when Langer died in 1994 (he was taken to his final resting place in a pink Chevrolet convertible). After a huge drugs raid in 1999, the club did re-open a couple of times, but never really took off again on the scene. Its disappearance off the clubbing radar pre-empted the clean up of nightclubs today. Gone are the days of being able to test your pill at every party. The result is that more than half (50% to 90%, depending on what study you read), of so-called ecstasy pills sold in Amsterdam lack the active ingredient MDMA.

If that fact brings out the activist in you, then head via Blauwbrug (the 'blue bridge') to **Waterlooplein** (p81), where you can research the old school anarcho-squat movement at the book and magazine store **Fort van Sjakoo** (Jodenbreestraat 24, www.sjakoo.nl), which was named after a local criminal who stole from the rich, but probably didn't pass on his takings to the poor. For further research on the current squat scene, visit the website **www.squat.net**.

Otherwise, you can take the Metro from Waterlooplein to Weesperplein station, then catch tram 7 or 10 to **Vondelpark** (p133). Here, you can reflect on how the 1970s were much simpler times: to entice people to visit Amsterdam, all you had to do was borrow KLM's advertising strategy. It published posters cajoling a long-haired American audience to 'Sleep in Hippie Park' – word of mouth did the rest. Even today, Vondelpark remains a magnet for the bongo-lovers among us.

However, the surrounding streets have witnessed the turbulent events of 1980, the most violent year since World War II in the Netherlands. In February that year, an organised group of squatters reclaimed a building from which they were previously evicted at Vondelstraat 72 by constructing barricades to a punk rock soundtrack. They drew supporters and disrupted local traffic until army tanks came in to disperse the crowds. On April 30 1980, the date of Queen Beatrix's inauguration, huge riots broke out and were only quashed by tear gas being used against the demonstrators. As a result, squatting became more highly politicised, with factions emerging and infighting taking place in groups. By the mid-1980s, the protest movement was in decline.

To step back in time, take the side-street Schoolstraat, which joins up the Vondelpark to **Overtoom**. This ramshackle squatted street remains in the same condition as the whole area was back in 1980. Then go up Overtoom and turn left to reach **OCCII** (Amstelveenseweg 134, 671 7778/www.occii.org) on the southern end of Vondelpark, which retains the old-school atmosphere with a volunteer staff and an alternative agenda of bands, DJs and queer nights. The adjoining squat

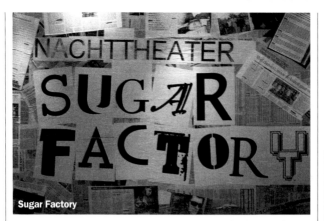

Sugar Factory

Binnenpret (Eerste Schinkelstraat 14-16, www.xs4all.nl/~binnenpr) celebrated its 25th anniversary in 2009 and still comes complete with €5 three-course vegetarian dinners several nights a week and the Info Café Bollox with its Anarchist Library. Their adjacent courtyard houses the entrance to the locally popular **Sauna Fenomeen** (http://saunafenomeen.nl), where a nudity rule is strictly enforced.

For a bit of peace and quiet, check into the John & Yoko room at the nearby Hilton Hotel (Apollolaan 138, 710 6000/www.hilton.com), where they came to have their week-long 'bed-in for peace' in 1969. If you do stay here, make sure that you pay tribute to legendary rocker and the nation's 'cuddle junkie' Herman Brood, who ended his speed-fuelled life by jumping off the roof in 2001.

For a more upbeat end to your trip, visit one of a cluster of music venues and clubs just outside the Vondelpark, around the Leidseplein. The former dairy **Melkweg** (p106), is home to music of all styles, with two decent-sized concert halls that offer an eclectic programme of club nights. Look

out for ex-RoXY DJ Joost van Bellen, who is still at the top of his game 20 years after playing at the legendary club. His RAUX nights at Melkweg are hugely popular and often feature the RoXY's original VJ Gerald van der Kaap. If you are feeling nostalgic for the '90s, look out for the 'Oud Hollandsch Acid Feest', hosted by Van Bellen's creative agency Meubel Stukken (www.meubelstukken.nl).

The **Paradiso** (p106) is a cornerstone of the live music and clubbing scene, often hosting several events in one day, whereas the **Sugar Factory** (p108) finds its niche as a 'night theatre'. Here, performance meets clubbing, with a line-up of wicked jazz and cutting-edge Electronation. Top acts from the worlds of '80s synthesiser electro play alongside current-day minimal techno, keeping the vibe fresh.

Although it may be the 21st century, and previous generations of hippies, squatters and clubbers have moved out or grown up, there are still plenty of opportunities to reminisce and relax with your friends in Amsterdam.

ITINERARIES

1000 ways to spend your weekends

From £12.99/ $19.95

Amsterdam by Area

De Waag

The Old Centre

The compelling Old Centre (aka Oud Centrum) surfs on a wave of contradiction. On one side, the surface delights of shops jostle with the fine pursuits of the mind, whereas on the other the trappings of sex jar against the icons of religion. Marked off by Centraal Station, Singel and Zwanenburgwal, the area is bisected by Damrak, which turns into Rokin south of Dam Square. The ancient Old Side (Oude Zijde) lies on the east, and the misleadingly titled New Side (Nieuwe Zijde) stretches along a gentle area to the west – the landmarks have actually been around for years, the most notable being Spui Square.

The Old Side

Straight up from Centraal Station, just beyond touristy Damrak and the **Beurs van Berlage**, lies **Dam Square**, the heart of the city since the first dam was built across the Amstel here in 1270. Once a hub

of social and political activities, today it's a convenient meeting point for tourists, the majority of whom convene under the erect **National Monument**, a 22 metre (70 foot) white obelisk dedicated to the Dutch servicemen who died in World War II. The west side of the square is flanked by the **Koninklijk Paleis** (Royal Palace), and next to it the 600-year-old **Nieuwe Kerk** stands proudly.

The root of Amsterdam's infamy is the nearby **Red Light District**, which is currently undergoing a 'clean up'. The city authorities are seeking to halve the number of prostitutes and coffeeshops in the hopes of attracting a classier line-up of cafés, shops and restaurants – and tourists. But while sex remains the main hook upon which the area hangs its reputation, it's actually secondary to window shopping. Even though people do buy an incredible amount here – sales are estimated to be worth around €500 million per year – most wander around, gazing at the live exhibits and taking in the history of the area at the **Erotic Museum** or Hash Marihuana Hemp Museum. And yet, in the centre of this illicit activity rises up the **Oude Kerk (Old Church)**, Amsterdam's oldest building, while the equally pious Museum Ons' Lieve Heer op Solder lies nearby.

At the bottom of Zeedijk, the castle-like **De Waag** (Weigh House) stands in the centre of terrace-rich Nieuwmarkt. Dating from 1488, it was built as a gatehouse and later contained an Anatomical Theatre (where Rembrandt painted his *Anatomy Lesson of Dr Nicolaes Tulp*). Yet more relative tranquillity exists on the Nes, home to many of the city's theatres and several charming cafés. When you reach the end of Nes, turn left and cross over a bridge to hunt down the **Oudemanhuis Book Market**. People have traded books, prints and sheet music here since the 18th century and it holds an enduring appeal for artists: Van Gogh chose to buy prints from the market to decorate his room.

Sights & museums

Allard Pierson Museum

Oude Turfmarkt 127 (525 2556/www. allardpiersonmuseum.nl). Tram 4, 9, 14, 16, 24, 25. **Open** 10am-5pm Mon-Fri; 1-5pm Sat, Sun. **Admission** €6.50; free-€3.25 reductions, MK. No credit cards. **Map** p65 D5 ❶

Established in Amsterdam in 1934, the Allard Pierson claims to hold one of the world's richest university collections of archaeological finds, gathered from ancient Egypt, Greece, Rome and the Near East. However, only those with a specific interest in such matters are likely not to be bored; many of the displays are dry, and will appeal just to scholars. With the exception of a few

accessible items, such as the full-size sarcophagi and the model of a Greek chariot, it's a frustrating experience.

Beurs van Berlage

Damrak 277, entrance at Beursplein 1 (530 4141/Artiflex tours 620 8112/ www.beursvanberlage.nl). Tram 4, 9, 16, 24, 25. **Open** *Exhibitions* 10am-6pm daily. *Café* 10am-6pm Mon-Sat, 11am-6pm Sun. **Admission** varies. No credit cards. **Map** p65 D2 ❷

Designed in 1896 by Hendrik Berlage as the city's stock exchange, the palatial Beurs paved the way for the Amsterdam School. Although some jaded critics thought it 'a big block with a cigar box on top', it is now considered one the country's most important architectural achievements. Built as a socialist statement, each of the nine million bricks was intended by Berlage to represent the individual, while much of the interior artwork warns against capitalism. It is now a classical concert hall, exhibition space and media centre, with its own café.

Dam Square

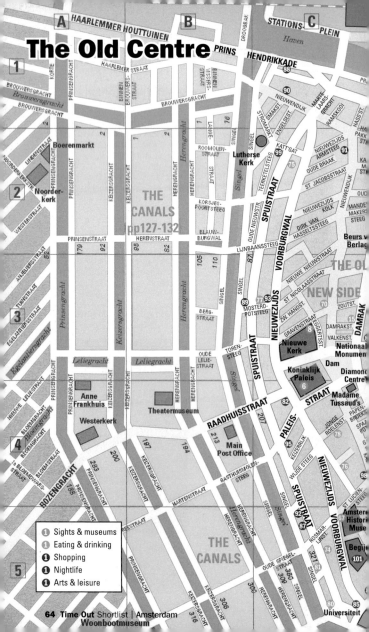

The Old Centre

A HAARLEMMER HOUTTUINEN **B** STATIONS **C** PLEIN

PRINS HENDRIKKADE

Haven

1

Boerenmarkt

Noorderkerk

2

THE CANALS
pp127-132

Lutherse Kerk

3

Leliegracht   Leliegracht

THE OLD NEW SIDE

THE OLD NEW SIDE

Beurs Berlag

Nieuwe Kerk

Nationaal Monumen

Koninklijk Paleis

Dam

Diamond Centre

4

Anne Frankhuis

Westerkerk

Theatermuseum

RAADHUISSTRAAT

Main Post Office

Madame Tussaud's

ROZENGRACHT

5

THE CANALS

THE CANALS

Amster Histori Muse

Begi

- ❶ Sights & museums
- ❶ Eating & drinking
- ❶ Shopping
- ❶ Nightlife
- ❶ Arts & leisure

Universiteit

Woonbootmuseum

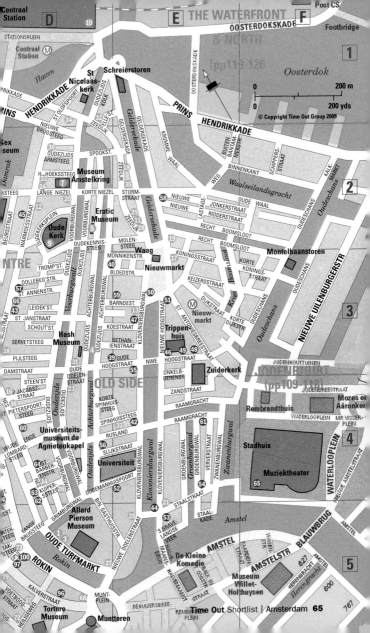

Old station, new hub

Centraal Station

Amsterdam is being ripped apart. The redevelopment activity is an attempt to right a wrong: the building of Centraal Station during 1882-89. Although it's impossible to imagine Amsterdam without its 'Old Holland'-style masterpiece (or its mirror-image, the Rijksmuseum), the building acted as a cultural marker, separating the city from its harbour and Amsterdam North across the IJ river – as well as its history as the world's richest city port during its 17th-century Golden Age.

With the scheduled completion of the Noord-Zuidlijn metro link in 2017, the north will be connected to the outlying south via Centraal Station, which is also undergoing total refurbishment. The station will finally become truly central, with two front sides: one will face across the waters towards a rapidly gentrifying north, and the other, traditional front side, will look out towards the Old Centre and the radiating horseshoe of canals with their gabled houses. It's hoped that the metro line will give a boost to the rising business centre Zuidas in the south, where many new office blocks are now lying largely empty.

Work on the 9.5 kilometre Noord-Zuidlijn started in 2003 and was always a point of controversy. Most of the aldermen responsible for initiating the project have now moved on, leaving the city with a legacy that's at best merely too expensive, and at worst out of control. The Noord-Zuidlijn has run considerably over its original budget – a staggering €1.8 billion – paid for by the council and the government. The whole project will cost the council over €600 million, not the estimated €314 million. Part of the problem lies in the difficulties of digging beneath a city built on poles; time-consuming processes had to be invented to construct tunnels 40 metres deep. Leaking walls and sinking old buildings stopped construction in March 2009, and at press time an independent commission was re-evaluating whether it was worth continuing. Watch this space: perhaps the nearly completed stations will be re-zoned as nightclubs with 24-hour opening permits by the time you arrive!

Bijzondere Collecties

Oude Turfmarkt 129 (525 7300/www.
uba.uva.nl/bijzondere_collecties). Tram 4,
9, 14, 16, 24, 25. **Open** 9.30am-5pm
Mon-Fri; 1-5pm Sat, Sun. **Map** p65 D5 ❸
They like their paper products at the
University of Amsterdam's 'Special
Collections': documents, prints, maps,
atlases, photos and endless rows of
books. The invaluable pre-1850 collection is especially strong on the history
of printing, Hebrew and Judaica stud-
ies, Protestantism and medicine; the
post-1850 collection focuses more on
meritorious design, with exhibitions of
ranging from Linnaeus prints to book
advertising from the 18th century.

Cannabis College

Oudezijds Achterburgwal 124 I (423
4420/www.cannabiscollege.com). Tram
4, 9, 14, 16, 24, 25/Metro Nieuwmarkt.
Open 11am-7pm daily. **Map** p65 D3 ❹
The college, occupying two floors in a
17th-century listed monument in the
Red Light District, provides the public
with an array of information about the
cannabis plant (including its medicinal
uses). The place is run by volunteers
and admission is free. However, staff
request a €2.50 donation if you wish to
wander around the indoor garden.

Erotic Museum

Oudezijds Achterburgwal 54 (624
7303). Tram 4, 9, 16, 24, 25/Metro
Nieuwmarkt. **Open** 11am-1am daily.
Admission €5. No credit cards. **Map**
p65 D2 ❺
The Erotic Museum resides in the heart
of the Red Light District, trying its best
to attract the punters, but it's not really sexy. Prize exhibits include an odd
bicycle-powered dildo and a few of
John Lennon's erotic drawings. Lovers
of Bettie Page will enjoy the original
photos of the S&M muse on display.

Koninklijk Paleis
(Royal Palace)

Dam (information 620 4060/tours 624
8698/www.koninklijkhuis.nl). Tram 1, 2,
4, 5, 9, 13, 14, 16, 17, 24, 25. **Open**
Jun-Aug 11am-5pm daily. *Sep-May*
noon-5pm Tues-Sun. **Admission** €7.50.
No credit cards. **Map** p64 C3/4 ❻
Originally erected in the 17th century
as the city hall, this classic building is
a symbol of the confidence that
Amsterdam felt at the beginning of its
Golden Age as the richest port in the
world. Famously built on a foundation
of 13,659 wooden piles sunk deep into
the sand, the Koninklijk Paleis was
thereby rated as the 'eighth wonder of
the world'. It was transformed into a
royal palace during harder times, after
Napoleon had made his brother,
Louis, King of the Netherlands in
1808; this era can be traced through
the fine collection of furniture on display inside. Until mid 2009, it was
closed for years of renovation, which
have clearly paid off.

Except for the statue of Atlas bearing his worldly load, which can be
seen at the back of the building, the
interior is far more impressive than
the exterior. The Citizen's Hall, with
its Baroque decoration in grand marble and bronze depicting a miniature
universe (with Amsterdam at its centre), is meant to make you feel about
as worthy as the rats carved into the
stone over the door of the Bankruptcy
Chamber. Gentler displays of creativity can be observed in the chimney
pieces, painted by the likes of
Ferdinand Bol and Govert Flinck,
pupils of Rembrandt (who had his
own sketches rejected). The building
became state property in 1936 and the
Dutch Royal family still use it for dinner parties when they feel the need to
impress international guests.

Museum Ons'
Lieve Heer op Solder

Oudezijds Voorburgwal 40 (624
6604/www.opsolder.nl). Tram 4,
9, 16, 24, 25. **Open** 10am-5pm
Mon-Sat; 1-5pm Sun. **Admission**
€7; free-€5 reductions, MK. No credit
cards. **Map** p65 D2 ❼

Nieuwe Kerk

AMSTERDAM BY AREA

has been renewed since. It is thought that the ornate oak pulpit and great organ were constructed sometime after 1645, when the building was gutted by the Great Fire. Behind the black marble tomb of naval hero Admiral de Ruyter (1607-76) – who helped to win the second Anglo-Dutch war by daringly sailing up the Medway in 1667 – is a white marble relief depicting the sea battle in which he died. Poets and Amsterdam natives including PC Hooft and Joost van den Vondel are also buried here. Bonus fact: the sundial on the tower was used to set all of the city's clocks until as recently as 1890. Today, the church hosts the occasional concert and regular, generally excellent, archaeological and modern art exhibitions.

Oude Kerk (Old Church)

Oudekerksplein 23 (625 8284/www. oudekerk.nl). Tram 4, 9, 16, 24, 25. **Open** 11am-5pm Mon-Sat; 1-5.30pm Sun. **Admission** €5; free-€4 reductions, MK. No credit cards. **Map** p65 D2 ❾

The Oude Kerk began life as a simple wooden chapel in 1306, but today rates as Amsterdam's most interesting church. It's easy to imagine the Sunday Mass chaos during its heyday in the mid-1500s, when it had 38 altars, each with its own guild-sponsored priest. Now it serves more as a radical contrast to the surrounding Red Light District, but still holds lessons: the inscription over the bridal chamber states 'marry in haste, mourn in leisure'. Keep your eyes peeled for the floor grave of Rembrandt's wife Saskia, who died in 1642. Also note the Gothic and Renaissance façade above the northern portal, and the stained-glass windows, parts of which date from the 16th and 17th centuries. For shock value, check out the carvings in the choir benches of men evacuating their bowels – they tell a moralistic tale. Occasional art shows exhibit a range of fascinating subjects, from contemporary Aboriginal art to the World Press Photo Exhibition.

Originally known as the Museum Amstelkring, this place is a well-kept secret. The main attraction is upstairs, and goes by the name: 'Our Sweet Lord in the Attic'. Built in 1663, this attic church was used by Catholics during the 17th century, when they were banned from worshipping after the Alteration. The altarpiece features a painting by the noted 18th-century artist Jacob de Wit. Meanwhile, the beautifully preserved rooms on the lower floor offer a realistic glimpse of what life was like during the 17th century. The museum will remain open during renovations which began in the summer of 2009, but there may be disruptions for visitors.

Nieuwe Kerk (New Church)

Dam (626 8168/recorded information 638 6909/www.nieuwekerk.nl). Tram 1, 2, 4, 5, 9, 13, 14, 16, 17, 24, 25. **Open** 10am-6pm Mon-Wed, Fri-Sun; 10am-10pm Thur. **Admission** varies. No credit cards. **Map** p64 C3 ❽

The sprightly Nieuwe Kerk dates from 1408, but due to a series of fires much

Eating & drinking

1e Klas

Line 2B, Centraal Station (625 0131/
www.restaurant1eklas.nl). Tram 1, 2,
4, 5, 9, 13, 16, 17, 24, 25, 26. **Open**
8.30am-11pm daily. €€€. **Café**. **Map**
p65 D1 ⑩

This former brasserie for first-class
commuters is now open to anyone who
wants to kill some time in style, while
waiting for their train – with a full meal
or just a snack. The delightful art nouveau interior will whisk visitors
straight back to the 1890s. Other great
eating options can be found in the west
tunnel: try Julia's (www.juliasophetsta-
tion.nl) for healthy pasta or Shakies
(www.shakies.nl) for organic juices,
coffees and bagels.

A Fusion

Zeedijk 130 (330 4068). Tram 4, 9, 16,
24, 25/Metro Nieuwmarkt. **Open** noon-
11pm daily. €€€. **Chinese**. **Map** p65
E2 ⑪

This laid-back, loungey affair looks as
though it's been taking notes from the
hipper, more happening side of NYC's
Chinatown. The dark and inviting interior harbours big screens playing Hong
Kong music videos, bubble teas
(lychee!), and some of the tastiest pan-
Asian dishes in town.

De Bakkerswinkel

Warmoesstraat 69 (489 8000/www.
bakkerswinkel.nl). Tram 1, 2, 4, 5, 9,
13, 16, 17, 24, 25, 26. **Open** 8am-6pm
Tue-Fri; 8am-5pm Sat; 10am-5pm Sun.
Café. **Map** p65 D2 ⑫

De Bakkerswinkel is a fantastic little
bakery and tearoom where you can
indulge lunchtime hunger pangs with
lovingly prepared sandwiches, hearty
soups and the most divine slabs of
quiche you've ever tasted. Check its
website for other branches around town.

De Bekeerde Suster

Kloveniersburgwal 6-8 (423 0112/www.
beiaardgroep.nl). Tram 4, 9, 16, 24,

Brasserie Harkema

25/Metro Nieuwmarkt. **Open** 3pm-1am
Mon-Fri; noon-2am Sat; noon-midnight
Sun. **Bar**. **Map** p65 E3 ⑬

Those shiny copper vats and gleaming
pipes aren't just for appearances: the
Amsterdam Steambrewery Company
has been making beer on site since
2002. Home brews include the refresh-
ing Witte Ros and seasonal *bocks*, as
well as a list of international beers that
leans heavily towards Belgium.

Brasserie Harkema

Nes 67 (428 2222/www.brasserie
harkema.nl). Tram 4, 9, 14, 16, 24, 25.
Open 11am-midnight daily. €€€.
French. **Map** p65 D4 ⑭

This former tobacco factory has titil-
lated the local scene with its sense of
designer space, excellent wines and a
kitchen that stays open late, serving
reasonably priced European classics.

Brasserie De Roode Leeuw

Damrak 93-94 (555 0666/www.
restaurantderoodeleeuw.com). Tram 4,
9, 14, 16, 24, 25. Open 7am-10.30pm
daily. €€€€. **Dutch**. **Map** p64 C3 ⑮

What's brewing?

Brouwerij de Prael

Who says that psychiatric patients and alcohol shouldn't mix? The new brewery and shop **De Prael** in the heart of the Red Light District is proving all the critics wrong, and its positive benefits to the local community are offering liquid food for thought. In the process, the project's two founders are putting their obsessions to good use.

Originating a decade ago in an industrial estate on the outskirts of town, De Prael was set up on the basis of its owners' background in mental healthcare and love of brewing to the sound of quirky local songs. By establishin De Prael as a 'social firm', with commercial objectives, they were able to invest all the earnings back into the foundation. Currently they employ 70 staff,

all of whom have a psychiatric condition: 80% are schizophrenic and the others suffer from borderline personality disorders. Yes, there are plenty of jokes, but the rules are simple: no drinking on the job and be on time.

All the beers from the De Prael brewery share their names with tears-in-your-beers singers. For instance, Mary is called after Mary Servaes (aka the Zangeres Zonder Naam) and as a triple, its strong alcohol content makes it as robust as the lady herself. Johnny, a blonde beer, was named after the fair-haired Johnny Jordaan; Heintje is as fresh and fruity as Hendrik (Hein) Nicolaas Theodoor Simons was reputed to be.

In stark contrast to the namesakes, the bottle labels are beautiful examples of understated design. Everything has been carefully thought out, down to the finest detail. And no doubt the bar will serve everyone's special needs, when it is unveiled by 2010. In the meanwhile, check out the store or join one of the daily tours.

Afterwards, perhaps you can keep up the theme by dining at the **Freud** (Spaarndammerstraat 424, 688 5548, www.restaurant freud.nl), a restaurant run by former psychiatric patients.

Brouwerij de Prael
Oudezijds Voorburgwal 30 (408 4470/www.deprael.nl). A five-minute walk from Centraal Station. **Open** *9am-4.30pm Mon-Fri.* **Store open** *12.30-5pm Mon; 10am-6pm Tues-Wed, Fri; 10am-9pm Thur, 11am-5pm Sat.*

This brasserie is housed in the oldest covered terrace in Amsterdam. As you might guess, it harks back to classier times, but what's more surprising is its embrace of the digital age as a Wi-Fi point. It specialises in pricey Dutch fare, and also boasts a range of wines from all over the Netherlands.

Bubbles and Wines
Nes 37 (422 3318/www.bubblesand wines.com). Tram 4, 9, 14, 16, 24, 25. **Open** 3.30pm-1am Mon-Sat; 2-9pm Sun. **Bar**. **Map** p65 D4 ⑯

A long, low-ceilinged room with the feel of a wine cellar, one with mood lighting and banquettes. There are more than 50 wines by the glass and 180 by the bottle; posh nosh includes Osetra caviar, truffle cheese and foie gras. The final bill is unlikely to suit the faint-hearted or light of wallet.

Café Bern
Nieuwmarkt 9 (622 0034). Tram 4, 9, 16, 24, 25/Metro Nieuwmarkt. **Open** 4pm-1am daily. **€€**. No credit cards. **Dutch**. **Map** p65 E3 ⑰

Despite its Swiss origins, the Dutch adopted the cheese fondue as a noted 'national dish' long ago. Sample its culinary conviviality at this suitably cosy bar that was allegedly established – oddly enough – by a nuclear physicist.

Café 't Mandje
NEW *Zeedijk 63 (622.5375/www.cafet mandje.nl). 4, 9, 16, 24, 25/Metro Nieuwmarkt.* **Open** 5pm-1am Mon, Tues; 4pm-1am Wed, Thur; 2pm-3am Fri, Sat; 2pm-1am Sun. No credit cards. **Café**. **Map** p65 E2 ⑱

This historical café open for more than 80 years, was the city's first (moderately) openly gay and lesbian bar. The proprietor Bet van Beeren, who died over 40 years ago, was legendary for her role aś (probably) the world's first lesbian biker chick. It was closed for years but reopened in 2008 after a renovation that suggests that, yes, time can stand still.

Café Stevens
Geldersekade 123 (620 6970). Tram 4, 9, 16, 24, 25/Metro Nieuwmarkt. **Open** 10am-1am Mon-Thur, Sun; 10am-3am Fri, Sat. No credit cards. **Bar**. **Map** p65 E2 ⑲

With a living-room feel, plenty of seats and views over De Waag, this is a perfect spot to while away a day. The patrons are mainly locals, with a good number of tourists and students drinking in the view and sinking a few with sandwiches and (excellent) thick chips.

Centra
Lange Niezel 29 (622 3050). Tram 4, 9, 14, 16, 24, 25. **Open** 1.30-10.30pm daily. **€€**. No credit cards. **Spanish**. **Map** p65 D2 ⑳

Good, wholesome, homely Spanish cooking with a suitably unpretentious atmosphere to match. The tapas, lamb and fish dishes are all great, and the place gets justifiably busy as a result.

De Doelen
Kloveniersburgwal 125 (624 9023). Tram 4, 9, 14, 16, 24, 25/Metro Waterlooplein. **Open** 9am-1am Mon-Thu; 9am-3am Fri, Sat; 10am-1am Sun. No credit cards. **Bar**. **Map** p65 E5 ㉑

An old-fashioned drinking hole – complete with gritted floors – on one of the main tourist drags. Rough edges are smoothed by sophisticated breakfasts (fruit smoothies, muesli), international snacks (houmous, tapenade) and frosty jugs of sangria in summer, along with bands on Sundays.

Getto
Warmoesstraat 51 (421 5151/www. getto.nl). Tram 1, 2, 4, 5, 9, 13, 16, 17, 24, 25, 26. **Open** 4pm-1am Tue-Thur; 4pm-2am Fri, Sat; 4pm-midnight Sun. **€€**. **Global**. **Map** p65 D2 ㉒

Cheap and cheerful food is served at Getto in surprisingly plush surroundings, catering to a mostly gay and lesbian crowd. On Wednesdays all burger dinners cost €10. Combined with the popular weekday cocktail

Snack attack

Street food is very popular in Amsterdam. As proof, note the success of noodle maestros Wagamama and the restaurant of club **Trouw Amsterdam** (see box p117). But there are cheaper options: the rolled 'pizzas' from Turkish bakeries, Dutch *broodjes* (sandwiches) from bakers and butchers, and the more spicy Surinamese *broodjes* from 'Chin-Indo-Suri' snack bars (see box p103).

Fast food can tell you a lot about the tastes of a nation. You simply must try a raw herring: the best time is between May and July when the *nieuw* (new) catch hits the stands, as it's then that their flesh is at its sweetest, since the high fat content has not yet been burned off by the arduous business of breeding. You don't need extras like onions or pickles, and they're cheap as chips.

Speaking of chips, the best are the chunky Belgian ones (*Vlaamse*), double-fried to ensure a crispy exterior and creamy interior. Enjoy them along with your pick of toppings, such as

oorlog (war): mayo, spicy peanut sauce and onions. **Vleminckx** (p75) and **Manneken Pis** (Damrak 41) are two of the best places to eat them.

The local term for a greasy snack – *vette hap* – is translated literally as 'fat bite', which says a lot for the honesty of the Dutch. At the ubiquitous Febo, you can put your change into a glowing *automaat* and, in return, get a hot hamburger, *bamibal* (a deep-fried noodle ball of vaguely Indonesian descent), or a *kaas soufflé* (a cheese treat). The most popular choice is the *kroket*, a mélange of meat and potato with a deep-fried skin, best served on a bun with hot mustard. The best place to try these is **Van Dobben** (Korte Reguliersdwarsstraat 5-9, 624 4200), just off Rembrandtplein. While this 1945-vintage late-night venue is the uncontested champion when it comes to the *kroket*, you can also find a more refined shrimp variation at nearby bakery **Holtkamp** (Vijzelgracht 15, 624 8757). That's right folks, just give grease a chance.

happy hours and two-for-one drinks between 11pm and midnight, this is the ideal place for an inexpensive date.

Greenhouse

Oudezijds Voorburgwal 191 (627 1739/www.greenhouse.org). Tram 4, 9, 14, 16, 24, 25. **Open** 9am-1am daily. No credit cards. **Coffeeshop**. Map p65 D4 ㉓

This legendary coffeeshop tenders highly potent weed with prices to match. It's won the Cannabis Cup over 30 times and, with the Grand Hotel next door, celebrities occasionaly stop by to get stoned with the best of them. The vibe inside has become a little commercial, but it's still worth a peek, if only to see the beautifully handmade interior, with sunken floors, ornate mosaic stones and elaborate blown-glass lamps.

Greenhouse Effect

Warmoesstraat 53-55 (624 4974/www. greenhouse-effect.nl). Tram 4, 9, 16, 24, 25. **Open** *Coffeeshop*: 9am-1am daily. *Bar* 9am-1am Mon-Thur, Sun; 9am-3am Fri, Sat. No credit cards. **Coffeeshop**. Map p65 D2 ㉔

This snug shop is shaped like a long, sleek train carriage, and features a polished interior and reliably high-quality ganja. It tends to fill up fast, but there's a separate space with the same name next door, where you'll discover a full bar as well as regular DJs. If the drink and dope combination renders you immobile, make a beeline for the hotel (p165) upstairs.

De Jaren

Nieuwe Doelenstraat 20-22 (625 5771/ www.cafe-de-jaren.nl). Tram 4, 9, 14, 16, 24, 25. **Open** 10am-1am Mon-Thur, Sun (kitchen closes 11pm); 10am-2am Fri, Sat (kitchen closes midnight). **Bar**. Map p65 E5 ㉕

An entire cross-section of Amsterdam – students, tourists, lesbigays, trendy mums and the fashion pack – come here for lunch, coffee or something stronger throughout the day, which can make it difficult to get a seat. Be prepared to fight for a spot on the popular Amstel-side outdoor terrace on sunny summer afternoons.

Kapitein Zeppos

Gebed Zonder End 5 (624 2057/www. zeppos.nl). Tram 4, 9, 14, 16, 24, 25. **Open** 12am-1am Mon-Thur, Sun; 12am-3am Fri, Sat. **Bar**. Map p65 D4 ㉖

A hidey-hole down the poetically named 'Prayer Without End' alley – a reference to the Santa Clara convent that stood here in the 17th century. Now it's a light-drenched, multifaceted café and restaurant with an understated Belgian theme: it's named after a 1960s Flemish TV detective, there's Belgian beer on tap and the most frequently heard soundtrack of choice is chanson.

Katoen

Oude Turfmarkt 153 (626 2635/www. goodfoodgroup.nl). Tram 4, 9, 14, 16, 24, 25. **Open** 9am-1am Mon-Thur; 9am-3am Fri, Sat; 10am-1am Sun. No credit cards. **Café**. Map p65 D5 ㉗

If shopping on Kalverstraat gets too much, run screaming across Rokin to this oasis of calm on the edge of the Old Centre. It has the stripped-down good looks of the 1950s (Formica tables, polished wood) and a satisfying but inventive lunch menu of salads, rolls and wraps.

Latei

Zeedijk 143 (625 7485/www.latei. net). Tram 4, 9, 16, 24, 25/Metro Nieuwmarkt. **Open** 8am-6pm Mon-Wed; 8am-10pm Thur, Fri; 9am-10pm Sat; 11am-6pm Sun. No credit cards. **Café**. Map p65 E2 ㉘

Packed with kitsch bric-a-brac and funky Finnish wallpaper – all of which, wallpaper included, is for sale – this little café serves up healthy juices and snacks all day, plus vegetarian dinners based around its immaculately prepared speciality couscous.

Nam Kee

Zeedijk 111-113 (624 3470/www.nam kee.nl). Tram 4, 9, 16, 24, 25/Metro Nieuwmarkt. **Open** noon-11pm Mon-Sat; noon-10pm Sun. **€€**. No credit cards. **Chinese**. Map p65 E2 ㉙

Cheap, terrific food has earned this Chinese joint a devoted following – the oysters in black bean sauce have achieved cult status. If it's busy, try the sister operation and dim sum maestro Nam Tin nearby (Jodenbreestraat 11-13, 428 8508), or neighbour New King (Zeedijk 115-117, 625 2180).

New Seasons

NEW *Warmoesstraat 19 (625 6125). Tram 1, 2, 4, 5, 9, 13, 16, 17, 24, 25, 26.* **Open** 1-11pm Tues-Sun. **€**. **Malaysian**. Map p65 D2 ㉚

While advertising itself as Malaysian, this simple restaurant also serves Chinese, Japanese and Indonesian dishes, and most are cooked to perfection. Prices are very reasonable.

Oriental City

Oudezijds Voorburgwal 177-179 (626 8352/www.oriental-city.nl). Tram 4, 9, 14, 16, 24, 25. **Open** 11.30am-11.30pm daily. **€€€**. **Chinese**. Map p65 D3 ㉛

The views from Oriental City are truly spectacular, overlooking Damstraat, the Royal Palace and the canals, plus the dim sum is among the best you'll find in Amsterdam.

Queen's Head

Zeedijk 20 (420 2475/www.queens head.nl). Tram 1, 2, 4, 5, 9, 13, 16, 17, 24, 25, 26. **Open** 4pm-1am Mon-Thur, Sun; 4pm-3am Fri, Sat. No credit cards. **Bar**. Map p65 D1 ㉜

The Queen's is a fun and attitude-free gay bar with a similarly minded clientele, plus a great view over a canal at the back. It holds regular special nights, with drag acts and DJs. It also hosts parties on Queen's Day (30 April), plus skin nights, football nights (during the cup season), Eurovision Song Contest nights and so on.

Rusland

Rusland 16 (627 9468). Tram 4, 9, 14, 16, 24, 25/Metro Nieuwmarkt/ Waterlooplein. **Open** 10am-midnight Mon-Thur, Sun; 10am-1am Fri, Sat. No credit cards. **Coffeeshop**. Map p65 E4 ㉝

Well known as the longest-running coffeeshop in the city, this 'Russian' den has hardwood floors and colourful cushions that complement an efficient multi-level design. The top floor has a bar which serves a selection of over 40 different loose teas and healthy fruit shakes; below is a decent pipe display. It's off the well-trodden tourist path, which means cheaper prices and smaller crowds for the punter.

Skek

Zeedijk 4-8 (427 0551/www.skek.nl). Tram 1, 2, 4, 5, 9, 13, 16, 17, 24, 25, 26. **Open** noon-1am Mon-Thur, Sun; noon-3am Fri, Sat. **Café**. Map p65 D1 ㉞

This café-cum-music joint is run by the student organisation that heads up the Filmtheater Kriterion, and it focuses on value and quality. While student visitors lap up the great discounts, other music lovers will probably get more out of the regular singer/songwriter and jazz shows on offer. They also serve nice, affordable lunches and dinners.

Thaise Snackbar Bird

Zeedijk 77 (snack bar 420 6289/restaurant 620 1442/www.thai-bird.nl). Tram 1, 2, 4, 5, 9, 13, 16, 17, 24, 25, 26. **Open** *Snack bar* 2-10pm daily. *Restaurant* 5-11pm daily. **€€€**. **Thai**. Map p65 E2 ㉟

Easily the most authentic Thai place in town. No doubt because of this, it's also the most crowded, but it's worth waiting for all the same, whether you drop by for *tom yum* soup or go for a full-blown meal. If you plan to linger, settle down in the restaurant (Zeedijk 72-74) across the street rather than the snack bar itself.

Betsy Palmer p77

Van Kerkwijk

Nes 41 (620 3316). Tram 4, 9, 14, 16, 24, 25. **Open** 11am-1am Mon-Thur, Sun; 11am-3am Fri, Sat. No credit cards. **Bar. Map** p65 D4 ❸
Far from the bustle of Dam square, though actually just a few strides away, Van Kerkwijk stands on one of Amsterdam's most charming streets. Airy by day, romantic and candlelit by night, it's equally good for group chats or tête-à-têtes. Lunch brings sandwiches and the evening more substantial food, although the emphasis is as much on genteel drinking. Take care on the almost vertical stairs leading down to the toilets if you've overindulged.

Vleminckx

Voetboogsteeg 33 (no phone). Tram 1, 2, 5. **Open** 11am-6pm Mon-Sat; noon-5.30pm Sun. **€**. No credit cards. **Chips**. **Map** p65 D5 ❸
Chunky Belgian chips served with your choice of toppings. Opt for the *oorlog* (war) variety: chips with mayo, spicy peanut sauce and onions.

Wynand Fockink

Pijlsteeg 31 (639 2695/www.wynand-fockink.nl). Tram 4, 9, 14, 16, 24, 25. **Open** 3-9pm daily. No credit cards.

Bar. Map p65 D3 ❸
Tucked away in a side alley behind the Krasnapolsky and largely unchanged since 1679, this tasting house has been a meeting place for Freemasons since the year dot, with past visitors including Churchill and Chagall. The menu of liqueurs and *jenevers* reads like a list of surrealist artworks: Parrot Soup; The Longer the Better; Rose Without Thorns.

Shopping

2PR

Oude Hoogstraat 10-12 (421 6329/www.2pr.eu). Tram 4, 9, 14, 16, 24, 25. **Open** noon-7pm Mon; 10am-7pm Tue, Wed, Fri, Sat; 10am-9pm Thur; noon-7pm Sun. **Map** p65 E3 ❸
This clever little number is just for the boys. Two shops side by side on Oude Hoogstraat offer urban streetwear and killer threads from the likes of Helmut Lang, Psycho Cowboy and D-Squared.

Absolute Danny

Oudezijds Achterburgwal 78 (421 0915/www.absolutedanny.com). Tram 4, 9, 16, 24, 25. **Open** 11am-9pm Mon-Sat; noon-9pm Sun. **Map** p65 D3 ❹

AMSTERDAM BY AREA

Free for all

Noordermarkt p132

Cheapskates, take note: you don't have to spend a fortune to have fun in Amsterdam. This list of activities shows just how easily budget visitors can have fun for free across the capital.

- The view from **NEMO**'s (p122).
- Complimentary coffee at various branches of **Albert Heijn** (p87).
- The **Rijksmuseum**'s garden on its west side (p134).
- Open-air concerts and the great outdoors of **Vondelpark** (p133).
- The **Civic Guard Gallery** at the Amsterdams Historisch Museum (p83), plus the neighbouring atmospheric inner courtyard **Begijnhof** (p81).
- **Noordermarkt** flea market on Monday mornings (p132).
- Tuesday lunchtime concerts at the **Muziektheater** (p109).
- Wednesday lunchtime concerts at the **Concertgebouw** (p141).
- Exploring the **hofjes** – courtyard almshouses – of the Jordaan.
- Tasting free samples of organic foodstuffs at the Saturday farmers' market on **Boerenmarkt** (p130).
- Smelling the flowers on sale at the **Bloemenmarkt** (p105).
- Checking the biggest barometer in the Netherlands; the neon light on the **Hotel Okura Amsterdam** (p177) tells you what tomorrow's weather will be like: blue for good; green for bad; white for changeable.
- Watching horseriding in Holland's **Manege** (Vondelstraat 140, 618 0942).
- Lounging at one of the city beaches like **Blijburg** (p123).
- Attending the opening of a new exhibition; Fridays at happening art hangout **Chiellerie** (p80).
- Going alternative queer clubbing monthly at **Hot Peper**, in the fabulous De Peper café (p137).
- Reading through the international papers and glossies at the brand new public library **Openbare Bibliotheek Amsterdam** (p122). And then proceeding to the top floor café to take in the view.
- Seeing top-notch bands recording for radio at **3voor12** (p80).
- Visiting the **City Archives** (Vijzelstraat 32, 2511 511).

Discover sexy accessories, ranging from rubber clothing to erotic toothbrushes at this fetish shop.

Betsy Palmer

Rokin 9-15 (422 1040/www.betsy palmer.com). Tram 4, 9, 14, 16, 24, 25. **Open** noon-6.30pm Mon; 10am-6.30pm Tue-Wed, Fri; 10am-9pm Thur; 10am-6pm Sat; 1-6pm Sun. **Map** p65 D4 ④
Tired of seeing the same shoes in every store, Dutch fashion buyer Gertie Gerards put her money where her mouth was and set up shop. Betsy Palmer is her in-house label, which sits alongside a huge variety of other labels that change regularly as they sell out.

Book Exchange

Kloveniersburgwal 58 (626 6266/www. bookexchange.nl). Tram 4, 9, 14, 16, 24, 25/Metro Nieuwmarkt. **Open** 10am-6pm Mon-Sat; 11.30am-4pm Sun. No credit cards. **Map** p65 E4 ④
The owner of this bibliophiles' treasure trove is a shrewd buyer who is willing to do trade deals. Choose from a range of second-hand English and American titles (mainly paperbacks).

Condomerie het Gulden Vlies

Warmoesstraat 141 (627 4174/www. condomerie.com). Tram 4, 9, 14, 16, 25. **Open** 11am-6pm Mon-Sat. **Map** p65 D3 ④
An astounding variety of innovative and imaginative rubbers of the non-erasing kind, designed to wrap up trouser snakes of all shapes and sizes.

Droog Design

Staalstraat 7A/B (523 5059/www. droogdesign.nl). Tram 4, 9, 14, 16, 24, 25. **Open** noon-6pm Tue-Sat. **Map** p65 E5 ④
This internationally acclaimed Dutch design collective has its own shop, with some of the wittiest ranges around: Jurgen Bey, Richard Hutten, Hella Jongerius and Marcel Wanders.

Geels & Co

Warmoesstraat 67 (624 0683/www. geels.nl). Tram 4, 9, 14, 16, 24, 25. **Open** 9.30am-6pm Mon-Sat. **Map** p65 D2 ④
Here you'll find coffee beans and loose teas, in addition to a wide range of coffee-making contraptions, brewing devices and decorative utensils. Head upstairs and you'll find a museum of hot beverage related equipment, open on Saturday afternoons.

Head Shop

Kloveniersburgwal 39 (624 9061/www. headshop.nl). Tram 4, 9, 14, 16, 24, 25/Metro Nieuwmarkt. **Open** 11am-6pm daily. **Map** p65 E3 ④
Land at the Head Shop, which opened 40 years ago, and you'll think Jimi, Janis and Jim are still around. It stocks pipes, bongs, jewellery, incense, books, mushrooms (actually 'truffles', since the law changed in 2009) and spores.

Jacob Hooy & Co

Kloveniersburgwal 12 (624 3041/www. jacobhooy.nl). Tram 4, 9, 14, 16, 24, 25/Metro Nieuwmarkt. **Open** 1-6pm Mon; 10am-6pm Tue-Fri; 10am-5pm Sat. **Map** p65 E3 ④
Sells a huge variety of medicinal herbs, teas, homeopathic remedies and cosmetics. The untouched 18th-century interior is worth a visit in itself.

Joe's Vliegerwinkel

Nieuwe Hoogstraat 19 (625 0139/www. joesvliegerwinkel.nl). Tram 4, 9, 14, 16, 24, 25/Metro Nieuwmarkt. **Open** noon-6pm Tue-Fri; 12am-5pm Sat. **Map** p65 E3 ④
Kites, kites and yet more kites. Also a quirky array of boomerangs, yo-yos and kaleidoscopes at this wonderfully colourful shop.

't Klompenhuisje

Nieuwe Hoogstraat 9A (622 8100/ www.klompenhuisje.nl). Tram 4, 9, 14/ Metro Nieuwmarkt. **Open** 10am-6pm Mon-Sat. **Map** p65 E3 ④

Delightfully crafted and reasonably priced children shoes, traditional clogs and handmade leather and woollen slippers are available here.

Nieuwmarkt Antique Market

Nieuwmarkt (no phone). Tram 4, 9, 14, 16, 24, 25/Metro Nieuwmarkt. **Open** *May-Oct* 9am-5pm Sun. **Map** p65 E3 ㊿

A few streets away from the ladies in the windows, this antiques and bric-a-brac market attracts browsers looking for other kinds of pleasures. Old books, furniture and objets d'art.

Oriental Commodities

Nieuwmarkt 27 (626 2797/www.orientalgroup.nl). Tram 4, 9, 14, 16, 24, 25/Metro Nieuwmarkt. **Open** 9am-6pm Mon-Sat; 10.30am-5pm Sun. No credit cards. **Map** p65 E3 ㉛

Visit Amsterdam's largest Chinese food emporium for the full spectrum of Asian foods and ingredients, ranging from shrimp- and scallop-flavoured egg noodles to fried tofu balls and fresh veg. You can also seek out a fine range of traditional Chinese cooking appliances and utensils.

Oudemanhuis Book Market

Oudemanhuispoort (no phone). Tram 4, 9, 14, 16, 24, 25. **Open** 9am-5pm Mon-Sat. No credit cards. **Map** p65 E4 ㉜

People have been buying and selling books, prints and sheet music from this shop since the 18th century.

Palm Guitars

s'Gravelandseveer 5 (422 0445/www.palmguitars.nl). Tram 4, 9, 14, 16, 24, 25. **Open** noon-6pm Wed-Sat. **Map** p65 E5 ㉝

Palm Guitars stocks new, antique, used and rare musical instruments (and their parts). If you're lucky, a roots musician may be around, jamming with a few locals.

Puccini Bomboni

Staalstraat 17 (626 5474/www.puccinibomboni.com). Tram 4, 9, 14/Metro Waterlooplein. **Open** noon-6pm Sun, Mon; 9am-6pm Tue-Sat. **Map** p65 E4 ㉞

Tamarind, thyme, lemongrass, pepper and gin are just some of the flavours of these delicious and imaginative handmade chocolates, all lacking in artificial ingredients. Business is going so well that Puccini Bomboni recently opened a second shop at Singel 184 (427 8341, open noon-6pm Mon; 11am-6pm Tue-Sat; noon-5pm Sun).

Tom's Skate Shop

Oude Hoogstraat 35-37 (625 4922/www.tomsskateshop.nl). Tram 4, 9, 16, 24, 25/Metro Nieuwmarkt. **Open** noon-6pm Mon; 10am-6pm Tue-Sat; noon-6pm Sun. **Map** p65 E3 ㉟

Dual-gender gear from the likes of Nike SB, Vans, Zoo York and local label Rockwell. Also in stock are limited edition trainers, sunnies by Electric and plenty of skateboards.

WonderWood

Rusland 3 (625 3738/www.wonderwood.nl). Tram 4, 9, 16, 24, 25. **Open** noon-6pm Wed-Sat. **Map** p65 D4 ㊱

The name says it all: wonderfully sculpted wood in the form of shopmade originals, re-editions of global classics and original plywood from the 1940s and '50s. Wonderful.

Nightlife

Winston Kingdom

Warmoesstraat 131 (623 1380/www.winston.nl). Tram 4, 9, 16, 24, 25. **Open** 9pm-3am Mon-Thur, Sun; 9pm-4am Fri, Sat. No credit cards. **Map** p65 D3 ㊲

An intimate venue that attracts a mixed crowd with its alternative rock and independent dance. Winston's yearly *Popprijs* (pop prize) gives hope to many student rock bands; Cheeky Mondays brings relief at the beginning

Red light blues

Are you a loud, obnoxious tourist prone to trawling through the Red Light District in a drunken pack? If so, your time is running out. In 2008, a plan was launched to clean up the infamous district. When he presented Project 1012, deputy mayor Lodewijk Asscher cited his inspiration as the clean-up of New York City by mayor Rudy Giuliani. What he didn't mention was the vast difference between the sizes of the two cities.

The city started by purchasing properties owned by 'Fat' Charles Geerts, a landlord who rented window spaces to prostitutes. New legislation has allowed the city to withdraw property rights from those suspected of criminal activities. Even the best-known 'gentleman's club', Yab Yum, has been closed down. The city aims to continue buying up windows, altering the zoning plan and replacing dubious businesses like coffeeshops, with galleries, high-end bars and restaurants.

For PR value, some windows are now 'fashion booths', as part of the intiative Red Light Fashion (www.redlightfashionamsterdam. nl), in which designers such as couture talent Jan Taminiau and streetwear whizz Bas Kosters, are offered former bordello rooms as affordable studios for a year. And a project running until late 2009 encourages artists to use vacated window spaces for studios on Korsjespoortsteeg and Bergstraat, (www.redlightartamsterdam.nl).

Furthermore, there is some flexibility: the mini Red Light District between the Singel and Spuistraat that was threatened by closure can stay open, since the prostitutes have proven they were offering a social service in the form of 'social single sex' to elderly local men.

Although most Amsterdammers support the idea of stamping out the criminal elements behind the sex and drug traffic, many say the plans will deter tourism. Others argue the area is already the closest thing to a happy safe sex Disneyland. But the area is certainly changing; drunken hordes may soon be a thing of the past.

fo the working week with jungle and drum 'n' bass; and other nights see everything in live music from garage to folk to funky ska.

Arts & leisure

Amsterdam Marionetten Theater

Nieuwe Jonkerstraat 8 (620 8027/www. marionettentheater.nl). Tram 1, 2, 4, 5, 9, 13, 16, 17, 24, 25, 26. **Map** p65 E2 ❺❽

Opera as you've never seen it before. Picture a scene with puppets wearing rich velvet costumes expert puppeteers and classic works by Mozart and Offenbach, and you'll have an idea of what the marionette theatre is all about. One of the last outposts of an old European tradition, the theatre also offers private lunches, dinners or high teas, to be taken while the puppets perform. Delightful.

Bethaniënklooster

Barndesteeg 6B (625 0078/www. bethanienklooster.nl). Tram 4, 9, 14, 16, 24, 25/Metro Nieuwmarkt. No credit cards. **Map** p65 E3 ❺❾

Hidden down a small alley between Damstraat and the Nieuwmarkt, this former monastery is a wonderful stage for new classical and jazz talent to cut its musical teeth. In between enjoying free public performances by Amsterdam's top music students, you'll also have the chance to tune into some reputable ensembles and quartets.

De Brakke Grond

Nes 45 (622 6866/www.brakke grond.nl). Tram 4, 9, 14, 16, 24, 25. No credit cards. **Map** p65 D4 ❻⓪

Belgian culture does stretch beyond beer, and De Brakke Grond is here to prove it. Mind you, some good Belgian beer will go down a treat after a fix of progressive Flemish theatre, and if you're lucky you might find an actor or two joining you at the bar of the adjoining café/restaurant.

3voor12

Raamgracht 58 (320 9448/www. chiellerie.nl). Metro Nieuwmarkt. No credit cards. **Open** 2-6pm daily (varies for exhibitions) **Map** p65 E4 ❻❶

This place is home to former 'Night Mayor' Chiel van Zelst. Boasting a new exhibition every week or two culled from members of the local arts scene, the gallery feels more like a hangout than mere art hangar.

Comedy Theatre

Nes 110 (422 2777/www.comedy theater.nl). Tram 4, 9, 14, 16, 24, 25. **Map** p65 D4 ❻❷

This old tobacco hall is now a comedy theatre on the city's most venerable theatre street. Hyping itself as the 'club house' for comedians, the programming combines politically hard-hitting performers with straightforward stand up. Expect to see local legends like Javier Guzman, as well as international ones such as Tom Rhodes or Lewis Black. To make sure that at least some of the acts are English-speaking on the night, it's best to phone the venue in advance.

De Engelenbak

Nes 71 (626 3644/www.engelenbak.nl). Tram 4, 9, 14, 16, 24, 25. **Map** p65 D4 ❻❸

Theatre productions by amateurs is what you get at De Engelenbak. The main draw is Open Bak, an open-stage event (10.30pm Tue) where anything goes: it's the longest-running theatre programme in the country, where everybody gets their 15 minutes of dramatic fame. Make sure you arrive half an hour early to get a ticket (€8.50), and on other nights bear in mind that the best groups tend to stage performances between Thursday and Saturday.

Frascati

Nes 63 (751 6400/tickets: 626 6866/ www.theaterfrascati.nl). Tram 4, 9, 14, 16, 24, 25. No credit cards. **Map** p65 D4 ❻❹

A cornerstone of progressive Dutch theatre since the 1960s, Frascati gives promising artists the chance to put their productions on one of its three stages. Their mission: to challenge the bounds of traditional theatre by teaming up professionalaly trained artists with those from the street, resulting in a variety of theatre and dance shows featuring MCs and DJs, such as the youthful Breakin' Walls festival. If you want to meet a thespian rather than just see one on stage, the adjoining café, Blincker, has plenty in permanent residence at its bar.

Muziektheater

Amstel 3 (625 5455/www.muziek theater.nl). Tram 9, 14/Metro Waterlooplein. **Map** p65 F4 **G5**
The Muziektheater is Amsterdam at its most ambitious. This plush, crescent-shaped building, which opened in 1986, has room for 1,596 people and is home to both the Dutch National Ballet and De Nederlandse Opera, although the stage is also used by visiting companies such as Nederlands Dans Theater and the latest Peter Sellars or Robert Wilson opera. On top of that, the lobby's panoramic glass walls offer impressive views out over the River Amstel.

W139

Warmoesstraat 139 (622 9434/www. w139.nl). Tram 4, 9, 16, 24, 25. **Open** 11am-7pm daily. No credit cards. **Map** p65 D3 **G6**
In its two decades of existence, W139 has never lost its squat aesthetics or sometimes overly conceptual edge, while a recent renovation has brought even more light and fresh inspiration.

The New Side

The Spui is the square that caps the three main arteries, which start down near the west end of Centraal Station: middle-of-the-road walking and shopping street Kalverstraat

(called Nieuwendijk before it crosses the Dam), Nieuwezijds Voorburgwal and the Spuistraat.

The nearby **Begijnhof** is a group of houses built around a secluded courtyard and garden. Established in the 14th century, it provided modest homes for the Beguines, a religious sisterhood. Nowadays its residents are still female and it's the best known of the city's many hofjes (almshouses). In the centre is the **Engelsekerk** (English Reformed Church), built in around 1400 and given over to Scottish Presbyterians living in the city in 1607. Also in the courtyard is a Catholic church, secretly converted from two houses in 1665 after the banning of open Catholic worship after the Reformation. And nearby is one of several entrances to the **Amsterdams Historisch Museum.**

The Spui Square plays host to many markets – the most notable being the book market on Fridays. You can leave Spui by going up Kalverstraat, Amsterdam's main shopping street, or Singel past Leidsestraat: both routes lead directly to the **Munttoren** (Mint Tower) at Muntplein. Right across from the floating flower market, this medieval tower was once the western corner of Regulierspoort, a gate in the city wall in the 1480s. The Munttoren is prettiest when it's floodlit at night, but daytime visitors may enjoy hearing its carillon ringing out at noon.

From here, walk down Nieuwe Doelenstraat past the **Hôtel de l'Europe** (a mock-up of which featured in Hitchcock's *Foreign Correspondent*). This street also connects with scenic Staalstraat, which is the city's most popular film location, having appeared in *The Diary of Anne Frank* and *Amsterdamned*. Walk up here and you'll end up in Waterlooplein.

Canal cruising

During a sojourn in the city, Hans Christian Andersen wrote, 'The view from my window, through the elms to the canal outside, is like a fairy tale.' Canals are what people imagine when they think of 'Amsterdam', and they continue to enchant visitors today. Like any other city built on water, Amsterdam is best seen from a boat. It has 75 kilometres (47 miles) of waterways and a total of 165 canals spanned by 1,400 bridges (more than Venice): look at the bottom right-hand corner of a bridge to see its number.

The tourist boats provide a doughty service, but they can't squeeze into the narrower waterways. Self-piloted hire boats are few and far between: in fact, there are only two such outfits, **Canal Motorboats** (Zandhoek 10A, 422 7007, www.canalmotorboats.com) on Realeneiland, and **Boaty** (Jozef Israëlkade, between Ferdinand Bolstraat & 2e Van der Helststraat, 06 2714 9493,

www.boaty.nl) on a dock outside Hotel Okura (p177) in the Pijp, which only rents silent electric motor boats. The boats of both firms have a capacity of six. If these don't suit, just befriend a boating local or charter a tour.

Amsterdam also has its own gondola service, **Stichting Battello** (686 9868, mobile 06 474 64545, www.gondel.nl), and it's suitably unique. Not only will you glide silently and comfortably along at an angle that reveals this city at its more picturesque, you'll also be chauffeured by one of two Guinness World Record holders: Hans, 'the tallest gondolier in the world', and Tirza, 'the only woman gondolier in the world'.

Best suited to lovey-dovey couples, a ride will cost a group of up to six people around €100 an hour. You can also bring along your own food or drink, or get them to arrange refreshments for a reasonable price. The standard course is around the Jordaan, but you are welcome to stipulate your own route should you desire.

Sights & museums

Amsterdams Historisch Museum

Nieuwezijds Voorburgwal 357 (523 1822/www.ahm.nl). Tram 1, 2, 4, 5, 9, 14, 16, 24, 25. **Open** 10am-5pm Mon-Fri; 11am-5pm Sat, Sun. **Admission** €10; free-€7.50 reductions, MK. No credit cards. **Map** p64 C5 ㊲
Amsterdam's municipal museum really does the city's rich history justice. Built on the site of a 1414 convent, the museum's current home dates from the 17th-century, and is itself a delight. The exhibits take visitors on a roughly chronological meander through Amsterdam's past, charting the city's rise from a fishing village to ecstasy capital. Expect archaeological artefacts (including recent finds from the dig of the NZ-lijn underground, see box p66), works of art (by the likes of Ferdinand Bol and Jacob Corneliszoon) and plenty of quirkier displays: tone-deaf masochists may care to play the carillon in room 10A, while lesbian barflies will want to pay homage to Bet van Beeren, late owner of the infamous Café 't Mandje (now reopened; p71). Upon exiting, don't miss the Civic Guard Gallery (free admission) that leads to the peaceful Begijnhof and Spui square.

Orange Football Museum

Kalverstraat 236 (0900 1437 premium rate/www.supportersclub-oranje.nl). Tram 4, 9, 14, 16, 24, 25. **Open** 11am-5pm Sat, Sun. **Admission** €5. No credit cards. **Map** p65 D5 ㊳
This enthusiastic museum has four floors of photos, art, songs and videos relating to the national football team.

Vodka Museum

NEW *Damrak 33 (528 6035/www.vodkamuseum.com) Tram 1, 2, 4, 5, 9, 14, 16, 24, 25.* **Open** 9am-10pm daily. **Admission** €7.50; €4-€6 reductions. **Map** p64 C2 ㊴
This new small museum is a bit of an oddity: a tribute to Russia's most legendary export. It covers the history, presents some advertising posters, features a shiny new bar and shows and serves many bottles of the stuff. But when in Rome, it's perhaps best to stick to the Dutch *jenever*.

Eating & drinking

Belgique

NEW *Gravenstraat 2 (625 1974/ www.cafe-belgique.nl). Tram 1, 2, 4, 5, 9, 14, 16, 24, 25.* **Open** noon-1am Mon-Thur; noon-3am Fri-Sat; 2pm-1am Sun. No credit cards. **Map** p64 C3 ㊹
One of the city's smallest bars packs in eight beers on tap, plus another 30 bottled brews – mainly from neighbouring Belgium. They sometimes even manage to squeeze in an eight-piece bluegrass band. A gem of a pub complete with dripping candles and hearty cheer.

Café de Dokter

Rozenboomsteeg 4 (626 4427/www.cafe-de-dokter.nl). Tram 1, 2, 4, 5, 9, 14, 16, 24, 25. **Open** 4pm-1am Tue-Sat. No credit cards. **Bar**. **Map** p65 D5 ㊷
Officially the smallest bar in all of Amsterdam, Café de Dokter is also one of the oldest, dishing out the cure for whatever ails you since 1798. Centuries of character and all kinds of charming gewgaws are packed into the compact space, giving it a unique old-world ambience. Whisky figures large (there's a monthly special) and the range of old-school bar snacks includes the likes of smoked *osseworst* with gherkins.

Dampkring

Handboogstraat 29 (638 0705/www.dedampkring.nl). Tram 1, 2, 4, 5, 9, 14, 16, 24, 25. **Open** 10am-1am Mon-Thur; 10am-2am Fri, Sat; 11am-1am Sun. No credit cards. **Coffeeshop**. **Map** p65 D5 ㊲
Known for its unforgettable (even bearing in mind temporary memory loss) interior, the visual experience of Dampkring's decor makes even a

Freedom of smoking

On 1 July 2008, all public spaces, including bars, live music venues, restaurants and clubs, became smoke-free in the Netherlands. But, due to the fact that 36% of the country's population are formally against the ban (the highest proportion in Europe), by 2009 the rebellion was in full swing.

The law is drawn up to protect the health of employees, so allows for separate non-service smoking areas. In short, in the great Dutch tradition, it is flexible, and thereby accommodates creativity. Storage rooms have become beer-tapping rooms, whereas the café itself has become the smoking area. Many have joined the 'Smoker's Church' (www.rokerskerk.nl), citing the freedom of religion as a reason to continue puffing. Some have asked for small donations from smokers in case they were ever fined. One club found Camel and Nicorette sponsorship to help fund their smoking area.

How the rule would apply to coffeeshops was the subject of much debate. After all, not being able to smoke in a coffeeshop is rather like being prohibited from going to the toilet in a public convenience. Much hilarity ensued, when the government claimed it had trained law enforcers to tell the difference between pure joints and those laced with tobacco. Consequently, many coffee shops are ignoring the smoking ban and offering herbal mixes as an alternative to tobacco. The vaporiser market is a growth industry: the gizmo vaporises THC (the active ingredient) at a low temperature so that the leaves stay uncombusted, resulting in a smokeless toke. At the end of the day, coffeeshop owners don't have that much to lose, with 85 per cent of sales being in takeaways.

However, smaller bars and cafés are being hit hard by the smoking ban, since they cannot spare the money or space to create designated smoking areas. In April 2009, a court ruling backed a café in Breda, agreeing that the law was indeed unfair. While awaiting a higher court ruling, many one-person run cafés decided to put the ashtrays back on the table. The debate looks set to continue for a while.

blowverbod
wegens overlast in de buurt
boete € 50,- art. 2.8 lid 4 APV

alcoholverbod
art. 2.8 lid 2 APV
uitgezonderd terras

mushroom trip look grey. Moulded walls and sculpted ceilings are covered in deep auburns laced with caramel-coloured wooden panelling, making a perfect location for watching the movie *Ocean's Twelve*. Monitors show the same George Clooney and Brad Pitt scene all day long.

Gartine

Taksteeg 7 (320 4132/www.gartine.nl). Tram 1, 2, 4, 5, 9, 14, 16, 24, 25. **Open** 8am-6pm Wed-Sun. €€. No credit cards. **Slow food**. Map p65 D5 ⑫

Open only for breakfast, lunch and a full-blown high tea, Gartine is a temple to slow food, served by a friendly couple who grow veg and herbs.

Harry's Bar

Spuistraat 285 (06 2155 8300/www. harrysbaramsterdam.com). Tram 1, 2, 4, 5, 9, 14, 16, 24, 25. **Open** 5pm 1am Mon-Thur, Sun; 5pm-3am Fri, Sat. **Bar**. Map p64 C5 ⑭

Small, dark and intimate, Harry's Bar is the perfect place to while away an afternoon lounging on a leather sofa.

There's everything here to suit all manner of movers and shakers, from Cristal to classic cocktails, expertly mixed.

Keuken van 1870

Spuistraat 4 (620 4018/www.keuken van1870.nl). Tram 1, 2, 5, 13, 17. **Open** 5-10pm Mon-Sat. €€. No credit cards. **Dutch**. Map p64 C2 ⑮

This former soup kitchen has been reinvented but retains a menu of authentic Dutch standards and, in a homage to its roots, a set three-course menu for €7.50. But be warned, it's so popular that diners often end up sharing tables.

Morningstar

NEW *Nieuwezijds Voorburgwal, opposite 289 (625 6542/www.morning-star.eu). Tram 1, 2, 5.* **Open** noon-6pm Mon-Wed, Fri-Sun; noon-9pm Thur. €. **Café**. Map p64 C4 ⑯

Conveniently located in a hipster bar zone, this former police post is now an organic snack bar. Greasy fries have been replaced with healthy snacks, burgers and meals; neon colours have made way for a funky warm interior.

Dampkring p83

OCEAN'S 12 HAZE

Supperclub

Prik

*Spuistraat 109 (320 0002/www.prik
amsterdam.nl). Tram 1, 2, 5, 13, 17.*
Open 4pm-1am Tue-Thur, Sun; 4pm-
3am Fri, Sat. No credit cards. **Bar**.
Map p64 C3 ⑰

'Queer or not, Prik is hot!' – so runs the
strap line of Prik, a popular gay haunt
which attracts a diverse crowd to enjoy
its delicious snacks and groovy sounds.

Supperclub

*Jonge Roelensteeg 21 (344 6400/www.
supperclub.nl). Tram 1, 2, 5, 13, 17.*
Open 7.30pm-1am Mon-Thur, Sun;
7.30pm-3am Fri, Sat. €€€€. **Global**.
Map p64 C4 ⑱

With its white decor, beds for seating,
irreverent food combos and wacky
acts, this is an arty joint. At the very
least, you'll remember your visit; the
owners even have their own cruise ship
that trawls the local waters offering
dinners a more dramatic backdrop.

Tokyo Café

*Spui 15 (489 7918/www.tokyocafe.nl).
Tram 1, 2, 4, 5, 9, 14, 16, 24, 25.*
Open 11am-11pm daily. €€€.
Japanese. **Map** p65 D5 ⑲

Thought to be haunted, this Jugendstil
monument now hosts its umpteenth
eaterie in the form of a Japanese café
complete with a lovely terrace, teppa-
nyaki pyrotechnics and a sushi and
sashimi bar– plus an 'all you can eat'
buffet. High-quality dishes may offer
little protection against local ghosts,
but will certainly keep hunger at bay.

Tweede Kamer

Heisteeg 6 (422 2236). Tram 1, 2, 5.
Open 10am-1am daily. No credit cards.
Coffeeshop. **Map** p64 C5 ⑳

Small and intimate, this shop embod-
ies the refined look and feel of vintage
jazz sophistication – which makes it an
extremely pleasant place to get stoned.
Aided by a bakery just around the corner, its spacecakes are delicious and
hugely effective. The house hash is
highly regarded, but seating inside is
limited; if there's no room, walk over to
nearby Dutch Flowers (Singel 387).

D'Vijff Vlieghen

*Spuistraat 294-302 (530 4060/www.
d-vijffvlieghen.com). Tram 1, 2, 5, 13,
17.* **Open** 6-10pm daily. €€€€.
Dutch. **Map** p64 C5 ㉛

The Five Flies achieves a rich Golden Age vibe – it even has a Rembrandt room, with etchings – but also works as a purveyor of kitsch. The food is best described as posh Dutch. Unique, and appropriately pricey.

Shopping

Albert Heijn

Nieuwezijds Voorburgwal 226 (421 8344/www.ah.nl). Tram 1, 2, 4, 5, 9, 13, 14, 16, 17, 24, 25. **Open** 8am-10pm daily. **Map** p64 C4 ⓷⓶

This massive shop, just behind Dam Square, is one of over 40 branches of Albert Heijn in Amsterdam. It contains virtually all the household goods you could ever need, though some of the range is unnecessarily expensive.

American Book Center

Spui 12 (625 5537/www.abc.nl). Tram 1, 2, 4, 5, 9, 14, 16, 24, 25. **Open** 11am-7pm Mon; 10am-8pm Tue, Wed, Fri, Sat; 10am-9pm Thur; 11am-6.30pm Sun. **Map** p64 C5 ⓷⓷

An Amsterdam institution since 1972, (it relocated a couple years back, two blocks from the old shop) the American Book Center stocks a truly enormous selection of English-language books and magazines from the US and UK. Check out the nearby ABC Treehouse (423 0967, Voetboogstraat 11) which regularly hosts various workshops, open-mic nights and author readings.

Artplein Spui

Spui (www.artplein-spui.nl). Tram 1, 2, 4, 5, 9, 14, 16, 24, 25. **Open** *Mar-Dec* 10am-6pm Sun. No credit cards. **Map** p64 C5 ⓷⓸

Oil paintings, acrylics, watercolours, graphic arts, sculpture, ceramics and jewellery are found at this small open-air (and therefore weather-dependent) Sunday arts and crafts market. There's a rotating system for the 60 or so artists, and buskers are usually on hand to lend a little atmosphere. The perfect place to take a Sunday stroll.

Albert Heijn

Athenaeum Nieuwscentrum

Spui 14-16 (bookshop 514 1460/news centre 514 1470/www.athenaeum.nl). Tram 1, 2, 4, 5, 9, 14, 16, 24, 25. **Open** *Bookshop* 11am-6pm Mon; 9.30am-6pm Tue, Wed, Fri, Sat; 9.30am-9pm Thur; noon-5.30pm Sun. *News centre* 8am-8pm Mon-Wed, Fri, Sat; 8am-9pm Thur; 10am-6pm Sun. **Map** p64 C5 ⓷⓹

This is where Amsterdam's highbrow literary browsers usually choose to hang out and chew the cultural fat. The Athenaeum Nieuwscentrum, as its name might suggest, also stocks newspapers from across the world, as well as a wide choice of magazines and periodicals in many languages.

De Bijenkorf

Dam 1 (0900 0919 premium rate/www. bijenkorf.nl). Tram 1, 2, 4, 5, 9, 13, 14, 16, 17, 24, 25. **Open** 11am-7pm Mon; 9.30am-7pm Tue, Wed; 9.30am-9pm Thur, Fri; 9.30am-6pm Sat; noon-6pm Sun. **Map** p64 C3 ⓷⓺

Amsterdam's most notable department store has a great household goods section and a decent mix of clothing (designer and own-label), kids' wear,

Athenaeum Nieuwscentrum p87

jewellery, cosmetics, shoes and accessories. The top-floor Chill Out department caters to funky youngsters in need of streetwear, clubwear, wacky foodstuffs and kitsch accessories.

Concrete Image Store

Spuistraat 250 (0900 2662 7383 premium rate/www.concrete.nl). Tram 1, 2, 5. **Open** noon-7pm Mon-Wed, Fri, Sat; noon-9pm Thur; 1-6pm Sun. **Map** p64 C5 ⑥⑦

This shop/gallery's concept is more loose and humorous than rigidly concrete: a cross-fertilisation of street fashion, artist-made dolls, limited-edition shoes, and exhibitions of photography and graphic design.

Dampkring

Prins Hendrikkade 10-11 (422 2137/ www.dampkringshop.com). Tram 1, 2, 4, 5, 9, 13, 14, 16, 17, 24, 25/ Metro Centraal Station. **Open** 10am-6pm Mon-Fri; 11am-5pm Sat. **Map** p64 C1 ⑧⑧

A new member of the green-fingered Dampkring family, this delightful emporium has everything you need to set up a cannabis grow centre at home: from hydroponics and organic equipment to bio-growth books and videos.

Female & Partners

Spuistraat 100 (620 9152/www. femaleandpartners.nl). Tram 1, 2, 5, 13, 17. **Open** 1-6pm Mon, Sun; 11am-6pm Tue, Wed, Fri, Sat; 11am-9pm Thur. **Map** p64 B3 ⑥⑨

The opposite of most enterprises here, Female & Partners welcomes women (and, yes, their partners) with an array of erotic clothes, videos and toys.

Hemp Works

Nieuwendijk 13 (421 1762/www.hemp works.nl). Tram 1, 2, 5, 13, 17. **Open** 11am-7pm Mon-Wed, Sun; 11am-9pm Thur-Sat. **Map** p64 C1 ⑨⓪

One of the first shops in Amsterdam to sell hemp clothes and products, and now one of the last, Hemp Works has had to diversify into seed sales and fresh truffles (since mushroom sales were banned in 2009) to keep its trade ticking over, and it's also been a notable Cannabis Cup winner for its homegrown strain of the stinky weed.

PGC Hajenius

Midtown

Nieuwendijk 104 (638 4252/www.mid-town.nl). Tram 1, 2, 4, 5, 9, 13, 14, 16, 17, 24, 25. **Open** noon-6pm Mon; 10am-6pm Tue, Wed, Fri, Sat; 10am-9pm Thur; noon-5pm Sun. **Map** p64 C2 ⑤

Dance music galore: gabber (the store was one of the original pioneers of the hardcore hybrid), trance, mellow house and garage are among the styles on the shelves. Midtown is also a good source for getting information and tickets for hardcore parties.

Paars

Spuistraat 242 (618 2828/www.paars lingerie.nl). Tram 1, 2, 5, 13, 17. **Open** 1-7pm Mon; 11am-7pm Tue, Wed, Fri; 11am-9pm Thur; 10am-6pm Sat; 1-6pm Sun.* **Map** p64 C5 ⑫

Easily the most sophisticated lingerie shop in Amsterdam, Paars' collections are high end and vary seasonally, making it interesting for true lingerie-lovers. Look for Galliano, Lise Charmel, Marlies Dekkers, Miss Bikini, Worth, La Perla, D&G, Malizia, Pain de Sucre and Roberto Cavalli, among others.

Patta Exclusive Sneakers

Nieuwezijds Voorburgwal 142 (528 5994/www.teampatta.nl). Tram 1, 2, 5, 13, 17. **Open** noon-7pm Mon-Wed, Fri-Sat; noon-9pm Thur; 1-6pm Sun. **Map** p64 C3 ⑬

Named ater the Surinamese slang for shoes, this store is where street trainer fetishists come to commune: all the expected brands, from Adidas to Vans, are here. Ground-floor shop Ben G provides synergy with its skateboards.

PGC Hajenius

Rokin 92-96 (623 7494/www.hajenius. com). Tram 4, 9, 14, 16, 24, 25. **Open** noon-6pm Mon; 9.30am-6pm Tue-Sat; noon-5pm Sun. **Map** p65 D4 ⑭

With its quaint deco interior, Hajenius has been a smoker's paradise (tobacco, not dope) for over 250 years, offering cigarabilia from Dutch pipes to cigars.

Vrolijk

Paleisstraat 135 (623 5142/www. vrolijk.nu). Tram 1, 2, 5, 13, 14, 17. **Open** 11am-6pm Mon; 10am-6pm Tue-Fri; 10am-5pm Sat; 1-5pm Sun. **Map** p64 C4 ⑮

AMSTERDAM BY AREA

Silence, please

Begijnhof

Noise kills. Aural disturbance can cause sleep loss, which leads to chronic stress and raised blood pressure. It is estimated that this causes the death of around 50 people in Amsterdam each year. Perhaps that's why two guidebooks to the city's quiet spots appeared in 2008. Finally, people are taking this not-so-silent threat seriously.

The British art critic and curator Siobhan Wall managed to find more than 140 spots for her book *Quiet Amsterdam* (ImageFound), after taking hundreds of photos of rarely seen landscapes and unusual interiors. The book itself, with its calm black-and-white photography, is a tribute to restfulness. Besides exploring classic spots of tranquillity, such as the back garden of the **Bijbels Museum** (p95) or the courtyard **Begijnhof** (p81), Wall searched out 'muzak-free' cafés and restaurants, and went further afield to parks such as Erasmus Park and Vijfhoek in Diemen.

Thom Breukel is a touch more methodical in his Dutch-language *Stil Amsterdam: Survivalgids voor de Stedeling* (Toth), which guides urbanites to 110 quiet spots. Breukel certainly knows his stuff, as the author of *The Big Silence Atlas of Amsterdam*, he is often spotted around town measuring decibels, recording his findings on www.amsterdam.nl/stilleplekken. He's a big fan of churches, courtyards and forgotten parks, and offers many escape routes: the **Fatih Mosque** – hidden from the bustle of Rozengracht, the courtyard of the **Amsterdams Historisch Museum** (p83), a quiet pocket of tranquillity that's a world away from the shopping masses of Kalverstraat; and **Oude Kerk** (p68), for when the buzz of the Red Light District get too much.

To elude the chaos of Leidseplein, he recommends sitting beneath the huge trees in **Leidsebosje**, a small corner park just south over the bridge from American Hotel (p170). If you lean against one of these giants, its sheer size absorbs all the background noise. And be sure to look up above your head at the witty sculpture of a man sawing off a branch – a charming addition to this quiet oasis.

The best selection of rose-tinted international reading – whether fiction or fact – you'll find in all of Amsterdam, in addition to a wide variety of CDs, DVDs and guides. It has a second-hand section upstairs, and also offers a range of novelty T-shirts, condoms and gifts that are always a big hit with tourists.

Vroom & Dreesmann

Kalverstraat 203 (0900 235 8363 premium rate/www.vroomen dreesmann.nl). Tram 1, 2, 4, 5, 9, 14, 16, 24, 25. **Open** 11am-8pm Mon; 10am-8pm Tue, Wed, Fri, Sat; 10am-9pm Thur; noon-8pm Sun. **Map** p65 D5 (96)

V&D means good quality products at prices that are just a small step up from those at the more ubiquitous HEMA. They stock a staggering array of toiletries, cosmetics, leather goods and watches, clothing and underwear for all the family, kitchen items, suitcases, CDs and videos. The bakery, Le Marché, sells delicious bread, quiches, shakes and sandwiches, while self-service restaurant La Place is a terrific option for a delicious and healthy lunch.

Waterstone's

Kalverstraat 152 (638 3821/www. waterstones.com). Tram 1, 2, 4, 5, 9, 14, 16, 24, 25. **Open** 9.30am-6.30pm Mon-Wed, Fri; 9.30am-9pm Thur; 10am-6.30pm Sat; 11am-6pm Sun. **Map** p65 D5 (97)

A mighty, if familiar, temple to literature in an area that's already bursting with bookshops. Thousands of books, magazines and videos, all of them in English, are on sale in this reputable store, and the children's section is especially delightful.

Zara

Kalverstraat 66-72 (530 4050/www. zara.com). Tram 1, 2, 4, 5, 9, 14, 16, 24, 25. **Open** 10am-6.30pm Mon-Wed, Fri-Sun; 10am-9pm Thur. **Map** p64 C4 (98)

Zara's winning formula of designer inspired gear alongside more traditional office wear, is as popular in Amsterdam as it is in every other international city. And if you want ubiquitous Euro-fashion, hot off the catwalks, you'll find it by the bucket load in Zara.

Nightlife

Bitterzoet

Spuistraat 2 (421 2318/www.bitterzoet. com). Tram 1, 2, 5, 13, 17. **Open** 8pm-3am Mon-Thur, Sun; 8pm-4am Fri, Sat. No credit cards. **Map** p64 C2 (99)

This busy, comfy and casual bar doubles as a venue for theatre and music. Bands and DJs embrace jazz, world and urban sounds, as demonstrated by once-a-monther Blue Note Trip: jazz for hipper literates.

Arts & leisure

Arti et Amicitiae

Rokin 112 (623 3508/www.arti.nl). Tram 4, 9, 14, 16, 24, 25. **Open** noon-6pm Tue-Sun. No credit cards. **Map** p65 D5 (100)

This marvellous old building houses a private artists' society, whose initiates regularly gather in the first-floor bar. Members of the public can climb a Berlage-designed staircase to a large exhibition space, home to some great temporary shows.

Engelse Kerk

Begijnhof 48 (624 9665/www.ercadam. nl). Tram 1, 2, 4, 5, 9, 14, 16, 24, 25. No credit cards. **Map** p64 C5 (101)

Nestled tightly within the idyllic courtyard of Begijnhof, the English Reformed Church has been hosting weekly concerts of baroque and classical music here since the early 1970s. Combined with a particular emphasis on the use of authentic period instruments, the church's acoustics are genuinely haunting. Its healthy evening schedule also raises funds to help secure the building's future.

De Kaaskamer p99

The Canals

Singel was the medieval city moat; other canals such as Herengracht, Keizersgracht and Prinsengracht, which follow its line outwards, were part of a Golden Age renewal scheme for the rich. The connecting canals and streets, originally home to workers and artisans, have a number of cafés and shops. Smaller canals worth seeking out include Leliegracht, Bloemgracht, Egelantiersgracht, Spiegelgracht and Brouwersgracht.

We've split venues on the canals into two: the Western Canal Belt (between Singel and Prinsengracht, south of Brouwersgracht, north and west of Leidsegracht); and the Southern Canal Belt (between Singel and Prinsengracht, running from Leidsegracht in a south-easterly direction towards the Amstel).

Western Canal Belt

Prinsengracht is easily the most charming of the canals in this area. Pompous façades have mellowed as shady trees, cosy cafés and some of Amsterdam's more funkadelic houseboats have grown in number here. There's some good shopping to be had; further north, the smart **Nine Streets** linking Prinsengracht, Keizersgracht and Herengracht all offer a diverse mix of speciality shops for browsing.

On your way up Prinsengracht, the tall spire of the 375-year old **Westerkerk** rears into view. Its tower is the tallest structure in this part of town, and climbing up it affords a good view of the **Anne Frank Huis**, now a museum of remembrance to the life of the aspiring diarist and other victims of the Holocaust. Fans of René Descartes – if you think, you therefore probably are – can pay tribute at his house around the corner at Westermarkt 6; and art lovers can admire the interiors of the **Bijbels Museum** (Bible Museum) and the photography foundation, **Huis Marseille**.

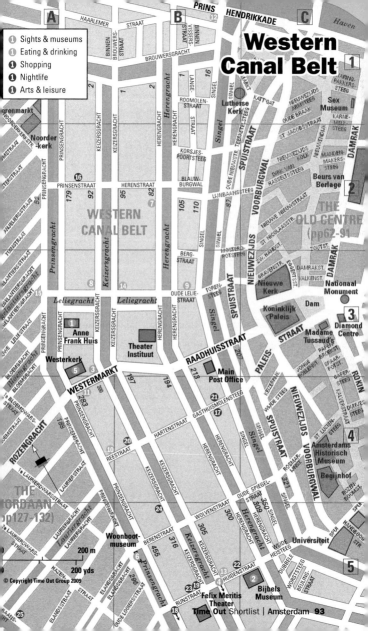

Western Canal Belt

Legend

- ❶ Sights & museums
- ❶ Eating & drinking
- ❶ Shopping
- ❶ Nightlife
- ❶ Arts & leisure

PRINS HENDRIKKADE

Haven

HAARLEMER STRAAT

BINNEN BROUWERSTRAAT

BROUWERSGRACHT

BINNEN VISSERSSTRAAT

Singel

KATTENGAT

Haarlemmerkt

Noorder-kerk

Luthese Kerk

Sex Museum

HARINGPAKKERS STEEG

LANGE NIEZEL

PRINSENSTRAAT

KEIZERSGRACHT

HERENGRACHT

ROOMOLENSTRAAT

KORSJES-POORTSTEEG

BLAUW-BURGWAL

OUDE NIEUWEZIJDS VOORBURGWAL

SINT JACOBSSTRAAT

KARNE-MELKSTEEG

NIEUWENDIJK

NIEUWEZIJDS KOLK

MANDEN-MAKERS-STEEG

Beurs van Berlage

WESTERN CANAL BELT

PRINSENSTRAAT 179 92

HERENSTRAAT 95 82

105 110

THE OLD CENTRE (pp62-91)

NIEUWEZIJDS VOORBURGWAL

NIEUWE NIEUWSTRAAT

SINT NICOLAASSTR.

DAMRAK

ZOUTST.

DIRK VAN HASSELTSTEEG

BERG-STRAAT

Singel

IJNBAANSSTEEG

NOORDER-POTSTEEG

ZW. HANDST.

GRAVENST.

Nieuwe Kerk

EGGERST.

DAMRAKST.

VALKENST.

Nationaal Monument

Leliegracht

OUDE LELIE-STRAAT

TOREN-STEEG

SPUISTRAAT

NIEUWEZIJDS VOORBURGWAL

Koninklijk Paleis

Dam

STRAAT

Madame Tussaud's

Diamond Centre

❶ Anne Frank Huis

Westerkerk

Theater Instituut

RAADHUISSTRAAT

Main Post Office

PALEIS-STRAAT

JONGE ROELENST.

PAPENBROEKST.

SPAAR-POTST.

PAPER-STEEG

ROKIN

KALVERSTRAAT

DUIFJES-STEEG

WESTERMARKT

WESTERMARKT

213

GASTHUISMOLENSTEEG

HARTENSTRAAT

KEIZERSGRACHT

HERENGRACHT

Singel

NIEUWEZIJDS VOORBURGWAL

ST. LUCIEN-STEEG

WIJDE STEEG

Amsterdams Historisch Museum

Begijnhof

THE JORDAAN (pp127-132)

ROZENGRACHT

PRINSENGRACHT

REESTRAAT

BERENSTRAAT

WOLVENSTRAAT

OUDE SPIEGEL-STRAAT

ROSMARIJN-STEEG

HEISTEEG

ROZEN-BOOMST.

SPUI

321 350 309

Universiteit

Woonboot-museum

KEIZERSGRACHT 316

455 305 300

HERENGRACHT

Singel

WIJDE HEISTEEG

DUBBELE

WORSTSTEEG

BEULING STR.

HANDBOOGSTR.

Felix Meritis Theater

Bijbels Museum

HUIDENSTRAAT

RUNSTRAAT

ELANDSGRACHT

200 m

200 yds

© Copyright Time Out Group 2009

Time Out Shortlist | Amsterdam **93**

Sights & museums

Anne Frank Huis

Prinsengracht 267 (556 7105/556 7100/www.annefrank.org). Tram 13, 14, 17. **Open** *Jan-Mar, Sept-Dec* 9am-7pm daily. *Apr-June* 9am-9pm Mon-Fri, Sun; 9am-10pm Sat. *July, Aug* 9am-10pm daily. **Admission** €8.50; free-€4 reductions. **Map** p93 A3 ❶

During World War II, the young Jewish diarist Anne Frank and her family hid for two years behind a bookcase in the back annexe of this 17th-century canalhouse. On 4 August 1944, the occupants were arrested and transported to concentration camps, where Anne died with sister Margot and their mother. Her father, Otto, survived, and decided that Anne's diary should be published. The rest is history: Anne fulfilled her dream of becoming a best-selling author with tens of millions of copies having since been printed in 55 languages. Today, more than a million visitors a year come to witness these sober unfurnished rooms. A new wing not only tells the story of Anne's family and the persecution of Jews, but also presents the difficulties of fighting discrimination of all types. You can book ahead online to avoid the queues.

Bijbels Museum

Herengracht 366-368 (624 2436/www. bijbelsmuseum.nl). Tram 1, 2, 5. **Open** 10am-5pm Mon-Sat; 11am-5pm Sun, public holidays. **Admission** €7.50; free-€3.75 reductions, MK. No credit cards. **Map** p93 C5 ❷

Housed in two handsome Vingboons canal houses, Amsterdam's own Bible Museum aims to illustrate life and worship in biblical times with archaeological finds from Egypt and the Middle East, including a remarkable mummy of an Israeli woman, models of ancient temples and a slideshow. There's also a splendid collection of Bibles, covering several centuries – look out for the rhyming Bible from 1271. A little dry in places, the museum attracts

folk who seek to admire the restored houses, splendid Jacob de Wit paintings and the sprawling gardens.

Homomonument

Westermarkt (www.homomonument.nl). Tram 13, 14, 17. **Map** p93 A3 ❸

Unveiled 20 years ago, Karin Daan's three-sectioned pink triangular monument to the memory of persecuted gays and lesbians was a world first. Flowers are often left on it for personal remembrance, especially during gatherings such as World AIDS Day. More information on gay and lesbian life is available from COC Amsterdam (p183).

Huis Marseille

Keizersgracht 401 (531 8989/www. huismarseille.nl). Tram 1, 2, 5. **Open** 11am-6pm Tue-Sun. **Admission** €5; free-€3 reductions. No credit cards. **Map** p93 B5 ❹

Located in a monumental 17th-century house, the walls of this photography foundation host the latest from hotshot snappers such as David Goldblatt, Valerie Belin and Jacqueline Hassink.

Westerkerk

Prinsengracht 277-279 (624 7766/tower 689 2565/www.westerkerk.nl). Tram 13, 14, 17. **Open** *Tower* Apr-Oct 10am-5.30pm Mon-Sat. **Admission** *Tower* €6. No credit cards. **Map** p93 A3 ❺

Before noise pollution, it was said that if you heard the bells of Westerkerk's tower, dating from 1631, you were in the Jordaan. The tower also offers a great view of this neighbourhood, provided you don't suffer from vertigo: the 85m (278ft) tower sways by 3cm (1.2in) in a good wind. It's thought that Rembrandt is buried in the church itself, although no one is quite sure where: Rembrandt died a pauper, and as a result, he is commemorated inside the building with a simple plaque. If queues for the tower are long, you can also enjoy expansive views at the Zuidertoren or the Ouderkerkstoren, which are both handled by the same office (689 2565).

Canal pride

Amsterdam Pride may be one of the lesbian and gay community's most anticipated events, but the extended weekend of crowded street parties, parades, vibrant drinking and noise draws thousands of spectators – straight and gay alike – all eager to join in.

The festival offers thousands of distractions, running the A to Z of camp: androgyny, barely clad boys, flirtation, leather, lesbians, Muscle Marys, PVC poseurs, and, of course, theatrics. They all take part in a genuinely non-stop playground.

Then there's the dizzying array of affiliated events: street parties, more street parties, singalongs, performances and Pride's apex, the awesome Saturday afternoon Canal Parade – the world's only floating Pride – which winds along the Prinsengracht and Amstel canal between 2pm and 6pm.

Canals spill over with topless mermaids, half-naked fire fighters, Marilyn Monroe lookalikes, pole dancers, Spartans, beauty queens, angels and wrestlers all waving from a hundred different boats. The Canal Parade draws thousands of onlookers – estimates put them at 350,000, and no one's clocking who's gay and who ain't. Then there are the politicians who hitch rides on these boats in the name of scoring canal-cred points.

As time goes on, everyone puts in overtime, cultivating the following day's hangover – although they've probably drunk their way through the first one, as the partying technically starts on Friday. Or Thursday, depending on who you ask. Either way, the closing party takes place during the late Sunday afternoon on Rembrandtplein, with a huge number of Dutch artists, DJs and those with enough energy left to sign off the celebration.

Like Queen's Day, when the city's population doubles and crams into the centre for the event, Pride is terribly Amsterdam. It's relaxed, tolerant, positive, outrageous and definitely worth celebrating.

Woonbootmuseum

Prinsengracht, opposite no. 296 (427 0750/www.houseboatmuseum.nl). Tram 13, 14, 17. **Open** *Jan, Feb, Nov, Dec* 11am-5pm Fri-Sun. *Mar-Oct* 11am-5pm Tue-Sun. Closed last 3wks Jan. **Admission** €3.50; €2.75 children under 152cm (5ft). No credit cards. **Map** p93 B5 ⑥

The Houseboat Museum is not just a museum about houseboats: it's actually located on one. Aside from a few explanatory panels, the *Hendrika Maria* is laid out exactly as a houseboat would be to help visitors imagine what it's like to live on the water. It's more spacious than you might expect and does a good job of selling the lifestyle afforded by its unique comforts. Until, that is, you notice the pungent scent of urine emanating from the public toilet or 'curlie' (as such facilities are called): it's right by the boat itself.

Eating & drinking

't Arendsnest

Herengracht 90 (421 2057/www.arendsnest.nl). Tram 1, 2, 5, 13, 17. **Open** 4pm-midnight Mon-Thur; Sun; 4pm-2am Fri, Sat. **Bar. Map** p93 B2 ⑦

A temple to the humble hop, the 'Eagle's Nest', in a lovely old canal house, sells mainly Dutch beer. Many of the customers are real ale types, but even amateurs will have a ball sampling the wares: 30 beers on draft and more than 120 bottled, from house ale Herengracht 90 to the aptly named Texelse Skuumkoppe. Also available are 100-plus Dutch *jenevers* and liquors, and several Dutch whiskies.

Brandon

Keizersgracht 157 (no phone). Tram 1, 2, 5, 13, 14, 17. **Open** 11am-1am Mon-Thur, Sun; 11am-3am Fri, Sat. No credit cards. **Bar. Map** p93 A3 ⑧

When the previous owners hung up their pinnies in the 1980s after 40 years behind the bar, they sealed up their café, retired upstairs and eventually passed away. Twenty years later, the new owners reopened this ghost bar just as they found it: furniture, photos, billiard room and all. A decidedly old-fashioned ambience lingers.

Grey Area

Oude Leliestraat 2 (420 4301/www.greyarea.nl). Tram 1, 2, 5, 13, 14, 17. **Open** noon-8pm daily. No credit cards. **Coffeeshop. Map** p93 B3 ⑨

Run by two blokes living the modern American dream: opening a stellar Amsterdam coffee shop, which offers some of the best weed and hash on the planet (try the Bubble Gum or Grey Mist Crystals). Also on offer are large glass bongs, a vaporiser and free refills of organic coffee. The owners are highly affable and often more baked than the patrons: sometimes they stay in bed and miss the noon opening time.

Hartenkaas

Reestraat 19 (626 5271/www.hartenkaas.nl). Tram 1, 2, 5. **Open** 9am-4pm Mon-Fri, 9am-5pm Sat. No credit cards. **Takeaway. Map** p93 ⑩

This takeaway shop rates its sandwiches as the best in the city, and aside from its cockiness, the claim is close to the truth. A mere €3.95 and an ability to make a choice from dozens of different toppings and tasty combinations is is all that you need for a hearty lunch in between patrolling the 'Nine Streets' shopping area.

Jet Lounge

NEW *Westermarkt 25 (624 7744/www.jetlounge.nl). Tram 13, 14, 17.* **Open** 6pm-1am Tues-Thur; 6pm-3am Fri; 8pm-3am Sat. No credit cards. **Cocktail bar. Map** p93 A4 ⑪

A friendly neighbourhood cocktail bar that knows how to make a newcomer feel like a regular. Cocktails are great, as are the DJs and occasional live band. An ideal place to sit back and lounge in style.

Brandon p97

activists often meet at this erstwhile Provo hangout to chew the fat, although it's a nice spot in which to relax, even if you aren't feeling in a cerebral mood.

Da Portare Via

NEW *Leliegracht 34 (no phone/www. houtovenpizza.nl). Tram 1, 2, 5, 13, 14, 17.* **Open** *5-10pm daily.* No credit cards. €. **Italian**. **Map** p93 B3 ⑭
This restaurant ties with Yam-Yam (see p130) for the best pizza in town contest. That's thanks to a very hot wood-fuelled oven, which pumps out crusty thin crusts in the best Italian style. You can only buy takeaway pizza, but there are plenty of canal-side benches nearby. Or ask politely at the neighbours Brandon (p97) if it's OK to eat there. They also have a second location in the Pijp (Frans Halsstraat 63).

Twee Zwaantjes

Prinsengracht 114 (625 2729/www. detweezwaantjes.nl). Tram 1, 2, 3, 5, 10, 13, 14, 17. **Open** *3pm-1am Mon-Thur, Sun; 3pm-3am Fri, Sat.* No credit cards. **Bar**. **Map** p93 A3 ⑮
Oom-pah-pah, oom-pah-pah – that's how it goes at this salt-of-the-earth bar when the locals are out in force and the air is filled with song. It's relatively quiet during the week, but weekends are real singalong, swingalong affairs, with revellers booming out tear-jerking tunes on such subjects as love, sweat and the Westerkerk.

Shopping

Blue Blood

NEW *Prinsenstraat 13 (320 2048/www. bluebloodbrand.com). Tram 1, 2, 5, 13, 14, 17.* **Open** *Winter noon-6pm Mon, Sun; 10am-6pm Tue-Wed, Fri; 10am-9pm Thur. Summer 11am-6pm Mon-Fri, 10am-6pm Sat.* No credit cards. **Map** p93 A2 ⑯
The third concept store for local high-end jeans icon Blue Blood focuses on the idea of 'love for denim'. It also has branches in other locations: Cornelis

Kobalt

Singel 2a (320 1559/ www.cafekobalt.nl). Tram 1, 2, 4, 5, 9, 13, 17, 24, 25, 26. **Open** *8am-1am Mon-Thur, Sun; 8am-3am Fri, Sat.* **Bar**. **Map** p93 B1 ⑫
This rather sophisticated bar near Centraal Station is a great way to beat the train delay blues. It has free Wi-Fi, round-the-clock food from breakfast to tapas to dinner, and any drink that you could name, from ristretto to champagne. DJs spin Friday nights, while Sunday afternoons are dedicated to slinky live jazz shows.

De Pels

Huidenstraat 25 (622 9037). Tram 1, 2, 5. **Open** *10am-1am Mon-Thur, Sun; 10am-3am Fri, Sat.* No credit cards. **Bar**. **Map** p93 B5 ⑬
The Nine Streets are littered with characterful bars, and this one is a lovely old-style, tobacco-stained example that has an intellectual bent. In fact, De Pels can justifiably claim a prime spot in Amsterdam's literary and political legacy: writers, journalists and social

Schuytstraat 18 is more of a vintage boutique whereas PC Hooftstraat 142 shamelessly embraces luxury.

Brilmuseum/Brillenwinkel

Gasthuismolensteeg 7 (421 2414/ www.brilmuseumamsterdam.nl). Tram 1, 2, 5, 13, 14, 17. **Open** 11.30am-5.30pm Wed-Fri; 11.30am-5pm Sat. No credit cards. **Map** p93 B4 ⓱
Officially, this 'shop' is an opticians' museum, but don't let that put you off. The fascinating exhibition features glasses throughout the ages, and if you like what you see then most of the pairs on display are also for sale.

Frozen Fountain

Prinsengracht 645 (622 9375/www. frozenfountain.nl). Tram 1, 2, 5, 7, 10. **Open** 1-6pm Mon; 10am-6pm Tue-Fri; 10am-5pm Sat. **Map** p93 B5 ⓭
The 'Froz' is a paradise for lovers of contemporary furniture . It stays abreast of innovative Dutch designers like Piet Hein Eek, the maestro of furniture made from recycled wood; it also sells stuff by the non-Dutch likes of Marc Newsom, plus modern classics and photography.

De Kaaskamer

Runstraat 7 (623 3483). Tram 1, 2, 5. **Open** noon-6pm Mon; 9am-6pm Tue-Fri; 9am-5pm Sat; noon-5pm Sun. No credit cards. **Map** p93 B5 ⓲
De Kaaskamer offers more than 200 varieties of domestic and imported cheeses, plus pâtés, olives, pastas and wines. Have fun quizzing shop staff on the cheese varieties and related trivia: they seriously know their stuff.

Kramer/Pontifex

Reestraat 18-20 (626 5274/ www.pontifex.kramer.googlepages.com). Tram 13, 14, 17. **Open** 10am-6pm Mon-Sat. **Map** p93 B4 ⓴
Broken Barbies and battered bears are restored to health by Mr Kramer, a doctor for old-fashioned dolls and teddies who has been here for 25 years. In the same shop, Pontifex is a candle seller.

De Kaaskamer

Nic Nic

Gasthuismolensteeg 5 (622 8523/www. nicnicdesign.com). Tram 1, 2, 5, 13, 14, 17. **Open** noon-6pm Mon- Fri; 11am-5pm Sat. **Map** p93 B4 ㉑
This shop sells wonderful kitsch: 1950s and '60s furniture, lamps, ashtrays and kitchenware, mostly in mint condition.

Pâtisserie Pompadour

Huidenstraat 12 (623 9554). Tram 1, 2, 5. **Open** 10am-6pm Mon-Fri; 9am-5pm Sat. **Map** p93 B5 ㉒
This fabulous bonbonnerie and tearoom with a delightful 18th-century interior imported all the way from Antwerp is likely to satisfy your sweet tooth, regardless of your age.

Skins Cosmetics

NEW *Runstraat 11 (528 6922/www. skins.nl). Tram 1, 2, 5.* **Open** 1-7pm Mon; 11am-7pm Tue-Wed, Fri; 11am-8pm Thur; 10am-6pm Sat; noon-5pm Sun. **Map** p93 B5 ㉓
The flagship store for Amsterdam's own skincare and fragrance empire has

expanded its offering, and now includes cosmetics by Ren, Dr Brandt, Leonor Greyl, Aveda and Le Labo. There's plenty of room in which to try the stock and beauty services. Drop in to sample some Révive, the skin care line containing the Nobel Prize-winning ingredient EGF.

Wella Warenhuis

Keizersgracht 300 (623 3766/www.wellawarenhaus.nl). Tram 1, 2, 5, 13, 14, 17. **Open** 1-6.30pm Mon-Wed, Fri, Sat; 1-8pm Thur. **Map** p93 B5 ❷
A vast canalside office-turned-warehouse stocks playful products from young Dutch designers, who take it in turns to man the cash register.

Nightlife

Maloe Melo

Lijnbaansgracht 163 (420 4592/www.maloemelo.com). Tram 7, 10, 13, 14, 17. **Open** 9pm-3am Mon-Thur, Sun; 9pm-4am Fri, Sat. **Map** p93 A5 ❷
Well, I woke up this morning, feeling Maloe Melowed. Yes, you've guessed it, this small, pleasantly pokey little juke joint is Amsterdam's native house of the blues. Quality rockabilly and roots acts play here on a regular basis, so shed your gloom and enjoy the tunes.

Southern Canal Belt

The Southern Canal Belt boasts two main squares: Rembrandtplein and Leidseplein. Rembrandtplein is unashamedly tacky and home to an array of tasteless (and worse) establishments, ranging from traditional striptease parlours to even seedier modern peepshow joints and nondescript cafés. Fortunately, there are a few exceptions to the prevailing tawdriness – places such as the grand café De Kroon (no.17), the art deco building Schiller (no.26) and HL de Jong's eclectic masterpiece, the **Pathé Tuschinski** on Reguliersbreestraat.

Also nearby is the floating flower market at the southern tip of Singel (the **Bloemenmarkt**). From the square, walk south along shopping and eating street Utrechtsestraat, or explore the picturesque Reguliersgracht and Amstelveld. Whichever you choose, you'll cross Herengracht on your journey. As the first canal to be dug in the glory days, Herengracht attracted the richest of merchants and is still home to the most overblown houses on any of Amsterdam's canals.

However, it's on the stretch built between Leidsestraat and Vijzelstraat, the **Golden Bend**, that things get out of hand. Around the corner on Vijzelstraat is the highly imposing city archive, the **Stadsarchief**. Nearby on Keizersgracht is the cutting-edge photography museum **Foam**.

Leidseplein, reached via the chaotic Leidsestraat or the gallery-filled strip of Nieuwe Spiegelstraat, is the tourist centre of Amsterdam. It's packed with merrymakers drinking at cafés and is dominated by the **Stadsschouwburg**, along with many cinemas, theatres and restaurants. Max Euweplein offers a route to the greener pastures of **Vondelpark**.

Sights & museums

Foam (Photography Museum Amsterdam)

Keizersgracht 609 (551 6500/www.foam.nl). Tram 16, 24, 25. **Open** 10am-6pm Mon-Wed, Sat, Sun; 10am-9pm Thur, Fri. **Admission** €7.50; free-€5 reductions. MK. **Map** p101 C2 ❷
Located in a tightly renovated canal house, this excellent museum displays a comprehensive array of talent, from rising stars (Ryan McGinley, Viviane Sassen) to big names (Weegee, Helen Levitt, Malick Sidibé and Richard Avedon). The café's food is a feast for the eyes as well as the stomach.

Southern Canal Belt

Sights & museums
Eating & drinking
Shopping
Nightlife
Arts & leisure

© Copyright Time Out Group 2009

Museum Geelvinck

NEW *Keizersgracht 633 (639 0747/ www.geelvinckhinlopenhuis.nl) Tram 16, 24, 25.* **Open** Fri-Mon 11am-5pm. **Admission** €6/free for MK holders. **Map** p101 C2 ㉗

This 17th-century canal house has four 'style rooms', including a library and a 'Red Room' from the Louis XV period, along with paintings by Pieter de Ring (1615-60). Despite such grandeur, the highlight is the classical back garden, which hosts regular concerts of chamber music.

Museum Willet-Holthuysen

Herengracht 605 (523 1822/www. willetholthuysen.nl). Tram 4, 9, 14. **Open** 10am-5pm Mon-Fri; 11am-5pm Sat, Sun. **Admission** €6; free-€4.50 reductions. **Map** p101 D1 ㉘

Upon the death in 1889 of Abraham Willet-Holthuysen, remembered as 'the Oscar Wilde of Amsterdam', his wife Sandrina Louisa, a hermaphrodite, left this 17th-century house and contents to the city on the condition that it was preserved and opened as a museum. The family found inspiration for the sumptuous decor in the neoclassical Louis XVI style. The French-style garden has a sundial, while the house contains an impressive collection of rare objets d'art, glassware, silver, china and paintings – including one of a shocked-looking Abraham (taken on his honeymoon perhaps?).

Stadsarchief Amsterdam

NEW *Vijzelstraat 32 (251 1511/www. stadsarchief.amsterdam.nl). Tram 16, 24, 25.* **Open** 10am-5pm Tue-Fri; 11am-5pm Sat-Sun. **Admission** free. **Map** p101 C2 ㉙

The city archives are located in an epic and decorative 1926 building that's shrouded in esoteric mists. The highly ornate structure was designed by architect KPC de Bazel, a practitioner of Theosophy – a spiritualist movement founded by the chain-smoking

Madame Blavatsky. The grand centrepiece is the Treasure Room. As embellished as Tutankhamen's Tomb, it displays the prizes of the collection. The archives also host exhibitions and film screenings. There is an excellent bookstore for browsing and a café.

Tassenmuseum Hendrikje

Herengracht 573 (524 6452/www. tassenmuseum.nl). Tram 4, 9, 14, 16, 24, 25. **Open** 10am-5pm daily. **Admission** €6.50; free-€5 reductions. **Map** p101 D1 ㉚

Bag habits are hard to break – so how about a bag break? This museum of bags and purses is the Western world's largest collection of its kind at a bag-gaga total of 3,500 items: anything from coin purses made of human hair to a Lieber rhinestone collectible named 'Socks' for Hillary Clinton's cat.

Eating & drinking

Bojo

Lange Leidsedwarsstraat 49-51 (622 7434/www.bojo.nl). Tram 1, 2, 5, 7, 10. **Open** 4pm-2am Mon-Thur; 4pm-4am Fri; noon-4am Sat; noon-2am Sun. **€€. Indonesian.** **Map** p101 B2 ㉛

Bojo is a fine Indo-eaterie, and one of very few places that stays open into the small hours. The price is right and the portions are large enough to glue your insides together before or after an evening of excess. Its sister operation at no.49 compensates for its earlier closing time by serving alcohol.

Ctaste

Amsteldijk 55 (622 335 366/www. ctaste.nl). Tram 3. **Open** 5.30-11pm Wed-Sun. **€€€. International.** **Map** p101 E2 ㉜

The interior is dark – very dark. After being welcomed with a snack and a drink and asked to choose between meat, fish or vegetarian, you'll be led into pitch black darkness by a blind person who will guide you through the meal. Keep claustrophobia at bay, and

Hot stuff

Blauw

In 1949, with Indonesian Independence, 180,000 residents of the 'Spice Islands' came to the Netherlands to become Dutch citizens. As a result, even the ubiquitous snackbar serves bastardised versions of their cuisine. A mirror image of an archipelago of more than 1,000 islands, with historical influences ranging from Chinese and Arabian to Portuguese and Dutch, Indonesian food mingles many cuisines with an almost infinite range of dishes.

To add to the confusion are the many **Chin-Indo-Suri** eateries, which serve up cheap dishes that have taken on the tones of the many immigrants from China (often via Indonesia) and Surinam, another former colony whose Caribbean style is usually represented by the pancake-like roti. The usual dishes on offer at these places are satay, *gado-gado* (steamed veg and boiled egg served with rice and satay sauce), *nasi goreng* (onion fried rice with meat, veg and egg) and *bami goreng* (the same but with noodles). While great for the monetarily-challenged, all visitors should stretch their funds to go to an official purveyor of *rijsttafel* (rice-table), which is a Dutch construct that nobly tries to include as many dishes as possible.

While in days gone by, connoisseurs would have sent you to The Hague for the most authentic Indonesian restaurants, Amsterdam now offers ample choices of its own. There's **Tempo Doeloe** (p104), quirky **Coffee & Jazz** (Utrechtsestraat 113, 624 58 51) and the haute **Blue Pepper** (Nassaukade 366/489 7039, www.restaurantbluepepper.com). Then there are the stellar cheap takeaways, such as **Toko Joyce** (Nieuwmarkt 38/427 9091, www.tokojoyce.nl) and **Sari Citra** (Ferdinand Bolstraat 52/675 4102) in De Pijp.

Top of the pile, however, is the perfectionist newcomer **Blauw** (Amstelveenseweg 158-160/675 5000, www.restaurantblauw.nl). The restaurant serves authentic dishes, but with a twist. Its 'rice-table' is a feast for the gods.

you'll learn how strongly taste is linked to vision; only on the way out can you ask what you've actually had.

Eat at Jo's

Marnixstraat 409 (638 3336). Tram 1, 2, 5, 7, 10. **Open** noon-9pm Wed-Sun. **€€**. No credit cards. **Global**. Map p101 B3 ❸❸

Each day brings a new menu to this cheap and eminently cheerful international kitchen, where fish, meat and vegetarian dishes are all lovingly prepared. Star spotters take note: whichever act is booked to play at the Melkweg may well eat here beforehand.

Flo Amsterdam

NEW *Amstelstraat 9 (890 4757/www. floamsterdam.com).* Tram 3. **Open** *lunch* noon-3pm Mon-Fri; *dinner* 5.30-11pm daily; *supper* 11-11.30pm Mon-Wed, Sun, 11pm-midnight Fri-Sat. **€€€**. **French**. Map p.101 D1 ❸❹

Part of a French brasserie chain, Flo stands for bourgeois cooking at its best, especially when it comes to classics such as steak tartar and its shellfish platter. It actually competes with its sister operations in Paris. A city first!

Hap Hmm

1e Helmerstraat 33 (618 1884/www. hap-hmm.nl). Tram 1, 3, 12. **Open** 4.30-8pm Mon-Fri. **€**. No credit cards. **Dutch**. Map p101 A3 ❸❺

Hungry but hard up? You need some of the Dutch grandma cooking served in this living-room style canteen, which packs famished punters with meat and potatoes for around €6.

Kamer 401

Marnixstraat 401 (620 0614/www. kamer401.nl). Tram 1, 2, 5, 6, 7. **Open** 6pm-1am Wed, Thur; 6pm-3am Fri, Sat. No credit cards. **Bar**. Map p101 A2 ❸❻

Art students and the terminally hip gather at this red-lacquered temple to pleasure, where there is no food or frippery, just booze, DJ-spun music and a party vibe. Nearby establishments Lux (Marnixstraat 403, 422 1412) and Weber (Marnixstraat 397, 622 9910) offer a similar formula.

Onder de Ooievaar

Utrechtsestraat 119 (624 6836/www. onderdeooievaar.nl). Tram 4. **Open** 10am-1am Mon-Thur, Sun; 10am-3am Fri, Sat. **Bar**. Map p101 D2 ❸❼

Here you have a highly uncomplicated venue for an evening's carousing among a mixed bunch of trendsetters, locals and a few visitors. Highlights include 't IJ beer on tap, the downstairs pool table and the rather lovely Prinsengracht-side terrace.

La Rive

InterContinental, Prof Tulpplein 1 (520 3264/www.restaurantlarive.com). Tram 7, 10/Metro Weesperplein. **Open** noon-2pm, 6.30-10.30pm Tue-Fri; 6.30-10.30pm Sat. Closed 1st 2 wks of Aug. **€€€€**. **French**. Map p101 E2 ❸❽

While Hôtel de l'Europe has Excelsior, it's La Rive at the InterContinental that overshadows the rest of the high-end competition, and it does so by serving chef Rogér Rassin's superb French cuisine without excessive formality. Perfect for stylish dining, if money is no object.

De Rokerij

Lange Leidsedwarsstraat 41 (622 9442/ www.rokerij.net). Tram 1, 2, 5, 7, 10. **Open** 10am-1am daily. No credit cards. **Coffeeshop**. Map p101 B2 ❸❾

A marvellous discovery on an otherwise hideously touristy street by Leidseplein, De Rokerij is a real Aladdin's cave: lit by wall-mounted candles and beautiful metal lanterns, it's decorated with colourful Indian art and a variety of seating (ranging from mats thrown on to the floor to formal, decorative thrones).

Tempo Doeloe

Utrechtsestraat 75 (625 6718/www. tempodoeloerestaurant.nl). Tram 4. **Open** 6-11.30pm daily. **€€€€**. **Indonesian**. Map p101 D2 ❹❿

Shoe Baloo p106

This cosy and rather classy Indonesian restaurant is widely thought to be one of the city's best and spiciest purveyors of rice table. Phone ahead, because reservations are required.

Van Dobben
Korte Reguliersdwarsstraat 5-9 (624 4200/www.vandobben.com). Tram 4, 9, 14, 16, 24, 25. **Open** 9.30am-1am Mon-Thur; 9.30am-2am Fri, Sat; 11.30am-8pm Sun. **€**. No credit cards. **Dutch**. **Map** p101 C1 ④
A kroket is the national version of a croquette: a mélange of meat and potato with a crusty, deep-fried skin best served on a bun with lots of hot mustard – and this 1945-vintage late-nighter is the uncontested champion.

Shopping

Bloemenmarkt (Flower Market)
Singel, between Muntplein & Koningsplein (no phone). Tram 1, 2, 4, 5, 9, 14, 16, 24, 25. **Open** 9am-6pm Mon-Sat; 11am-5.30pm Sun. No credit cards. **Map** p101 B1/C1 ㊷

This fascinating collage of colour is the world's only floating flower market, with 15 florists and garden shops (although many also hawk rather cheesy souvenirs these days), all permanently ensconced on barges along the southern side of Singel. A good investment as the plants and flowers usually last well.

Concerto
Utrechtsestraat 52-60 (623 5228/ www.concerto.nl). Tram 4, 9, 14. **Open** 10am-6pm Mon-Wed, Fri, Sat; 10am-9pm Thur; noon-6pm Sun. **Map** p101 D2 ㊸
Head here for classic Bach recordings, obscure Beatles items or that beloved old Diana Ross album that got nicked at your party. There are also second-hand 45s and new releases at very reasonable prices.

Daryl van Wouw
NEW *Prinsengracht 705a (428 6374/ www.darylvanwouw.com). Tram 4, 9, 14.* **Open** noon-7pm Mon; 11am-7pm Tue-Wed, Fri; 11am-9pm Thur; 10am-6pm Sat; noon-6pm Sun. **Map** p101 B2 ㊹

Local young fashion designer and Project Catwalk judge Daryl van Wouw – an expert in how to apply street trends to the catwalks – finally has his own boutique. It may be small but shows off his playful style to the max.

Lambiek

Kerkstraat 132 (626 7543/www. lambiek.net). Tram 1, 2, 5, 16, 24, 25. **Open** 11am-6pm Mon-Fri; 11am-5pm Sat; 1-5pm Sun. **Map** p101 B2 ⑮
Lambiek, founded in 1968, claims to be the world's oldest comic shop and has thousands of books from around the world; its on-site cartoonists' gallery hosts exhibitions every two months.

Rituals

NEW *Leidsestraat 62 (625 2311/www. rituals. com). Tram 1, 2, 4, 5, 9, 14, 16, 24, 25.* **Open** noon-6pm Mon; 10am-6pm Tue, Wed, Fri, Sat; 10am-9pm Thur; noon-6pm Sun. **Map** p101 B2 ⑯
We all have to brush our teeth and do the dishes, and this franchise has gizmos to ritualise those daily grinds. And just as it cleverly mixes products for body and home, this outlet ingeniously integrates with the minimum space it has. The original flagship store is also nearby: Kalverstraat 73.

Shoe Baloo

Koningsplein 7 (626 7993/www.shoe baloo.nl). Tram 1, 2, 4, 5, 9, 14, 16, 24, 25. **Open** 10am-6pm Mon-Wed, Fri, Sat; 10am-9pm Thur; 1-6pm Sun. **Map** p101 B1 ⑰
A space age men's and women's shoe shop with a glowing Barbarella-pod interior. Über cool, but well worth taking the time to cruise for Miu Miu, Costume Nationale and Patrick Cox.

Nightlife

Jimmy Woo's

Korte Leidsedwarsstraat 18 (626 3150/ www.jimmywoo.com). Tram 1, 2, 5, 7, 10. **Open** 11pm-3am Thur, Sun; 11pm-4am Fri, Sat. **Map** p101 B2 ⑱

Amsterdam has never seen anything quite so luxuriously cosmopolitan as club Jimmy Woo's. Now you too can marvel at the lounge area filled with a mixture of modern and antique furniture, and confirm for yourself the merits of its bootylicious light design and sound system. If you have problems getting inside thanks to the crowds, cool off across the street at its sister bar, the swanky Suzy Wong (Korte Leidsedwarsstraat 45, 626 6769).

Melkweg

Lijnbaansgracht 234A (531 8181/ www.melkweg.nl). Tram 1, 2, 5, 7, 10. **Open** hours vary. No credit cards. **Map** p101 A2 ⑲
A former dairy (the name translates as 'Milky Way'), Melkweg has become world renowned as an always innovative home to live music of all styles. The complex also hosts a theatre, cinema, art gallery and café, and holds weekend club nights to boot, so it's no surprise it's a key cultural beacon in the centre of the city. Membership is compulsory for anyone wanting in.

Paradiso

Weteringschans 6-8 (626 4521/ www.paradiso.nl). Tram 1, 2, 5, 7, 10. **Open** varies. No credit cards. **Map** p101 B3 ⑳
A cornerstone of the live music and clubbing scene and a name synonymous with quality shows across the city, this former church is in such demand that it often hosts several events in one day. The main hall has a rare sense of grandeur, with multiple balconies and stained-glass windows peering down upon performers and DJs. The smaller hall upstairs is a fantastic place to catch new talent. Membership is compulsory.

Studio 80

Rembrandtplein 17 (521 8333/www. studio-80.nl). Tram 4, 9, 14, 16, 24, 25. **Open** 10am-4pm Wed, Thur, Sun; 11pm-5am Fri, Sat. **Map** p101 C1 ㉑

Man to man

Church

Not all the gays have been married off and are hanging out in mellow joints such as Getto (p71) and Prik (p86). The more extrovert side of the gay spectrum got a fresh injection of energy when **Church**, the first new cruising club in 10 years, opened late in 2008.

Of course the **Cockring** (Warmoesstraat 96, 623 9604/ www.clubcockring.com) and **the Web** (Sint Jacobsstraat 6, 623 6758) have been keeping the torch for all things leathery and naughty alight, behind their impossibly photogenic exteriors. In general, public cruising areas, most notably the hugely popular Nieuwe Meer – which is good for sunbathing and even swimming in summer, along with round-the-clock man-to-man action – have been made less attractive by the cutting of bushes, police patrols and the introduction of Highland cattle to scare off the fun-seekers. However, after a brief media kerfuffle in 2008 over the nightly cruising around the rose garden in Vondelpark, the police do condone the discreet shaking of bushes.

Nonetheless, there's something to say for the safety of indoors, and Church has it all plus more: a bar with Greek-style columns, a stage perfect for drag-queen acts and a great sound and light system. For those who dare to go deeper, there's a glory hole room, a sling chamber, dark room, showers and even douche facilities. Opened by the Gala Foundation, the same folks who organised the hugely popular safe sex parties (Z)onderbroek (word play combining underpants with 'without pants'), Church also has a reputation for its cheeky theme nights: 'Amen', 'Oriental Dance', 'Naked Bar', 'Suits in the City', 'Who's Your Daddy?' and 'Mr B Heaven' (a reference to the popular leather and bondage shop on Warmoesstraat). In short, don't be surprised if you have to check in your underpants at the door.

Church

Kerkstraat 52 (no phone/www. clubchurch.nl). **Open** 8pm-midnight Wed-Thur; 10pm-4am Fri-Sat; 4-8pm Sun.

In the midst of Rembrandt Square lurks this former radio studio, a black pearl waiting to be discovered. Dirty disco, deep electronic acid and hip hop are shown off at very reasonable prices. The city's progressive techno and minimal crowds find their home here and bring their record bag- and synthesiser-wielding friends from across Europe.

Sugar Factory

Lijnbaansgracht 238 (626 5006/ www.sugarfactory.nl). Tram 1, 2, 5, 7, 10. **Open** 9pm-4am Thur, Sun; 9pm-5am Fri, Sat. No credit cards. **Map** p101 A2/B2 **62**

This 'night theatre' club has found its niche as a place where performance meets clubbing, catering to both beat freaks and more traditional music fans at the same time. Discocult cuts things up with resident DJs Guerilla Speakerz while WickedJazzSounds livens up Sunday evenings with live musicians and even bona fide big bands. And as bonus, the club won a 'Golden Gnome' in 2009 for best smoking area.

Arts & leisure

De Balie

Kleine Gartmanplantsoen 10 (553 5151/www.debalie.nl). Tram 1, 2, 5, 7, 10. No credit cards. **Map** p101 B3 **63**

Theatre, new media, photography, cinema and literary events sit alongside lectures, debates and discussions about social and political issues at this influential centre for the local intelligentsia. Throw in a café and you've got healthy food for both mind and body.

Boom Chicago

Leidseplein Theater, Leidseplein 12 (423 0101/www.boomchicago.nl). Tram 1, 2, 5, 7, 10. **Map** p101 B2 **64**

This American improv troupe is one of Amsterdam's biggest success stories. With several different shows running nightly (except Sundays in winter), all in English, the group offers a mix of improvisation and sketches.

Koninklijk Theater Carré

Amstel 115-125 (0900 252 5255 premium rate/www.theatercarre.nl). Tram 7, 10/Metro Weesperplein. **Map** p101 E1 **65**

It's the dream of many to perform in this glamorous space, formerly home to a circus and recently refurbished in a very grand style. The Carré hosts some of the best Dutch cabaret artists and touring operas, as well as the odd big music name. If mainstream musical theatre is more your thing, this is the place to come to see and hear Dutch versions of popular blockbusters like *Grease* and *Cats*.

Mediamatic

Vijzelstraat 68 (638 9901/www. mediamatic.net). Trams 16, 24, 25. **Open** times vary. No credit cards. **Map** p101 C2 **66**

This cutting-edge organisation is dedicated to the outer reaches of technology and multimedia, and covers such tricky subjects as multiculturalism and death.

Pathé Tuschinski

Reguliersbreestraat 26-34 (0900 1458/ www.pathe.nl). Tram 4, 9, 16, 24, 25. **Map** p101 C1 **67**

This exuberant cinema is named after Abraham Tuschinski, the city's most illustrious cinematic entrepreneur, who built the structure in 1921 as a 'world theatre palace'. The interior and exterior are a striking combination of rococo, art deco and Jugendstil.

Stadsschouwburg

Leidseplein 26 (624 2311/www.stads schouwburgamsterdam.nl). Tram 1, 2, 5, 7, 10. **Map** p101 B3 **68**

The Stadsschouwburg (or Municipal Theatre) is an impressive 19th-century building. Constructed in a traditional horseshoe shape, it seats 950 and is known for its progressive theatre and opera productions – occasional contemporary music performances are also held. It's currently being renovated, and will link up with the Melkweg in 2010.

Waterlooplein p118

Jodenbuurt, the Plantage & the Oost

Located south-east of the Red Light District, Amsterdam's Jewish quarter is a mix of old and new architectural styles. Enter the skull-adorned gateway between Sint Antoniesbreestraat 130 and 132 to discover the **Zuiderkerk** (South Church); for the more energetic, its tower affords a great view of the whole neighbourhood.

Crossing the bridge at the end of Sint Antoniesbreestraat leads you to the **Rembrandthuis**. Immediately before this, however, are steps to the **Waterlooplein** flea market, dominated by the **Stadhuis-Muziektheater** (the City Hall-Music Theatre). Also close at hand are the **Joods Historisch Museum** (Jewish Historical Museum) and **Hermitage Amsterdam** (see box p113).

Stroll down Muiderstraat to discover the largely residential Plantage area that lies south-east of Mr Visserplein. The attractive **Plantage Middenlaan** winds past the Hortus Botanicus, near the **Verzetsmuseum** (Museum of Dutch Resistance), and along the edge of **Artis**, the city zoo, towards the **Tropenmuseum**.

Jews began to settle here more than 200 years ago, and the area soon grew with the investment of 19th-century diamond money (see box p115). The Plantage is still wealthy, with graceful buildings and tree-lined streets, although its charm has sadly faded somewhat. The area has seen extensive redevelopment, as witnessed along **Entrepotdok**, where post-hippie houseboats and views of Artis create a pleasant contrast to the apartment buildings.

Further south of Mauritskade is **Amsterdam Oost** (East), where the Arena hotel complex nestles on the edge of Oosterpark. Disaster

Artis

of all sexual orientations, Artis has an indoor 'rainforest' for nocturnal creatures and a 120-year-old aquarium with a simulated canal, complete with eels and bike wrecks. Further attractions include a planetarium, savannah land, a geological museum and, for kids, a petting zoo and playgrounds. During the summer months, they extend their Saturday opening hours until sunset and host special concerts, performances and tours.

Hollandsche Schouwburg

Plantage Middenlaan 24 (531 0340/ www.hollandscheschouwburg.nl). Tram 9, 10, 14. **Open** 11am-4pm daily. **Admission** free. **Map** p111 C2 ➋
In 1942, this grand theatre became a main point of assembly for some 70,000 of the city's Jews, before being taken to the transit camp at Westerbork. It's now a monument with a small but poignant exhibition, and a memorial hall displaying 6,700 surnames by way of tribute to the 104,000 Dutch Jews who were exterminated. The façade is intact, with most of the inner structure removed to make way for a memorial.

Hortus Botanicus

Plantage Middenlaan 2A (625 9021/ www.hortus-botanicus.nl). Tram 9, 14/Metro Waterlooplein. **Open** *Jan, Dec* 9am-4pm Mon-Fri; 10am-4pm Sat, Sun. *Feb-June, Sept-Nov* 9am-5pm Mon-Fri; 10am-5pm Sat, Sun. *Jul, Aug* 9am-7pm Mon-Fri; 10am-7pm Sat, Sun. **Admission** €7; free-€3.50 reductions. No credit cards. **Map** p111 B3 ➌
The Hortus has formed a peaceful oasis here since 1682, although it was originally set up more than 50 years earlier when East India Company ships brought back tropical plants and seeds to supply doctors with medicinal herbs (as well as coffee plant cuttings, one specimen of which continued to Brazil to kickstart the South American coffee industry). Other highlights include a massive water lily, the *Victoria Amazonica,* which blooms only once a

tourists, take note: near the corner of Oosterpark and Linneaustraat is the spot where filmmaker Theo van Gogh was brutally murdered by an Islamic extremist in 2004 after making a film deemed to be offensive to Muslims. A sculpture in Oosterpark, *The Scream,* was unveiled in 2007 in his memory.

Sights & museums

Artis

Plantage Kerklaan 38-40 (0900 278 4796/www.artis.nl). Tram 9, 10, 14. **Open** *Summer* 9am-6pm daily. *Winter* 9am-5pm daily. **Admission** €17.70; free-€16.50 reductions. No credit cards. **Map** p111 C2 ➊
The first zoo in mainland Europe (and the third oldest in the world) provides a relaxing day out for children and adults. It's so chilled here that if the weather is nice, they allow you to stay beyond closing hours. On special occasions they even give gay animal tours – those pink flamingos are outlandish! Along with the usual animals

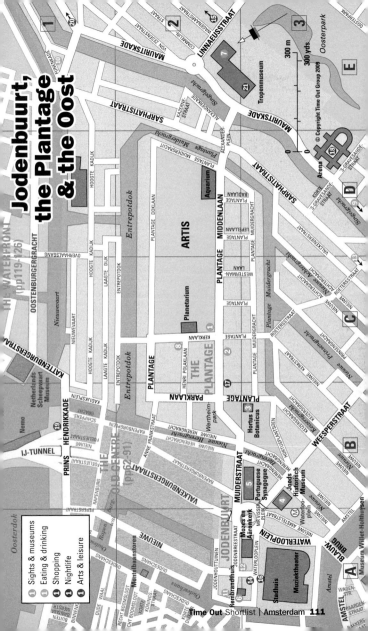

Jodenbuurt, the Plantage & the Oost

THE WATERFRONT (pp119-126)

Oosterpark

Oosterdok

Oosterpark

THE OLD CENTRE (p62-91)

JODENBUURT

- Sights & museums
- Eating & drinking
- Shopping
- Nightlife
- Arts & leisure

© Copyright Time Out Group 2009

300 m

300 yds

Tropenmuseum

Aquarium

ARTIS

Planetarium

THE PLANTAGE

Netherlands Scheepvaart Museum

Nemo

IJ-TUNNEL

PRINS HENDRIKKADE

Hortus Botanicus

Portuguese Synagogue

Joods Historisch Museum

Mozes en Aäronkerk

Rembrandthuis

Mantelbaanstoren

Stadhuis

Muziektheater

Museum Willet-Holthuysen

Arena

BLAUW-BRUG

year, and the oldest potted plant in the world, a 300-year-old cycad – on display in the 1912 palm greenhouse. Other conservatories maintain desert, tropical and sub-tropical climates and a butterfly greenhouse sets hearts of all ages aflutter.

Joods Historisch Museum (Jewish Historical Museum)

Nieuwe Amstelstraat 1 (531 0310/ www.jhm.nl). Tram 9, 14/Metro Waterlooplein. **Open** 11am-5pm daily. Closed Jewish New Year & Yom Kippur. **Admission** €7.50; free-€4.50 reductions, MK. **Map** p111 B3 ④

Housed since 1987 in four synagogues in the old Jewish quarter, the Jewish Historical Museum is full of religious items, photographs and paintings detailing the history of religious practice and Dutch Jewish culture in the Netherlands. There's a real sense of warmth here, especially in the interactive children's section. Temporary exhibitions are also generally excellent, such as the recent 'Superheroes and Schlemiels', exploring the relationship between comics and Jewish memory.

Portuguese Synagogue

Mr Visserplein 3 (624 5351/guided tours; 531 0380/www.esnoga.com). Tram 9, 14/ Metro Waterlooplein. **Open** Jan-Mar, Nov, Dec 10am-4pm Mon-Thur, Sun; 10am-2pm Fri. *Apr-Oct* 10am-4pm Mon-Fri, Sun. Closed Yom Kippur. **Admission** €6.50; free-€5 reductions. No credit cards. **Map** p111 B3 ⑤

Architect Elias Bouwman's mammoth synagogue, one of the largest in the world and reputedly inspired by the Temple of Solomon, was inaugurated in 1675. It's built on wooden piles and surrounded by smaller annexes (offices, archives, the rabbinate and one of the world's oldest libraries). A renovation in the 1950s restored the synagogue to it original form, and interesting tours of its noteworthy interior can be organised through the Jewish Historical Museum. The synagogue holds occasional concerts and candlelight specials at different times of the year.

Rembrandthuis

Jodenbreestraat 4 (520 0400/www. rembrandthuis.nl). Tram 9, 14/ Metro Waterlooplein. **Open** 10am-5pm daily. **Admission** €8 (incl. audio guide); free-€1.30 reductions, MK. **Map** p111 A2/3 ⑥

You can't help but admire the skill and effort with which craftsmen have tried to recreate this house, purchased by Rembrandt in 1639 for 13,000 florins (about €6,000), a massive sum at the time, and occupied by the artist until bankruptcy forced him to move out in 1656. The presentation is, however, dry and unengaging on the whole. Nagging at you is the knowledge that this isn't actually Rembrandt's house, but rather a mock-up of it – which lends an unreal air that's only alleviated when guest artists are allowed to use the studio. There's a remarkable collection of Rembrandt's etchings, which show him at his most experimental, but if it's his paintings you're after, head to the Rijksmuseum (p134).

Tropenmuseum

Linnaeusstraat 2 (568 8200/www. tropenmuseum.nl). Tram 9, 10, 14/bus 22. **Open** 10am-5pm daily. **Admission** €7.50; free-€6 reductions, MK. **Map** p111 E2 ⑦

Visitors to this handsome building get a vivid glimpse of daily life in the tropical and subtropical parts of the world (a strange evolution for a museum originally erected in the 1920s to glorify Dutch colonialism), including Southeast Asia, Oceania, West Asia, North Africa, Latin America and a series called Man and Environment. Exhibits – from religious items and jewellery to washing powder and vehicles – are divided by region. Temporary exhibitions, covering everything from Bollywood to Voodoo, are also consistently excellent.

St Pete's on the Amstel

Hermitage Museum, Phase 2

In June 2009, an outpost of St Petersburg's Hermitage museum opened in Amsterdam with a star-studded, 30-hour ceremony, attended by Queen Beatrix and Russian president Dmitri Medvedev.

Set in a former 19th-century hospital complete with 17th-century courtyard, the building has two vast exhibition spaces, a concert hall and a restaurant. The museum promises to mount two exhibitions a year, borrowing items from the three million-strong collection of its prestigious Russian parent.

The Hermitage's riches owe much to the collecting obsession of Peter the Great (1672-1725), who came to Amsterdam to learn shipbuilding and the art of building on waterlogged ground – the latter knowledge he applied to his pet project, St Petersburg. Peter befriended local doctor Frederik Ruysch, perhaps the greatest ever anatomist and preserver of body parts and mutants in jars. Ruysch enjoyed constructing ghoulish collages with gall and kidney stones piled up into landscapes; dried veins woven into lush shrubberies and testicles crafted into pottery. The scenes were animated with dancing foetus skeletons. After kissing the head of a preserved baby, Peter paid Ruysch 30,000 florins for the lot (much of it is still on display in St Petersburg's Kunstkammer collection). With any luck, some of Peter's prized souvenirs – including Rembrandts – will return for a visit.

The opening exhibition, 'In the Russian Court', features 1800 objects spanning the 19th century, with future shows to include 'The Roots of Modern Art: Braque, Matisse and Picasso' (spring to autumn 2010) and 'Alexander the Great and the Way East' (from autumn 2010).

Hermitage Amsterdam

Nieuwe Herengracht 14 (530 8755/www.hermitage.nl). Tram 4, 9/Metro Waterlooplein. **Open** 10am-5pm daily. **Admission** €8; €5 reductions. No credit cards. **Map** p111 B3.

Brouwerij 't IJ

Verzetsmuseum (Museum of Dutch Resistance)

*Plantage Kerklaan 61 (620 2535/www.
verzetsmuseum.org). Tram 9, 14/Metro
Waterlooplein.* **Open** 11am-5pm Mon,
Sat, Sun; 10am-5pm Tue-Fri. **Admission**
€6.50; free-€3.50 reductions, MK. No
credit cards. **Map** p111 C2 ❽

The Verzetsmuseum tells the story of
the Dutch Resistance during World
War II through a series of artefacts:
false ID papers, clandestine printing
presses and illegal newspapers, spy
gadgets and an authentic secret door
behind which Jews hid. The exhibits
explain how the Dutch people survived
Nazi occupation, and are interspersed
with moving personal testimonies.
Regular temporary exhibitions inves-
tigate wartime themes and modern-day
forms of oppression, and there's a
small research room too. Although a lot
of the information is in Dutch, staff are
often only to happy to give you a per-
sonalised tour.

Eating & drinking

Amstelhaven

*Mauritskade 1 (665 2672/www.
amstelhaven.nl). Tram 3, 7, 10/Metro
Weesperplein.* **Open** *Summer* 11am-
1am Mon-Thur, Sun; 11am-3am Fri,
Sat. *Winter* 4pm-1am Wed, Thur, Sun;
4pm-3am Fri, Sat. **Bar. Map** p111 D3 ❾

Occupying a prime spot on an arterial
canal of the Amstel, this freshly refurbished bar's cavernous insides are
filled with yuppies chowing down on
posh Dutch food and grooving to weekend DJs. But that's not the point.
Amstelhaven's raison d'être is summer
days spent sprawled on the vast deck's
sofas and beanbags, watching boats
bob in the water as staff serve the
resident salty dogs in situ.

Brouwerij 't IJ

*Funenkade 7 (320 1786/www.
brouwerijhetij.nl). Tram 10, 14/
bus 22.* **Open** 3-8pm daily. **Bar.**
Map p111 E1 ❿

A girl's best friend

Amsterdam is famous for its
diamond trade, something it
owes largely to the Jewish
population in and around the
Jodenbuurt area. Indeed, It's
a heritage that's still marketed
heavily to this day; the city's
sparkler shops are as much
tourist attractions in their own
right as they are retail outlets.

To experience an aspirational
brush with luxury, take a tour
around any one of them; for
example, the **Amsterdam
Diamond Center** (Rokin 1-5, 624
5787, www.amsterdamdiamond
center.nl) in the Old Centre,
or the relatively new **Diamant
Museum Amsterdam** (Paulus
Potterstraat 8, 305 5300, www.
diamantmuseumamsterdam.nl)
near Museumplein.

However, the best of the
bunch stands, in fact, near the
Jodenbuurt: **Gassan Diamond**
has an epic building that once
housed 357 polishing machines,
when it was the biggest diamond
processing plant in the world.
Get in the mood by upgrading
from the free tour to one which
includes champagne. But just
remember: falling in love with
a piece of compressed carbon is
the easy part – working out how
you're going to pay for it may
prove to be a little more tricky.

Gassan Diamond

*Nieuwe Uilenburgerstraat 173-5,
(622 5333/www.gassandiamond.
com). Metro Waterlooplein/Tram
9, 14.* **Open** 9am-5pm daily.

Café de Sluyswacht

The famous tasting house at the base of the Gooyer windmill, where wares from award-winning local brewery 't IJ can be sampled. Inside is bare (still retaining the look of the municipal baths it once was) and seating is minimal, so if the weather permits, plonk down on the pavement outside. Its standard range of tipples is available for sampling behind the bar, from pale Plzen to the darker, head-poppingly strong brew, known as Columbus.

Café de Sluyswacht

Jodenbreestraat 1 (625 7611/www. sluyswacht.nl). Tram 9, 14/ Metro Nieuwmarkt. **Open** 11.30am-1am Mon-Thur; 11.30am-3am Fri, Sat; 11.30am-7pm Sun. **Bar**. **Map** p111 A2 ⓫
Listing precariously, the building housing this wooden-framed bar has been around since 1695, when it began life as a lock-keeper's cottage. Inside it's snuggly and warm, whereas outside you can enjoy great views of Oude Schans. A spacious smoking area attracts a lot of students.

The Coffee Gallery

NEW *Jodenbreestraat 94 (06 535 25929/www.thecoffeegallery.nl). Tram 9, 14/Metro Waterlooplein.* **Open** 9am-3pm daily. **Café**. No credit cards. **Map** p111 A3 ⓬
Remember Seinfeld's 'Soup Nazi'? Well, meet the 'Coffee Nazi'. There are many rules to follow here and the proprietor will not be rushed, but it's all a small price to pay for some of the city's best coffee – and a mere €1.10 for a takeaway cappuccino. You might want to do the same with his sandwiches, pastas and risottos.

De Hogesluis

Sarphatistraat 23 (624 1521/www. hogesluis.nl). Tram 3, 7, 10/Metro Weesperplein. **Open** 11am-1am daily. **Bar**. **Map** p111 C3 ⓭
From the Taittinger poster and the glowing fittings to the midnight-blue leather seats, this place oozes understated class, although fortunately it's not in the least bit snooty, and welcomes visitors of all ages and

Eastern block parties

Breaking news: city's hottest clubs make themselves at home in two former newspaper offices in Amsterdam Oost.

The **Volkskrantgebouw** (Wibautstraat 150, www.volks krantgebouw.nl) was launched in 2007 as a new concept, with a group negotiating to take over the building until June 2012 and fill it with creative industries and artists. The icing on the cake is **Canvas op de 7e** (www.canvasopde7e.nl, open noon-1am Sun-Thur, noon-3am Fri-Sat), a rooftop café/restaurant/cocktail bar/club on the seventh floor, with a stellar view of the city.

However, Canvas is merely the lo-fi little brother when compared to the operation across the street. Established in 2009 by the same people behind the already legendary Club 11, **Trouw Amsterdam** (Wibautstraat 131, 463 7788, www.trouwamsterdam.nl, open Wed-Sat, times vary) continues to combine progressive rogramming and good food. In its opening month alone, Trouw booked Kode 9, The Whitest Boy Alive, Flying Lotus, Jazzanova and Tony Allen, and also established a monthly club night for wacky local DJ/artist collective Pips: lab (www.pipslab.nl). The restaurant (open 7-11pm Tue-Sat) serves up reasonably priced global street foods (pad thai, tortillas and saoto soup). And there's even an excellent smoking room with a view over the dance floor.

inclinations. Half of the large space overlooking the river is given over to a (pricey) restaurant, but it's best used as the perfect spot for an indulgent sundowner in the summer months.

Shopping

290 Square Meters

NEW *Houtkopersdwarsstraat 3 (419 2525/www.290sqm.com). Tram 9, 14/ Metro Waterlooplein.* **Open** 11am-6pm Tues-Sat. **Map** p111 A3 ⑭

In its former space, this shop/agency/gallery's claim to fame was that it was the first place in the world where people could purchase customised Nikes. Now, in a more spacious former bank vault, it offers a spectrum of goods, ranging from bikes to fashion, limited-edition books and scents.

Dappermarkt

Dapperstraat (694 7495/www. dappermarkt.nl). Tram 3, 7, 9. **Open** 9am-5pm Mon-Sat. No credit cards. **Map** p111 E2 ⑮

Voted best market of the Netherlands, Dappermarkt is a locals' market, which means that prices don't rise with visitor numbers. It sells all the usual market fodder, plus plenty of cheap clothes.

Waterlooplein

Waterlooplein (552 4074/www. waterloopleinmarkt.nl). Tram 9, 14/ Metro Waterlooplein. **Open** 9am-5pm Mon-Sat. No credit cards.
Map p111 A3 **⑯**
Amsterdam's top bazaar is basically a huge flea market with the added attraction of loads of brand new clothes stalls (although gear can be a bit pricey and, at many stalls, a bit naff). Bargains can be found, but they may be well hidden.

Nightlife

Club 3VOOR12

Studio Desmet, Plantage Middenlaan 4A (www.3voor12.nl). Tram 9, 14. **Open** *Airs between* 10pm-1am Thur. **Admission** free. **Map** p111 B2 **⑰**
This old film theatre bursts into life on Thursday nights to coincide with a live national radio and TV show. Each broadcast throws up a diverse line-up – one week it's three little-known local acts, the next it's international superstars in town for their sold-out gig. Entry is free, but there's limited capacity, so you must reserve a place at http://3voor12.vpro.nl/gastenlijst. The catch is not necessarily knowing what you're signing up for, which – obviously – can make for a surprising evening.

Hotel Arena

's Gravesandestraat 51 (850 2400/ www.hotelarena.nl). Tram 3, 7, 9, 10, 14. **Open** 10pm-4am Fri-Sun. No credit cards. **Map** p111 D3 **⑱**
Once an orphanage, then a youth hostel, the Arena is now finding its feet as a trendy hotel, bar and restaurant. Big city folk already used to trekking long distances will no doubt laugh in the face of its (relative lack of) accessibility, but Amsterdammers tend to forego the small detour eastwards, making it hard for the Arena to truly kick clubbing butt. That said, monthlies like Salsa Lounge, with its funky Latin bias, provide notable exceptions.

Arts & leisure

ARCAM

Prins Hendrikkade 600 (620 4878/ www.arcam.nl). Bus 22, 42, 43. **Open** 1-5pm Tue-Sat. **Admission** free. No credit cards. **Map** p111 B1 **⑲**
The gallery here at the Architecture Centrum Amsterdam is obsessed with the promotion of Dutch contemporary architecture – from the early 20th-century creations of the world-famous Amsterdam School to more modern designs – and as a result organises forums, lectures, its own series of architecture books and exhibitions in its fresh 'silver snail' location.

Studio K

Timorplein 62 (ticket office 692 0422/ restaurant 06 1702 7407/www.studio-k.nu). Tram 14/bus 43. **Open** 11am-1am Mon-Thur, Sun; 11am-3am Fri, Sat. **Map** p111 E1 **⑳**
Opened late in 2007, this former school turned cultural centre is, like mother ship Kriterion, entirely run by students. The place has a distinctive festival feeling as it puts on films, theatre, debates, exhibitions, comedy, club nights and food and drink.

Tropentheater

Kleine Zaal Linnaeusstraat 2; Grote Zaal Mauritskade 63 (568 8500/www. tropentheater.nl). Tram 3, 7, 9, 10, 14/bus 22. **Map** p111 E3 **㉑**
The Tropentheater, next door to the Tropenmuseum, puts on shows influenced by non-Western culture. The programme encompasses everything from Indian dance to salsa concerts, and Turkish films to African drumming. Tropentheater prides itself on offering performances that are as engaging as they are culturally enlightening.

Bimhuis p126

The Waterfront

Amsterdam's historic wealth owes a lot to the waterfront: it was here that goods were unloaded, weighed and prepared for storage in the local warehouses. At the time, the harbour and its arterial canals formed a harmonious whole with the city itself. But a drop in commerce slowly destabilised this unity and the building of Centraal Station in the late 19th century served as a final marker of a change in the industrial mindset. This neo-Gothic monument to modernity blocked both the city's view of the harbour and its own past.

Directly south, the Schreierstoren or 'Weeping Tower' is the most interesting relic of Amsterdam's medieval city wall. Built in 1487, it was from this point, on 4 April 1609, that Henry Hudson departed in search of shorter trade routes to the Far East, and in failing discovered New Amsterdam, which later became known as Manhattan.

An eye-opener along the way is the Renzo Piano-designed **NEMO**, a science museum whose green building dominates the horizon. It dwarfs the silver shell-shaped **ARCAM** architecture gallery and the nautically inclined **Nederlands Scheepvaartmuseum** (www. scheepvaartmuseum.nl), which is closed for renovations and scheduled to reopen in late 2010. The area is thus about sailing forwards (see itinerary p52). One recent success story is the opening of the largest library in the country, **Openbare Bibliotheek Amsterdam**, just east of Centraal Station (CS).

Equally ambitious is its neighbour, the city's **Music Conservatory**. De Architekten Cie designed the building according to Japanese *engawa* principles: the hallways are placed on the exterior to maximise soundproofing for the practising students, yet create a transparency that invites passers-by in to listen to a recital. Meanwhile, the work

I want to ride my fietsicle

Bicycles may be taken for granted, but as 'iron horses that need no feeding' they are functional and proud creatures whose invention has transformed modern life as much as the commercial flight. The *fiets*, as the Dutch call bicycles, have democratised personal movement in an affordable way. Thanks to their mechanical nudity – the artist Saul Steinberg called the bike an 'X-ray of itself' – they are easy to maintain. And did we mention their eco-friendly nature?

The Dutch love the humble bike; they buy 1.5 million annually and then, in Amsterdam alone, steal 150,000 of them. It has been calculated that if the 540,000 bikes in the city were lined up, they would cover the Vondelpark twice. The city is full of cycling visionaries. **VMX Architect** has built a shed for 2,500 bicycles, pile-driven in a canal just west of Central Station. Local squatters have invented 'tall bike jousting' (http://squat.net/hogefiets), a recreation using bikes made of spare parts, available at **Recycled Bicycles** (Spuistraat 84a, www.recycledbicycles.org).

Visiting parties may want to hire a **Fietscafe** (www.fietscafe.nl), a mobile pub, which allows up to 17 people to drink beer and pedal in synchrony. And the **Fietsfabriek** (1e Jacob van Campenstraat 12, www.fietsfabriek.nl) continues its quest to bring cargo bikes to the world with ten 'factories' in Holland and four beyond.

The Amsterdam-based American kinetic artist Eric Staller (www.conferencebike.com), famed for his *Lightmobile* (1985), a Volkswagen Beetle covered with 1,659 computerised lights, has embraced the bicycle as a long-term muse. He has sold hundreds of his **Conference Bike**, where seven people sit in a circle elbow to elbow. In a similarly inspired vein, a few 'dream bike festivals' (www.mebike.org) have taken place in recent years.

Amsterdam cyclists are rightfully proud, or perhaps even a little smug, about their rights to the road. So they should be, since bikes play a key role in achieving the long-term sustainability of our planet. So happy pedalling!

The Waterfront

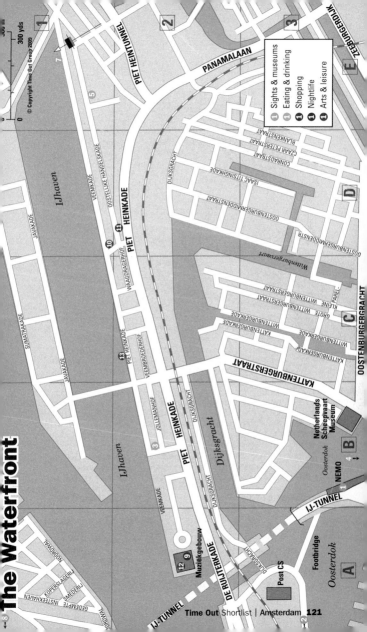

© Copyright Time Out Group 2009

300 yds

IJhaven

PIET HEINTUNNEL

PANAMALAAN

Sights & museums
Eating & drinking
Shopping
Nightlife
Arts & leisure

CONRADSTRAAT
CZAAR PETERSTRAAT
BLANKENSTRAAT

ISAAC TITSINGKADE

OOSTENBURGERMIDDENSTRAAT

OOSTENBURGERMIDDENSTR.

DIJKSGRACHT

PIET HEINKADE

VEEMKADE

OOSTELIJKE HANDELSKADE

WAAGDRAGERHOF

Wittenburgervaart

KLEINE WITTENBURGERSTRAAT

GROTE WITTENBURGERSTRAAT

PAREL

OOSTENBURGERGRACHT

SUMATRAKADE

JAVAKADE

KATTENBURGERKADE

WITTENBURGERKADE

KATTENBURGERKADE

KATTENBURGERSTRAAT

PIET HEINKADE

VEEMBRIDGEHOF

JOLLEMANHOF

DIJKSGRACHT

Dijksgracht

Netherlands
Scheepvaart
Museum

NEMO

Oosterdok

IJ-TUNNEL

IJhaven

VEEMKADE

PIET HEINKADE

DIJKSGRACHT

Muziekgebouw

DE RUIJTERKADE

DIJKSGRACHT

IJ-TUNNEL

Footbridge

Post CS

Oosterdok

KOPERSLAGERIJ
SMEDERIJ
GEMPTE INSTEEKHAVEN
NORDKAAL

continues on residential housing, offices, a massive City Inn hotel and De Blub, a blob-shaped bar and restaurant designed by London's Future Systems, all of which is pencilled for completion by 2011. If all this momentum gets too much, you can always visit the pagoda-shaped floating restaurant, Sea Palace, which will stay docked in kitsch contrast opposite.

Sights & museums

NEMO

Oosterdok 2 (531 3233/www.e-nemo. nl). Bus 32, 33, 34, 35. **Open** 10am-5pm Tue-Sun (daily Dutch school holidays). **Admission** €12.50; free-€6.50 reductions. **Map** p121 B3 ❶
NEMO opened in 1997 and since then has built a strong reputation as a child-friendly science museum. It eschews exhibits in favour of hands-on trickery, gadgetry and tomfoolery (in English and Dutch): you can play DNA detective games, blow mega soap bubbles or explode things in a 'wonderlab'. Log on to the internet to watch the animated film Growing Pains, which was produced for their Teen Facts exhibit, and you'll discover how pleasantly busy they are. On top of that, Renzo Piano's mammoth structure (resembling the reflection of the tunnel below) never fails to raise a gasp from people who are setting eyes on it for the first time. The outdoor café, DEK5, is a lovely place in which to while away an afternoon reading and relaxing. The roof is generally freely accessible whenever it's not a virtual beach or host to the Jazz op het Dak festival.

Openbare Bibliotheek Amsterdam

NEW *Oosterdokskade 143 (523 0900/ www.oba.nl).* **Open** 10am-10pm daily. **Map** p121 A3 ❷

Hotel De Goudfazant

Boats and beaches

Enjoy an alternative holiday at these revamped venues.

Pont 13

Blijburg
Bert Haanstrakade 2004 (416 0330/www.blijburg.nl). Tram 26/ bus 359. **Open** *varies.* €€€. No credit cards. **Global**.
Amsterdam is great for a beach holiday, now the IJburg is covered in sand, and Blijburg is on hand with bands and barbecues. It will close in October 2009 and re-open further up the coast in 2010.

Hotel De Goudfazant
Aambeeldstraat 10H (636 5170/ www.hoteldegoudfazant.nl). Ferry from Centraal Station/Bus 38, 105, 109. **Open** 6pm-1am Tue-Sun. **Global**.
This post-industrial restaurant offers fine French cuisine and seafood at affordable prices.

Kaap Kot aan de Amstel
NEW *Korte Ouderkerkerdijk 30 (463 7158/www.kaapkot.nl). Metro Spaklerweg.* **Open** *May-Oct 11-1am daily. Winter opening hours vary.* €€. **Global**.
Head up the Amstel river to this aluminum prefab shed near the

main city jail and the Hells Angels clubhouse. Simple dishes such as pumpkin soup and baked Dorade fillet combine with excellent wines.

Pont 13
Aparandadam 50 (770 2722/ www.pont13.nl). Bus 22, 48. **Open** 6-10pm daily. €€€. **Global**.
This revamped ferry in the western havens is intriguing. Simple, hearty fare is prepared with genuine flair.

NDSM
TT Neveritaweg 15 (330 5480/ www.ndsm.nl). Ferry from Centraal Station/bus 35, 37, 38, 91, 94.
A shipbuilding yard-turned-cultural complex, which hosts small-scale workshops and performances that are popular with local artists.

Wilhelmina-Dok
Noordwal 1 (632 3701/www. wilhelmina-dok.nl). Ferry from Centraal Station. **Open** 11am-midnight. €€€. **Mediterranean**.
Devour soup and sandwiches by day and Mediterranean dishes by night in this scenic cubic building.

As one of Europe's largest public libraries, this big city landmark opened on 07-07-07. Designed by Jo Coenen, the building treats arriving visitors to a soaring view up to its seventh floor café-restaurant, which, in turn, offers a spectacular view over Amsterdam. With walnut floors and white walls and shelves, the interior is eminently low key; colour comes from the books and the mixed bag of people using the free Wi-Fi – or the polyester study 'pods' (which make an ideal spot for a nap). The place was much praised when it opened, though critics have posed pertinent questions such as 'Um, where exactly are all the books?'

Eating & drinking

Fifteen

Pakhuis Amsterdam, Jollemanhof 9 (0900 343 8336 premium rate/ www.fifteen.nl). Tram 25, 26. **Open** noon-3pm, 5.30pm-1am Mon-Sat. **€€€€**. **Global**. No credit cards. **Map** p121 B2 ❸

This culinary franchise of sorts belonging to Jamie Oliver seeks to transform challenged street kids into a well-oiled kitchen brigade. It's inspired by his love for dishes honest and fresh, offering a pre-set four course tasting menu, which changes weekly.

Kilimanjaro

Rapenburgerplein 6 (622 3485/www. restaurantkilimanjaro.com). Bus 22, 42, 43. **Open** 5-10pm Tue-Sun. **€€€**. **African**. **Map** p121 B3 ❹

This relaxed and friendly pan-African eating place offers a reliable assortment of traditional recipes from as far afield as Senegal, the Ivory Coast, Tanzania and Ethiopia. Once you've eaten your way from the east all the way through to the west coast of Africa, you'll probably need some swift refreshment in the cooling form of either fruity cocktails or the seriously potent regional beers.

Koffiehuis KHL

Oostelijke Handelskade 44 (779 1575/ www.khl.nl). Tram 10, 26/Bus 41. **Open** 11am-10pm Tue-Fri; noon-10pm Sat, Sun. No credit cards. **Bar**. **Map** p121 E1 ❺

This beautiful, light-flooded interior harks back to the days in the early 20th century when it was a canteen serving staff of the Royal Holland Lloyd shipping line. Now it's a café-cum-meeting space serving the local community, with plenty to attract new visitors. There is art on the walls and regular live music for lifting spirits.

Nevy

NEW *Westerdoksdijk 40 (334 6409/ www.nevy.nl). Tram 3/bus 48.* **Open** noon-1am daily. **€€€**. **Bar/Seafood**. **Map** p121 A1 ❻

Nevy is a sophisticated dining spot, with sleek lines, burnished marbles, a voluptuous lounge and a view over the IJ. The Michelin-starred chef Robert Kranenborg acts as an adviser to the kitchen, which dedicates itself to cooking wonderful seafood dishes. What more could you ask for? But, if your appetite isn't sated, try Nevy's sister operations Vyne and Envy.

Odessa

Veemkade 259 (419 3010/www.de-odessa.nl). Tram 10, 26/bus 41. **Open** 6pm-1am Mon-Fri; 6pm-3am Sat, Sun. **€€€**. **Global**. **Map** p121 E1 ❼

More dedicated trendsters regularly make the trek to the unlikely environs of an old Ukrainian fishing boat for Odessa's fusion food and tastefully revamped interior – the vibe is 1970s James Bond filtered through a modern lounge sensibility. On warmer nights, you can dine on the lit deck. DJs raise the tempo by spinning party tunes from 10pm on weekend evenings.

Open!

Westerdoksplein 20 (620 1010/www. open.nl). Tram 3/bus 18, 21, 22, 48. **Open** 10am-1am Mon-Thur, Sun; 10am-3am Fri, Sat. **Map** p121 A1 ❽

The rejuvenation of Siberia

NDSM

There was a time when Amsterdam North was called the Siberia of the city. Even in centuries past, the land on the other side of that body of water called the IJ was known for being little more than the spot that even the Romans overlooked, and where later the remains of freshly executed criminals were hung for public display. There was scant interest to draw short-term visitors northwards – except perhaps cycling routes towards such painfully scenic fishing villages as Volendam and Marken, or the trip on the free ferry from the back of Centraal Station. But if the **Noord-Zuidlijn** metro link (p66) actually gets built, this will finally unite this once isolated area with the rest of Amsterdam.

Meanwhile, redevelopment plans continue. A new branch of the **Filmmuseum** (p141) is being built just west of the Shell Tower, behind Centraal Station. From late 2009, the surrounding grounds and pavilion Tolhuistuin (www.tolhuistuin.nl) will be designated a cultural destination for festivals, exhibitions, dining and music. With **Paradiso** (p146) doing the musical booking, it's looking very promising indeed.

Already the former shipping yard **NDSM** (p123) has been transformed into a huge creative space with artists' studios, a skate hall and a slew of singular spaces. It sports a wonderful post-apocalyptic vibe that's ideal for parties, concerts and wacky theatre festivals like **Over het IJ** (p42) and **Robodock** (p44). It has a surrounding district of student container dwellings, a 'clean energy' exhibition, restaurant and café (www.noorderlichtcafe.nl), and boasts regular visits from the alternative party boat Stubnitz (www.stubnitz.com), a floating zone that books bands, DJs and artists.

This ground zero for Dutch subculture is also home to the Benelux headquarters of MTV networks, which moved into a wildly revamped former woodwork factory. It's the aspiration of the powers-that-be to reinvigorate Amsterdam as a 'creative capital'. Only time will tell whether they realise their dream.

Set in a box of steel and glass atop an unused railway bridge, this is one of the more attractive restaurants in town. Its open kitchen pumps out simple classics for lunch and dinner, all at reasonable prices: try the steak tartare or steak béarnaise. For further regeneration, take a walk along the adjoining residential housing project that will lead to Prinseneiland.

Nightlife

Bimhuis

Piet Heinkade 3 (788 2188/www. bimhuis.nl). Tram 25, 26. **Open** most shows start 8.30pm. **Map** p121 A2 **9**
The name Bimhuis is familiar to jazz fans all over the world , and musicians queue up for a chance to grace its stage. Even its move to a bizarre glass box jutting oddly out of the Muziekgebouw complex (pX16) hasn't tarnished its reputation. Instead, the eye-catching building and familiar interior layout have provided the Bimhuis with a healthy future.

Café Pakhuis Wilhelmina

Veemkade 576 (419 3368/www.cafe pakhuiswilhelmina.nl). Tram 10, 26; bus 42. **Open** hours vary Wed-Sun. No credit cards. **Map** p121 D1 **10**
Wilhelmina is still often overlooked by casual clubbers. Is it the club's IJ location? The absence of bouncers? Or the bottles of beer for only €2? Regardless, don't miss it if your heart lies with today's leftfield music scene. Professor Nomad does weekly improv and theme nights, regular nights drop dubstep and filthy drum 'n' bass, and every first Thursday of the month brings the always enjoyable Hardrockkaraoke.

Panama

Oostelijke Handelskade 4 (311 8686/ www.panama.nl). Tram 10, 26. **Open** 9pm-3am Thur, Sun; 10pm-4am Fri, Sat. **Map** p121 D2 **11**
Rising star on the Amsterdam nightlife scene, restaurant/theatre/club Panama overlooks the IJ in one of the city's most booming areas. Most nights mix up Dutch DJ talent with big international names, such as Danny Howells, Sander Kleinenberg and John Digweed. On Sunday, enjoy live music, mostly jazz and latin tunes.

Arts & leisure

Muziekgebouw

Piet Heinkade 1 (788 2010/tickets 788 2000/www.muziekgebouw.nl). Tram 25, 26. **Map** p121 A2 **12**
Designed by the internationally renowned Danish architectural practice 3xNielsen, the Muziekgebouw is one of the most innovative musical complexes anywhere in Europe, befitting its previous incarnation, the IJsbreker's long-lasting ethos to promote modern variants of classical, jazz and world music. Never afraid to take risks, the centre's weekly schedule bustles with delights ranging from cutting-edge multimedia works to celebrations of composers from the last 150 years. It is also home to the Klankspeeltuin (www.klankspeeltuin.nl), where seven-to 12-year-olds can play with an inspired selection of musical machines, installations and computers.

Pakhuis de Zwijger

NEW *Pakhuis de Zwijger, Piet Heinkade 179 (788 4440/www. dezwijger.nl). Tram 25, 26.* **Map** p121 C2 **13**
Welcome to a hip cultural venue. Pakhuis de Zwijger is a former warehouse that has been refitted to house various media organisations. It also hosts a cutting-edge array of events, including readings, workshops and gatherings of the design, new media and creative industries; it's all about innovation. Particularly inspired are VJ visionaries Beamlab (www.beamlab.nl) and street fashion guerrillas Streetlab (www.streetlab.nl). There's also a great IJ-side café that is open weekdays from 9am to 11pm.

Boerenmarkt p130

The Jordaan

The Jordaan emerged when the city was extended in the 17th century. It was originally designated an area for the working classes and industrial enterprises (it also provided a haven for victims of religious persecution, such as the Jews and Huguenots). However, despite such proletarian origins, its properties are now highly desirable. While many residents are fiercely community-spirited, the nouveaux riches have moved in to gentrify the area.

The Jordaan has no major sights; it's a place in which you stumble across things. The area north of the shopping-dense **Rozengracht**, the Jordaan's approximate mid-point, is picturesque, whereas the area to the south is more commercial. As you explore, you may chance upon some of Amsterdam's more unusual galleries (see box p131).

Between scenic coffee breaks and decadent daytime beers, browse in the specialist shops tucked away on these adorable side streets. You'll find many outdoor markets nearby: Monday morning's Noordermarkt and Saturday's organic foodie paradise Boerenmarkt take place around the **Noorderkerk**, the city's first Calvinist church, built in 1623. Adjacent to the Noordermarkt lies the Westermarkt, and another general market fills Lindengracht on Saturdays.

Between Brouwersgracht and the postcard-pretty Westelijk Eilanden, quirky shops can be found on Haarlemmerstraat and its westerly extension Haarlemmerdijk, where you'll see Haarlemmerpoort city gate, built in 1840. Behind it lies the wonderful **Westerpark**, which in turn connects to the arts complex Westergasfabriek.

Eating & drinking

Amsterdam

Watertorenplein 6 (682 2666/www.cra dam.nl). Tram 10/Bus 21. **Open** 11am-midnight Mon-Thur, Sun; 11am-1am Fri, Sat. €€€. **Dutch**. Map p129 A2 ●

Kitsch Kitchen p130

This spacious monument to industry just west of the Jordaan pumped water from the coast's dunes for around a century. Now it pumps out honest Dutch and French dishes – from *kroketten* to caviar – under floodlights rescued from the old Ajax stadium.

Café Chris

Bloemstraat 42 (624 5942/www.cafe chris.nl). Tram 10, 13, 17. **Open** 3pm-1am Mon-Thur; 3pm-2am Fri, Sat; 3-9pm Sun. No credit cards. **Bar.** **Map** p129 C4 **2**

Not much has changed since 1624 at the oldest bar in town, where builders from the Westerkerk would come to receive their pay. It remains popular among local workers as an unpretentious place to unwind, surrounded by charming bric-a-brac.

Foodware

Looiersgracht 12 (620 8898/www.food ware.nl). Tram 7, 10, 17. **Open** noon-9pm Mon-Sat. **€€**. No credit cards. **Takeaway. Map** p129 C5 **3**

This takeaway (with a few chairs) offers soups, sandwiches, salads and meals; ask for a fork and make for a canalside bench. Order an Italian *bollen* and you are likely to come back for more.

La Oliva Pintxos y Vinos

NEW *Egelantiersstraat 122-4 (320 4316).* Tram 3, 10. **Open** noon-10pm, Tue, Wed; noon-11pm, Thur-Sat; 1-10pm Sun. **€€€**. **Spanish**. **Map** p129 B4 **4**

From yuppies to genuine Spaniards, many praise La Oliva's authentic food and tapas, as well as the rich selection of wines by the glass. If it's too full (and there's a good chance it will be), there are plenty of other options along this strip, recently nicknamed 'Little Italy'.

Proust

Noordermarkt 4 (623 9145/www.good foodgroup.nl). Tram 3/Buses 18, 21, 22. **Open** 9am-1am Mon; noon-1am Tue-Fri, Sun; 9am-3am Sat. **Bar.** **Map** p129 C2 **5**

Still trendy after all these years, and great for market pitstops or bar crawl kick-starts. The style is sleek and pared down. If full, try heading over to Finch next door; on warm days both bars' terraces merge into one convivial whole.

Semhar

Marnixstraat 259-261 (638 1634/www. semhar.nl). Tram 3, 10. **Open** 4-10pm Tue-Sun. **€€**. **African**. **Map** p129 B5 **6**

A great spot to tuck into the *injera* (tasty sourdough pancake) and veg-friendly food of Ethiopia (best washed down with a calabash of cold beer).

Small World Catering

Binnen Oranjestraat 14 (420 2774/ www.smallworldcatering.nl). Tram 3/ Bus 18, 21, 22. **Open** 10.30am-8pm Tue-Sat; noon-8pm Sun. No credit cards. **Café. Map** p129 B2 **7**

The base for this catering company is a tiny deli. Besides the superb coffee and fresh juices, you can enjoy a range of salads, lasagnes and sandwiches.

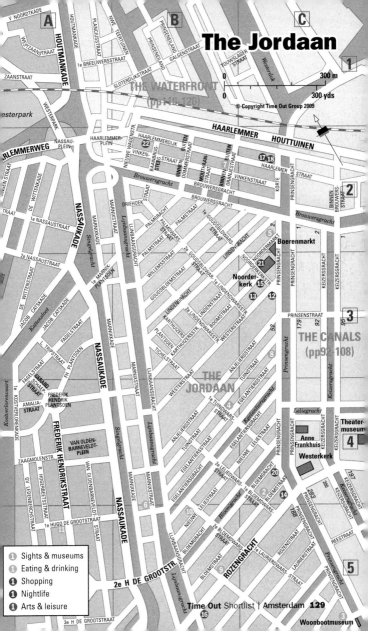

The Jordaan

0   300 m
0   300 yds
© Copyright Time Out Group 2009

THE WATERFRONT
(pp118-126)

HAARLEMMER HOUTTUINEN

THE CANALS
(pp92-108)

THE JORDAAN

Boerenmarkt

Noorder-
kerk

Anne
Frankhuis

Westerkerk

Theater-
museum

Time Out Shortlist | Amsterdam **129**

Woonbootmuseum

1 Sights & museums
1 Eating & drinking
1 Shopping
1 Nightlife
1 Arts & leisure

't Smalle

*Egelantiersgracht 12 (623 9617/www.
t-smalle.nl). Tram 3, 10, 13, 14, 17.*
Open 10am-1am Mon-Thur, Sun;
10am-2am Fri, Sat. No credit cards.
Bar. Map p129 C3 ⑧
This charming bar boasts one of the
most scenic terraces along one of the
prettiest canals in the city, so it's hardly
surprising that waterside seats are
snared early in the day. Its gleaming
brass and candles hark back to the
18th century, when it functioned as the
Hoppe distillery.

Struik

NEW *Rozengracht 160 (no phone/www.
myspace.com/bar_struik), Tram 10,
13, 14, 17.* **Open** 5pm-1am Mon;
10am-1am Tue-Thu; 10am-3am Fri;
11am-3am Sat; 11am-1am Sun. **Bar.
Map** p129 B5 ⑨
A chilled bar for creatives who like
their music cool and their design street.
The friendly neighbourhood café feeling is enhanced by *econo* daily dinner
specials. Later on, the DJ kicks in.

SPRMRKT p132

De Vliegende Schotel

*Nieuwe Leliestraat 162-168 (625 2041/
www.vliegendeschotel.com). Tram 10,
13, 14, 17.* **Open** 4-11.30pm daily.
€€. Vegetarian. Map p129 B5 ⑩
The 'Venerable Flying Saucer' serves up
a splendid array of meat-free dishes in
a buffet format. If the restaurant is full,
try nearby De Bolhoed (Prinsengracht
60-62, 626 1803) for tasty vegan dishes.

Yam-Yam

*Frederik Hendrikstraat 88-90 (681
5097/www.yamyam.nl). Tram 3, 10.*
Open 6-10pm Tue-Sat; 5.30-10pm Sun.
€€. Italian. Map p129 A5 ⑪
With tasty, inexpensive pastas and pizzas served in a hip and atmosphere, it's
no wonder that Yam-Yam is a favourite
among pre-clubbers and locals alike.

Shopping

Boerenmarkt

*Westerstraat/Noorderkerkstraat (no
phone/www.boerenmarktamsterdam.nl).
Tram 3, 10.* **Open** 9am-4pm Sat.
No credit cards. **Map** p129 C3 ⑫
Every Saturday, the Noordermarkt
turns into an organic farmers' market.
Groups of singers or medieval musicians can make a visit feel more like a
day trip than a grocery shop.

Delicious Food

Westerstraat 24 (320 3070). Tram 3.
Open 10am-6.30pm Mon, Wed-Fri;
9am-6pm Sat. **Map** p129 C3 ⑬
Organic produce has reached a pinnacle of urban 'rustic' chic at what can
only be described as a bulk food boutique. An enticing spread of the finest
pastas, nuts, spices, oils and vinegars.

Kitsch Kitchen

*Rozengracht 8-12 (622 8261/www.kitsch
kitchen.nl). Tram 13, 14, 17.* **Open**
10am-6pm Mon-Sat. **Map** p129 C4 ⑭
Mexican Mercado with a twist. Even
the hardiest denouncers of tat will love
the colourful culinary and household
objects, wacky wallpapers included.

Art crossing

Serieuze Zaken

You could easily fill a holiday by trawling through the 40-odd Jordaan galleries. Since they occupy former homes or shops, they are pleasantly compact spaces. The best time to visit is during the afternoons between Wednesday and Saturday, when most galleries are open.

For a taste of the international, try **Serieuze Zaken** (Lauriersgracht 96, 427 5770, www.serieuze zaken.info). Owner Rob Malasch is famed for who he knows on the art scene. He championed now-celebrated Chinese artists such as Hui Xin early on and is developing a collection of works by LA artists. The gallery's neighbour **Torch** (Lauriergracht 94, 626 0284, www. torchgallery.com) has built up a quirky reputation by exhibiting the likes of Jake & Dinos Chapman, Anton Corbijn, Richard Kern and Micha Klein. And the **Stedelijk Museum Bureau Amsterdam** (Rozenstraat 59, 422 0471, www. smba.nl) is often hipper than its mothership, with subversive shows by locally based rising stars.

Across Rozengracht (where one can pay one's respects at the

house in which Rembrandt died at No.184), is **Galerie Fons Welters** (Bloemstraat 140, 423 3046, www.fonswelters.nl). Doyen of the Amsterdam gallery scene, Fons Welters likes to 'discover' local talent and has shown remarkable taste in the fields of photography and installation, providing a home for Dutch artists Jennifer Tee and Berend Strik. A visit to his gallery is worth it for the Atelier van Lieshout entrance alone.

For straightforward iconography, head to **Rockarchive** (110 Prinsengracht, 423 0489, www. rockarchive.com), owned by photographer Jill Furmanovsky, where there is usually a savvy selection of rock prints.

Then there's the curious **KochxBos Gallery** (1e Anjeliersdwarsstraat 3, 681 4567, www.koch xbos.nl), which specialises in art from the dark sides of 'low-brow' artists such as Ray Caesar.

If you are fascinated by what lies behind closed doors, then visit Open Ateliers Jordaan (www.open ateliersjordaan.nl) in May, when around 70 artists' studios open their doors to the public.

Noordermarkt

Noordermarkt (no phone). Tram 3, 10. **Open** 7.30am-1pm Mon. No credit cards. **Map** p129 C3 ⑮

North of Westermarkt, Noordermarkt is frequented by serious shoppers. The stacks of (mainly second-hand) clothes, shoes, jewellery and hats need to be sorted with a grim determination, but there are real bargains to be had.

SPRMRKT

Rozengracht 191-193 (330 5601/www. sprmrkt.nl). Tram 10, 13, 14, 17. **Open** noon-6pm Mon, Sun; 10am-6pm Tue, Wed, Fri, Sat; 10am-8pm Thur. **Map** p129 B5 ⑯

A whopping 450 square metres of cool threads. The prize is the shop-within-the-shop, SPR+, which features picks from Margiela, Acne Jeans, Peachoo + Krejberg. There's also a selection of 1960s and '70s furniture.

Unlimited Delicious

Haarlemmerstraat 122 (622 4829/ www.unlimiteddelicious.nl). Tram 3/bus 18, 21, 22. **Open** 9am-6pm Mon-Sat. **Map** p129 C2 ⑰

Known for such twisted treats as a caramel-balsamic-chocolate pie with a brownie bottom, Unlimited Delicious also offers courses in bonbon-making.

Vlaamsch Broodhuis

Haarlemmerstraat 108 (528 6430/ www.vlaamschbroodhuys.nl). Tram 3/ bus 18, 21, 22. **Open** 11am-6.30pm Mon; 8.30am-6.30pm Tue-Fri; 9am-5pm Sat. No credit cards. **Map** p129 C2 ⑱

The name might be a bit of a mouthful, but it's worth a visit to wrap your gums around the tasty sourdough breads, fine French pastries and fresh salads, among other treats.

Nightlife

Flex Bar

Pazzanistraat 1 (486 2123/www.flex bar.nl). Tram 3, 10/bus 18, 21, 22. **Open** times vary. **Map** p129 A2 ⑲

Electronic sounds are provided by local DJs such as Rednose Distrikt, Fight-club and Beat Dimensions Crew. Flex-bar consists of two spaces, often with different programmes.

Arts & leisure

Bibliotheca Philosophica Hermetica

NEW *Bloemstraat 15 (625 8079/www. ritmanlibrary.nl). Tram 3, 10.* **Open** Mon-Fri 9.30am-12.30pm, 1.30-5pm. No credit cards. **Map** p129 C4 ⑳

This library holds more than 20,000 manuscripts and volumes of Christian-Hermetic tradition. You'll find that it's the perfect place for factchecking the *Da Vinci Code* or discovering small but illuminating exhibitions.

Noorderkerk

Noordermarkt 44 (626 6436/www. noorderkerkconcerten.nl). Tram 3, 10. No credit cards. **Map** p129 C3 ㉑

Although the wooden benches in this early 17th-century church are a little on the hard side, all is soon forgiven thanks to its programme of recitals. Reservations recommended.

The Movies

Haarlemmerdijk 161 (638 6016/www. themovies.nl). Tram 3/bus 18, 21, 22. **Map** p129 B2 ㉒

The oldest cinema in the city continues to exude a genteel atmosphere. The adjoining Wild Kitchen serves decent set dinners costing between €27 and €35; prices include a ticket for a film.

Westergasfabriek

Haarlemmerweg 8-10 (586 0710/www. westergasfabriek.com). Tram 3, 10/bus 18, 21, 22. **Map** p129 A2 ㉓

With a plethora of industrial areas being reinvented as performance and exhibition spaces, this former gasworks is evolving into one of the city's premier cultural hubs. It's also the new home of Cosmic (www.cosmictheater.nl), an inspired theatre troupe.

Rijksmuseum p134

The Museum Quarter, Vondelpark & the South

The heart of the late 19th-century Museum Quarter lies in Museumplein, the city's largest square, bordered roughly by the Concertgebouw, the **Rijksmuseum**, the Stedelijk Museum of Modern Art and the **Van Gogh Museum**. However, with the Rijksmuseum partially closed until 2013, and the **Stedelijk Museum** scheduled to reopen in spring 2010, the heart is beating more faintly at present (see box p142). Museumplein itself is not really an authentic Amsterdam square, but it does have plenty of grass, a wading pool that turns into a skating ramp and a pleasant café.

As you would expect in such cultural surroundings, property doesn't come cheap and the affluence is apparent. Housing covers more than its fair share of elegant 19th-century mansions, whereas Van Baerlestraat and PC Hooftstraat are as close as Amsterdam gets to Rodeo Drive, their boutiques offering solace to ladies who might otherwise lunch alone with their poodles.

Vondelpark is the city's largest and most central park, and the last few years have witnessed much renovation as the park has sunk two to three metres since it was first built – some of the larger trees are, in fact, 'floating' on huge blocks of styrofoam, or are slyly reinforced with underground poles. There are several ponds and lakes, along with play areas and cafés, the most pleasant of which are 't Blauwe Theehuis and Café Vertigo at the **Nederlands Filmmuseum**. Vondelpark gets fantastically busy on sunny days and Sundays, when bongos abound, dope is toked and football games take up any space that happens to be left over. Films, plays and public concerts are also staged, with a festival of free open-air performances taking place during the summer months.

Stretching out in the shape of a ring beneath Vondelpark is a fairly indeterminate region known as Nieuw Zuid (New South), which is itself bordered to the north by Vondelpark, to the east by the Amstel and to the west by the 1928 Olympisch Stadion (www.olympisch-stadion.net).

Sights & museums

House of Bols

Paulus Potterstraat 14 (570 8575/ www.houseofbols.nl). Tram 2, 3, 5, 12. **Open** noon-6pm Mon, Wed-Sun. **Admission** €11.50 (over-18s only, includes free cocktail). **Map** p135 D2 ❶
The Bols were among the first producers of fine *jenever* – the original gin – and began it all in 1575. Besides a 'World of Bartending', their centre also features a 'Hall of Taste', which promises a fun, synaesthetic experience. You may even get a free cocktail in the 'Mirror Bar' after the tour. It's too bad that it doesn't serve absinthe – that might combine nicely with a visit to the Van Gogh Museum across the street.

Rijksmuseum

Jan Luijkenstraat 1 (674 7000/ www.rijksmuseum.nl). Tram 2, 5, 7, 10, 16, 24, 25. **Open** 9am-6pm Mon-Thur, Sat, Sun; 9am-8.30pm Fri. **Admission** €11; free reductions, MK. **Map** p135 D2/E2 ❷
Designed by PJH Cuypers and opened in 1885, the nation's 'treasure house' is home to 40 Rembrandt and four Vermeer paintings. With the country's largest collection of art and artefacts, it holds up a mirror to Centraal Station, built by the same architect. However, most of the museum's million exhibits will be hidden from view until after the summer of 2013, while it gets a €227 million facelift. The closure is, in fact,

something of a blessing in disguise: rather than overdosing on the vast collection, visitors can focus on the masterpieces among 400 fine works in the Philips Wing. If you do want to see the interior as it transforms, you can join one of the museum's regular 'Hard Hat Tours'. Some parts of the collection will also be featured in shows organised by other museums throughout the Netherlands and its outpost at the Schiphol Airport. In short: there are still plenty of Golden Age artworks to gaze at, but it's advisable to check the museum's excellent website before you visit.

Stedelijk Museum of Modern Art

Paulus Potterstraat 13 (573 2911/www. stedelijk.nl). Tram 2, 3, 5, 12. **Open** 10am-6pm daily. **Admission** €9; free-€4.50 reductions, MK. **Map** p135 D3 ❸
After enjoying a temporary home in the Post CS building near Centraal Station, the Stedelijk Museum is scheduled to return to its old haunt on Paulus Potterstraat in April 2010 . In the meanwhile, Stedelijk in de Staat (Stedelijk in the City) is holding various exhibitions around town. Check the website to get the latest information. Wherever it is, the museum has an amazing and diverse collection to draw from. Pre-war highlights include works by modern masters Cézanne, Picasso, Matisse and Chagall, plus a collection of paintings and drawings by the Russian constructivist Kasimir Malevich. Among post-1945 artists in the collection are Minimalists Donald Judd, Barnett Newman and Frank Stella, Pop artists Roy Lichtenstein, Sigmar Polke and Andy Warhol, Abstract Expressionists Karel Appel and Willem De Kooning, and conceptual artists Jan Dibbets, Jeff Koons and Bruce Nauman.

Van Gogh Museum

Paulus Potterstraat 7 (570 5200/www. vangoghmuseum.nl). Tram 2, 3, 5, 12. **Open** 10am-6pm Mon-Thur, Sat, Sun; 10am-10pm Fri. **Admission** €12.50;

The Museum Quarter, Vondelpark & the South

VIJZELGRACHT

Heineken Experience

THE PIJP (pp145–148)

THE CANALS (pp92–109)

HOBBEMAKADE

Boerenwetering

HOBBEMAKADE

MUSEUM QUARTER

Pieter de Hoochstraat

Vermeerstraat

V. Miereveld straat

Rijksmuseum

Van Gogh Museum

MUSEUM-PLEIN

Stedelijk Museum

VAN BAERLESTRAAT

Concertgebouw

STADHOUDERSKADE

Footbridge

LEIDSEPLEIN

Stadsschouwburg

American Hotel

Casino

Bellevue

Melkweg

OVERTOOM

CONSTANTIJN HUYGENSSTRAAT

Nederlands Filmmuseum

ROEMER

VAN BAERLESTRAAT

Vondelpark

NASSAUKADE

OVERTOOM

OVERTOOM

Polikliniek

W.Y. PLEIN

BILDERDIJKSTRAAT

DE CLERCQSTRAAT

Bilderdijkgracht

Singelgracht

Jacob van Lennepkade

Da Costakade

300 m

300 yds

© Copyright Time Out Group 2009

Sights & museums
Eating & drinking
Shopping
Nightlife
Arts & leisure

Vondelpark p133

free-€2.50 reductions, MK. *Temporary exhibitions* prices vary. **Map** p135 D2 **4**
An excellent collection of more than 200 paintings and 500 drawings by everyone's favourite troubled genius occupies this Gerrit Rietveld-designed building on a permanent basis. Meanwhile, the relatively new wing by Japanese architect Kisho Kurokawa is usually home to temporary exhibitions that focus on Van Gogh's contemporaries and his influence upon other artists. These shows are assembled from both the museum's own extensive archives and private collections. Try to visit around midday (from 11am) or late afternoon (around 4.30pm): the queues at other hours can be frustratingly long, and the gallery unbearably busy. It's worth noting that there's a programme of lectures, concerts and films on Friday evenings. You can book online to avoid the line-ups at the museum.

Eating & drinking

Bagels & Beans
Van Baerlestraat 40 (675 7050/www. bagelsbeans.nl). Tram 2, 3, 5, 12. **Open** 8am-6pm Mon-Fri; 9.30am-6pm Sat, Sun. **Café. Map** p135 D3 **5**
An Amsterdam success story, this branch of B&B also boasts a wonderfully peaceful back patio. Perfect for an economical breakfast, lunch or snack; sun-dried tomatoes are a speciality, always employed with particular skill.

't Blauwe Theehuis
Vondelpark 5 (662 0254/www.blauwe theehuis.nl). Tram 1, 2, 3, 5, 12. **Open** 9am-5pm Mon-Wed; 9am-11pm Thur; 9am-2am Fri; 9am-1am Sat; 9am-10pm Sun. **Bar. Map** p135 C3 **6**
One of the few local landmarks that allows you to nestle inside with a beer, HJAB Baanders' extraordinary 1930s teahouse – a sort of UFO-hat hybrid – is a choice spot for fair-weather drinking. In summer, there are DJs and barbecues, although it's a romantic spot for dinner and drinks all year round.

Eetcafé I Kriti
Balthasar Floriszstraat 3 (664 1445/ www.ikriti.nl). Tram 3, 5, 12, 24. **Open** 4pm-1am daily. **€€€. Greek. Map** p135 E3 **7**
Eat and party Greek style in this evocation of Crete. On a lucky night, the owner and chef Yannis steps out of the kitchen between squid grillings to sing and play guitar for guests, sometimes boosted by plate-lobbing antics.

Kashmir Lounge
Jan Pieter Heijestraat 85-87 (683 2268/www.kashmirlounge.com). Tram 7, 17. **Open** 10am-1am Mon-Thur; 10am-3am Fri, Sat; 11am-1am Sun. No credit cards. **Coffeeshop. Map** p135 A3 **8**
Illuminated with candlelight, Kashmir may seem too dark at first, but once your eyes adjust, you'll discover an opulent cavern of Indian tapestries, ornate tiles, hand-carved walls and cushions swathed in zebra and cheetah prints. Turning a multitude of obscure corners and partially enclosed tables, you can feel like a VIP at no extra charge. Along with a terrace and regular DJs and live music, this is a gem of a coffeeshop.

De Peper
Overtoom 301 (412 2954/www.de peper.org). Tram 1. **Open** 6pm-1am Tues; 6pm-3am Fri; 6pm-1am Sun. **€**. No credit cards. **Vegetarian. Map** p135 B3 **9**
This purveyor of the cheapest and best vegan food in town is a collectively organised, non-profit project mingling culture with an awesome kitchen – well, depending on who's volunteering that night. Book ahead. It's part of OT301 (p141).

Peperwortel
Overtoom 140 (685 1053/www.peper wortel.nl). Tram 1, 3, 12. **Open** 4-9pm Mon-Fri; 3-9pm Sat, Sun. **€€**. No credit cards. **Global. Map** p135 C2 **10**
You could survive for weeks on takeaways from Pepper Root (which, if you

follow the name's Jewish Amsterdam roots, translates into Horse Radish), with its range of dishes embracing everything from Dutch to Mexican, as well as Indian and Spanish cuisines.

Riaz

Bilderdijkstraat 193 (683 6453/www.riaz.nl). Tram 3, 7, 10, 12, 17. **Open** 11.30am-9pm Mon-Fri, Sun. **€€**. No credit cards. **South American**. **Map** p135 B1 ⓫

A Surinamese joint where you might be lucky enough to bump into Ruud Gullit; it's where he scores his rotis when he happens to be in town.

Wildschut

Roelof Hartplein 1-3 (676 8220/www.goodfoodgroup.nl). Tram 3, 5, 12, 24. **Open** 9.30am-1am Mon-Fri; 10am-3am Sat, Sun. **Bar**. **Map** p135 E3 ⓬

A stunning example of Amsterdam School architecture, this semi-circular building drips with elegant nouveau detail. The menu mirrors the upmarket surroundings, as does the regular clientele, which includes flush locals, loud yuppies and art-weary tourists.

Shopping

Azzurro Due

Pieter Cornelisz Hooftstraat 138 (671 9708/www.azzurrofashiongroup.nl). Tram 2, 3, 5, 12. **Open** 1-6pm Mon; 10am-6pm Tue, Wed, Fri; 10am-9pm Thur; 10am-6pm Sat; noon-5pm Sun. **Map** p135 D2 ⓭

If you've got to splurge on cutting-edge fashion, this is as good a spot as any. Saucy picks from Marni, Miu Miu, Chloé and Stella McCartney attract the usual hordes of mediacrities.

Intertaal

Van Baerlestraat 76 (575 6760/www.intertaal.nl). Tram 2, 3, 5, 12, 16, 24. **Open** 10am-6pm Tue-Fri; 10am-5pm Sat. **Map** p135 D3 ⓮

Dealing in language books, CDs and teaching aids, Intertaal will be of use to all learners of a new foreign language, whether they're grappling with basic Dutch or improving their English.

Lairesse Apotheek

Lairessestraat 40 (662 1022/www.delairesseapotheek.nl). Tram 2, 3, 5, 12, 16, 24. **Open** 8.30am-6pm Mon-Fri; 10am-5pm Sat. **Map** p135 D3 ⓯

One of the largest suppliers of alternative medicines in the country, from chemist Marjan Terpstra. The shop is out of the way if you're just popping in for haemorrhoid cream, but the interior is inspiring enough to be on any design junkie's must-see list.

Marlies Dekkers

NEW *Cornelis Schuytstraat 13 (471 4146/www.marliesdekkers.nl). Tram 2.* **Open** noon-6pm Mon, 10am-6pm Tues-Fri, 10am-5pm Sat. **Map** p.135 C3 ⓰

Amsterdam's globally-acclaimed lingerie designer has her own store on the posh shopping strip of Cornelis Schuytstraat. She also has a boutique in the Nine Streets area (Berenstraat 18).

Marqt

NEW *Overtoom 21 (422 6311/www.marqt.com). Tram 1, 3, 12.* **Open** 8am-9pm Mon-Sat; 11am-7pm Sun. **Map** p135 C2 ⓱

This sleek health supermarket stocks local and organic products. The whole set-up, including the minimalist milk packaging, comes across as a fine piece of branding. You may even have trouble paying by cash – it's that futuristic. A second branch is set to open up late in 2009 near Rembrandtsplein.

Pied-à-Terre

Overtoom 135-137 (627 4455/www.piedaterre.nl). Tram 1, 3, 12. **Open** 1-6pm Mon; 10am-6pm Tues, Wed, Fri; 10am-9pm Thur; 10am-5pm Sat. No credit cards. **Map** p135 C2 ⓲

In this store, you can find travel books, guides and maps for active holidays. Adventurous walkers can seek advice from helpful staff for out-of-town trips.

Street art

You don't need to go indoors to get your fix of art and culture: Amsterdam has an active street art scene, which means that you can see it on every corner of town, from freehand graffiti to stencils, sculptures, tags and stickers.

One of the prolific practitioners is Laser 3.14. Dubbed Amsterdam's 'guerrilla poet', his words of wisdom are dotted all over town; 'Swallowed by your own introspective vortex' and 'She fears the ghouls that reside in her shadow' are two cryptic examples. Another familiar sight, notably in the Pijp, is a cluster of spray-painted stereos and electricity poles, courtesy of Morcky. Sticker artist DHM has a different approach, glueing tribal tattoo-style animals all over the urban jungle.

Arguably the most well-known group of artists from the street scene is The London Police (TLP). The collective, started by three British men, specialises in 'lads': simple-looking black-and-white blob characters that popped up on electricity boxes around town, but later found their way into galleries.

Like many urban galleries around the world, Amsterdam's have seized upon street art. Studio Apart (Prinsengracht 715, 06 141 71881/www.studioapart.com) represents a number of designers and artists with a background in graffiti, and holds exhibitions by the likes of Ottograph, Juice, and the collective KMDG. Street clothing shops such as Hanazuki (Vijzelstraat 87, 422 9563/www.hanazuki.com), Wolf & Pack (Spuistraat 232, 427 0786/www.wolfandpack.com) and Henxs (St Antoniebreestraat 136, 638 9478/www.henx.com) also host exhibitions. At Henxs, the sticker-covered front porch is a kind of who's who of the street scene.

A short walk from here is the city's oldest graffiti site. The 'House with the Bloodstains' at Amstel 216 was home to former mayor Coenraad van Beuningen (1622-93). After seeing visions of fireballs and coffins above the Reguliersgracht, he scrawled graffiti of sailing ships and stars, and wrote his and his wife's name with his own blood. Or so the story goes.

Get your skates on

It's 9pm on a Friday night. Most locals are slumped in front of the telly or drinking in a bar – but not the people currently assembling in the Vondelpark. Unless it's raining, every Friday a group of skating fanatics meets to snake the 20-kilometre, three-hour-long Friday Night Skate through central Amsterdam (www.fridaynightskate.com).

It all started in 1997, when three friends decided to do something special to kick off the weekend. Ten years later, that same group varies from a small handful of die-hards in winter to hundreds in summer, but whatever the cause they all have one thing in common: a love of skating around the city. Forget tracing circles around boring parks – it's high bridges, car parks, tunnels and noisy roads this lot are after.

Things never get stale. Each week there is a new route, but the start and finish is always in Vondelpark, by the red bench opposite the Filmmuseum (p141). And they are not adverse to a good theme such as 'red' or 'Santa'. There are teams of 'blockers', who block the roads, so cars and cyclists can't get in the way, plus 'flying nurses' who'll come to your assistance if you ever have an unscheduled meeting with the hard tarmac. Some skaters even carry sound systems on their backs, providing tunes to help people move with purpose. It's free, it's fun and it's a great way to make new friends.

Rivièra Maison

NEW *Van Baerlestraat 2-4 (471 1699/ www.rivieramaison.com). Tram 1, 2, 3, 5, 12.* **Open** 11am-6pm Mon; 10am-6pm Tues-Wed, Fri-Sat; 10am-9pm Thur; noon-5pm Sun. **Map** p 135 C2 ⓳
At this two-storey concept store, cool interiors collide with stylish lifestyle products – right up to the latest design books, fragrances and candies. Where IKEA offers a cheap breakfast to lure its punters, here you'll find complementary coffee and a wine bar instead.

Waterwinkel

Roelof Hartstraat 10 (675 5932/ www.springwater.nl). Tram 3, 5, 12, 24. **Open** 10am-6pm Mon-Fri; 10am-5pm Sat. **Map** p135 E3 ⓴
The variety of native and imported water in this unusual store will charm many. The source of life indeed.

Nightlife

The Mansion

Hobbemastraat 2 (616 6664/www.the-mansion.nl). Tram 2, 5, 7, 10. **Open** *restaurant* 7-11pm Mon-Thur; 7pm-midnight Fri, Sat. *Bar* 6.30pm-1am Mon-Thur; 6.30pm-3am Fri, Sat. *Club* 9pm-3am Fri, Sat. **Map** p135 D2 ㉑
This restaurant/bar/club is like a gentleman's club with ladies allowed. The staff are decked out in designer outfits, and the decor is plush chinoiserie. Expect to dance to the tunes of DJs and to burn a hole in your wallet.

Arts & leisure

Concertgebouw

Concertgebouwplein 2-6 (reservations 671 8345/24hr information in Dutch & English 573 0511/www.concertgebouw.nl). Tram 2, 3, 5, 12, 16, 24. **Map** p135 D3 ㉒
With its beautiful architecture and crystal clear acoustics, this is a favourite venue of many of the world's top musicians, and is home to the world-famous Royal Concertgebouw Orchestra. As you would expect, the sound in the Grote Zaal (Great Hall) is excellent. The Kleine Zaal (Recital Hall) is perhaps less comfortable, but is the perfect size for both chamber groups and soloists.

Gasthuis Werkplaats & Theater

Marius van Bouwdijk Bastiaansestraat 54 (616 8942/www.theatergasthuis.nl). Tram 1, 3, 12. No credit cards. **Map** p135 B2 ㉓
The Gasthuis emerged from a group of squatters who became critical darlings in just a few years. Even when their home, a former hospital, was threatened with demolition, their arty activities contributed a great deal towards the building's ultimate salvation. Now tied directly to Frascati (p80), the rolling programme is, as you might expect, mainly youthful and experimental. Some productions are in English; make sure you check the website beforehand to guarantee a comprehensible evening's entertainment.

Nederlands Filmmuseum (NFM)

Vondelpark 3 (589 1400/www.film museum.nl). Tram 1, 2, 3, 5, 6, 12. No credit cards. **Map** p135 C2 ㉔
This stylish building overlooking the Vondelpark is a cinema and a museum. The most important centre of cinematography in the Netherlands, it collects films and restores copies that have been ravaged by the passage of time. It regularly screens silent films to the authentic accompaniment of an old-fashioned pianola, and specialises in major retrospectives and edgier contemporary movies. In summer, be sure to take in an outdoor screening on the terrace of the Café Vertigo while you can – it will be moving to a new location in Amsterdam North in 2011.

OT301

NEW *Overtoom 301, (779 4913/http:// ot301.nl).* Tram 1, 6. No credit cards. **Map** p135 B3 ㉕

Where are all the museums?

The city of Amsterdam is not big on planning. Every museum is closed – or so it seems. The Dutch Shipping Museum is shut until late 2010, and the Stedelijk Museum of Modern Art (p134) lost its home in Post CS in 2008 – at least its renovation on Museumplein is on schedule.

But the real story is the renovation of the **Rijksmuseum** (p134). It closed in 2003, with a plan to reopen in 2008 after its facelift by architect Cruz y Ortiz; now it emerges that it will not reopen until 2013. In February 2008, the only remaining contractor (BAM) presented its estimate to complete the project: €222 million, €88 million over budget. Minister of Culture and Education Ronald Plasterk announced that he would not be 'held hostage', and split the project into smaller portions so that more museums could participate. BAM denied taking advantage of its singular position, and instead blamed the stressed construction industry, the time frame and the historical nature of the building.

The Rijksmuseum continues to run a satellite programme: it's holding exhibitions at Schiphol Airport and lending out parts of its collection to other museums. The 'best of' exhibition in the Philips Wing is actually more than enough for the average human to absorb in one day. Sometimes it's good to have focus. Besides, the city is already one big museum anyway.

The former Dutch film academy building has been transformed by squatters into a cultural 'breeding ground', which includes a club, a radio station, a vegan restaurant (see De Peper, p137) and an art house cinema.

Smart Project Space

Arie Biemondstraat 101-11 (427 5951/ www.smartprojectspace.net). Tram 3, 7, 12, 17. No credit cards. **Map** p135 B2 ㉖
Located in a former pathology lab, the sprawling Smart dedicates its vast exhibition spaces to 'hardcore art'. But it also has three cinemas that screen arthouse films, a media centre, a lecture hall and a decent in-house café/restaurant Lab111 for hungry Bohos.

Vondelpark Openluchttheater

Vondelpark (428 3360/www.open luchttheater.nl). Tram 1, 2, 3, 12. No credit cards. **Map** p135 C3 ㉗
Theatrical events have been held in Vondelpark since 1865, and the tradition continues each summer. Wednesdays offer a lunchtime concert and a mid-afternoon children's play; Thursday nights find a concert on the bandstand; Friday evenings bring theatre performances and Saturday and Sunday afternoons promise child-friendly events. The theatre gets especially packed in the summer, but since experiencing funding problems for 2009, it may be forced to cut back its programming.

Vondeltuin

Vondelpark 7 (06 2756 5576/www. vondeltuin.nl). Tram 1, 2. No credit cards. **Map** p135 C3 ㉘
Rollerblades, skates and accessories are rented to those looking to make the most of the area's potential for concrete cruising. If you're seeking less sedate thrills, make a beeline for ramp-happy Skatepark Amsterdam (www.skatepark amsterdam.nl) at the NDSM yard (p123), which offers skating lessons for beginners, competitions for the more experienced and plenty of all-in rail riding.

Albert Cuypmarkt p148

The Pijp

Although it's hardly a treasure trove of historical sights, the Pijp is rooted firmly in the present. Well over 150 different nationalities keep its global village alive, and many upmarket restaurants and bars have flourished here in recent years. The gentrification process is firmly underway and over the next decade the construction of the Metro's controversial **Noord-Zuidlijn** (p66) will take place pretty much directly beneath bustling Ferdinand Bolstraat.

The Pijp is the best known of the working-class quarters built in the late 19th century. Harsh economic times necessitated a plan of long, narrow streets, leading to its apt nickname, 'the Pipe'. High rents forced tenants to sublet rooms to students and artists, lending the area its bohemian character.

Today, the Pijp is home to a mix of halal butchers, Surinamese, Spanish and Turkish delicatessens, and restaurants offering authentic Syrian, Moroccan, Thai, Pakistani, Chinese and Indian cuisine. This makes the Pijp one of the best spots in town to buy quality snacking treats, the many ingredients for which are almost always bought fresh from the single largest daily market anywhere in the Netherlands: **Albert Cuypmarkt**. The market attracts thousands of customers every day to the junctions of Sweelinckstraat, Ferdinand Bolstraat and 1e Van der Helststraat, north into the lively Gerard Douplein, and also south towards Sarphatipark. Another pretty street, which is rich with cafés and bars, is Frans Halsstraat.

Sights & museums

Heineken Experience

Stadhouderskade 78 (523 9222/www. heinekenexperience.com). Tram 7, 10, 16, 24, 25. **Open** 11am-7pm (last entry 5.30pm) daily. **Admission** €15. **Map** p145 A4 ❶

Heineken Experience p143

If you're after green hoodies emblazoned with logos of your favourite beer, this is the place to come (or head straight to the Heineken store; Amstelstraat 31, www.heinekenthecity.nl). As one might expect, it's all very light-hearted – where else could you take a virtual reality ride from the perspective of a Heineken bottle? And you get two free beers, though that's a come-down from the old days: when Heineken stopped its brewing operations in this building back in 1988, a tour cost a mere two guilders (less than €1), followed by as much of the fizzy stuff as you could consume.

Eating & drinking

Bazar
Albert Cuypstraat 182 (675 0544/ www.bazaramsterdam.nl). Tram 4, 16, 24, 25. **Open** 11am-1am Mon-Thur; 11am-2am Fri; 9am-2am Sat; 9am-midnight Sun. €€. **North African**. **Map** p145 B4 ②
If you fail to find Bazar, look up at the sky and search for an angel. This former church, now downgraded to an Arabian kitsch café, is one of the real glories of Albert Cuypmarkt. Sticking

to the winning formula set by its Rotterdam mothership, it boasts a menu that travels the world but lingers lovingly in the environs of North Africa. Whether it's for breakfast, lunch or dinner, Bazar is a real winner.

Bloemers
Hemonystraat 70 (400 4024). Tram 3, 4, 25. **Open** 10am-1am Mon-Thur, Sun; 10am-3am Fri, Sat. **Bar**. **Map** p145 C3 ③
A justifiably popular neighbourhood bar on the eastern fringes of the Pijp, with a dark wood interior enlivened by old posters and chandeliers. The kitchen serves well-priced and tasty international classics for lunch and dinner. Capacity doubles when the terrace, complete with swing seats, opens during the summer.

Burger Meester
Albert Cuypstraat 48 (670 9339/www. burgermeester.eu). Tram 3, 12, 16, 24. **Open** noon-11pm daily. €€. **Burgers**. No credit cards. **Map** p145 A5 ④
A specialist in designer burgers. Order your beef, lamb, tuna or falafel burger with toppings that include wild mushrooms, wasabi, grilled peppers or

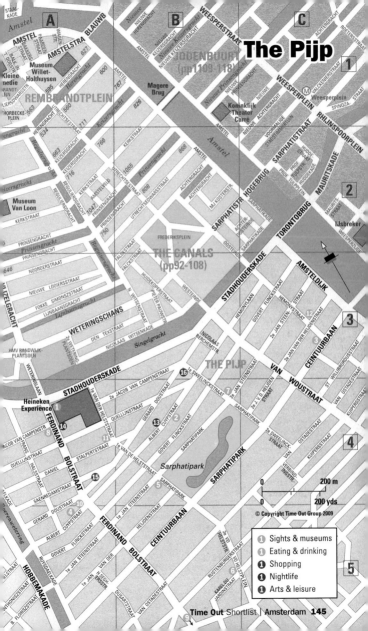

The Pijp

AMSTEL

REMBRANDTPLEIN

Museum Willet-Holthuysen

JODENBUURT
(pp109-118)

Magere Brug

Koninklijk Theater Carré

Museum Van Loon

THE CANALS
(pp92-108)

FREDERIKSPLEIN

WETERINGSCHANS

HMV RANDWIJK PLANTSOEN

THE PIJP

Heineken Experience

Sarphatipark

SARPHATIPARK

		200 m
0		
		200 yds
0		

© Copyright Time Out Group 2009

- ① Sights & museums
- ① Eating & drinking
- ① Shopping
- ① Nightlife
- ① Arts & leisure

Bazar p144

match Pizza – heavily loaded but with a delicious crispy crust – is the house speciality, popular with all ages, but a real hit with kids.

Le Restaurant
NEW *2e Jan Steenstraat 3 (379 2207/ www.le-restaurant.nl)*. Tram 3, 4, 25. **Open** 7-10pm Tue-Sat. €€€€. No credit cards. **Map** p145 B4 ⑦
Acclaimed chef Jan de Wit returned home after a two-star restaurant adventure in Vreeland. His formula is simple: five courses inspired by French cuisine and what's in season, changing on a monthly basis. It's already earned him the first 10/10 review from feared local critic Johannes van Dam.

De Taart van m'n Tante
Ferdinand Bolstraat 10 (776 4600/ www.detaart.com). Tram 3, 12, 25. **Open** 10am-6pm daily. No credit cards. **Café**. **Map** p145 A4 ⑧
The café – affectionately known as My Aunt's Cake – began its existence as a purveyor of over-the-top cakes (which it still produces) before becoming the campest tearoom in what can be a very camp town. Set in a glowing pink space filled with charmingly mismatched furniture, it's particularly gay friendly (try the Tom of Finland cake). It also features a delightful and welcoming B&B (www.cakeundermypillow.com).

Twenty Third Bar
NEW *Ferdinand Bolstraat 333 (678 7111/www.okura.nl)*. Tram 16, 24. **Open** 6pm-1am daily. **Bar**. **Map** p145 B5 ⑨
On the 23rd floor of Hotel Okura (p177), this cocktail bar offers fantastic views of the Pijp and the compact Amsterdam School architecture (see box p147) of the Rivierenbuurt. Be prepared to pay for the view – and the 17 different varieties of champagne on offer.

Warung Spang-Makandra
Gerard Doustraat 39 (670 5081/www. spangmakandra.nl). Tram 16, 24.

pancetta – and it will arrive complete with a baked potato or a tasty salad. They also have a new Jordaan branch (Elandsgracht 130, 423 6225).

Café Krull
Sarphatipark 2 (662 0214). Tram 3, 16, 24, 25. **Open** 9am-1am daily. **Bar**. **Map** p145 B4 ⑤
Light from the windows floods this delightful locals' café, which is busy at all hours, with laptop holders taking advantage of Wi-Fi, parents treating their offspring to a hot chocolate, and – later on – evening imbibers of every stripe. The barman's music choice is exquisite (disco, Motown, easy listening, rockabilly), plus the outdoor picnic tables are a dream in summer.

Renato's Trattoria
Karel du Jardinstraat 32 (673 2300/ www.renatotrattoria.nl). Tram 3, 12, 25. **Open** 6-10pm daily. €€. No credit cards. **Italian**. **Map** p145 B5 ⑥
Dropping in here is like briefly stepping into Italy itself, with hearty hospitality and raw kitchen action to

The Amsterdam School

The city's own modernist moment.

Museum Het Schip

Amsterdam's architectural monuments are not the products of imperial minds, but rather the living homes of merchants and working men and women. Many were designed by the expressionist Amsterdam School, which imbued their Gaudí-esque buildings with a socialist vision during the interwar years of the early 20th century.

While credit can be given to the stonemasons, who had to practise non-geometrical brickwork when repairing houses slowly sinking into the mud, it was Hendrik Berlage who pioneered the architectural movement. He rejected the ornate styles that had defined 19th-century Dutch homes, and facilitated an experimental era of building in the shape of the urban development, Plan Zuid – which provided much-needed housing for the working classes.

Although the Amsterdam School was short-lived due to its lack of funding, stylistic examples remain liberally dotted around the city.

Located along the waterfront, the epic **Scheepvaarthuis** (Prins Hendrikkade 108-114) is usually considered to be the school's first work; it is now the Hotel Amrâth (p165). Its playground lies at Plan Zuid. Josef Israelkade, between 2e Van der Helststraat and Van Woustraat, is a pleasant stretch along the Amstelkanaal. Enter PL Takstraat and then circle Burg Tellegenstraat, popping into the Cooperatiehof courtyard on the way, to see the school at its best.

If you backtrack and cross the Amstelkanaal, then walk down Waalstraat, you'll find that later examples of the school's work exhibit greater restraint. It's still worth visiting the Spaarndammer neighbourhood. The Ship is home to the **Museum Het Schip** (Spaarndammerplantsoen 140, 418 2885, www.hetschip.nl, 1-5pm Wed-Sun; pictured), which operates Amsterdam School boating and walking tours, and boasts an exhibition space devoted to its architectural legacy.

Open 11am-10pm Tue-Sat; 1-10pm Sun. **€**. **Global**. Map p145 A4 ⓾

An Indonesian-Surinamese restaurant serving tasty and addictive Javanese *rames*. The decor is very simple, but the relaxed vibe and beautifully presented dishes will make you want to linger for a while over your meal, rather than take it away.

Wijnbar Boelen & Boelen

1e Van der Helststraat 50 (671 2242/ www.wijnbar.nl). Tram 7, 10, 16, 24, 25. **Open** 6pm-midnight Tue-Thur, Sun; 6pm-1am Fri, Sat. **Bar**. Map p145 A4 ⓫

Many of the regulars come here just to sample the Frenchified food, but as the name implies, the wine's the real star of the show at this compact yet airy bar, located on the edge of the Pijp's main nightlife strip. The emphasis is on old world tipples, but there are also well-edited selections from Australia, New Zealand, and North and South America. The friendly owners can offer suggestions for those of you who are less well versed in wine-drinking.

Yo-Yo

2e Jan van der Heijdenstraat 79 (664 7173). Tram 3, 4, 25. **Open** noon-7pm Mon-Sat. No credit cards. **Coffeeshop**. Map p145 C3 ⓬

Located on a leafy residential street near Sarphatipark and the Albert Cuypmarkt, this chill-out spot lacks the commercialism and crowds found in other more central shops. The herb here is all-organic, and the place is run by a pleasant lady who bakes her own fresh apple pie every day – a delicious cure for the chronic munchies if ever there was one.

Shopping

Albert Cuypmarkt

Albert Cuypstraat (no phone/www. albertcuypmarkt.com). Tram 3, 12, 16, 24, 25. **Open** 9am-6pm Mon-Sat. No credit cards. Map p145 B4 ⓭

The country's largest general market sells all kinds of things, from pillows to prawns, at great prices. The clothes tend to be run-of-the-mill cheap threads.

Dirk van den Broek

Marie Heinekenplein 25 (673 9393/ www.lekkerdoen.nl). Tram 7, 10, 16, 24. **Open** 8am-9pm Mon-Sat. Map p145 A4 ⓮

Not a glamorous supermarket, for a time Dirk van den Broek was extraordinarily fashionable: its red bags were must-haves for Amsterdam's designer lemmings and have even been spotted on the arms of the fashion ratpack overseas. Dirk remains cheaper than Albert Heijn, while its choice has improved.

Sid Lee Collective

NEW *Gerard Doustraat 72-80 (662 3030/www.sidleecollective.com).* Tram 16, 24. **Open** *gallery/store* noon-6pm Mon-Wed, Sun; noon-9pm Thur-Fri; 10am-6pm Sat. *Bar* noon-11pm Mon-Thur, Sun; noon-midnight Fri, 10am-midnight Sat. Map p145 A4 ⓯

The Montreal-based ad agency that established this funky satellite office/ gallery/store/café/bar sells everything from Canadian fashion labels, such as Team Macho and Renata Morales, to exhibitions by the likes of NYC street artist Dan Witz. Entry for the bar/café is at Albert Cuypstraat 101.

Nightlife

Badcuyp

1e Sweelinckstraat 10 (675 9669/www. badcuyp.nl). Tram 3, 4, 12, 16, 24, 25. **Open** 11am-1am Tue-Thur, Sun; 11am-3am Fri, Sat. Map p145 B3 ⓰

Small and friendly, this popular nightspot focuses on playing world music and jazz. Besides the intriguing range of international talents in the main hall, the cute café plays host to regular salsa, African, jazz and open jam evenings. The café/restaurant downstairs is also quite nice with free Wi-Fi and an increasing number of dinner shows.

Nieuwe Kerk p150

Day Trips

There's more to the Netherlands than just the capital city, of course, and for a relatively compact country it boasts an astonishing variety of landscapes, from sandy beaches and windswept dykes to thick woods and leafy forests, along with real urban jungles. Amsterdam itself is part of one of the world's most densely populated areas: no fewer than 40 per cent of the country's entire population inhabit the built-up sprawl known as the Randstad or 'Edge City' – which is named for its coastal location on the Netherlands' western edge.

This region is made up of Delft, Haarlem, the Hague, Leiden and Utrecht, as well as bitter urban rivals Amsterdam and Rotterdam. The area's road, rail and waterway networks are impressive, making for a pleasant journey from the city to the countryside. All the destinations in this chapter can easily be explored on day trips, but they also stand up to more leisurely and sustained exploration.

Delft

Imagine a miniaturised Amsterdam, with canals reduced to dinky proportions, bridges narrowed and merchants' houses in miniature, and you have the essence of Delft. Even though it's small and often scoffed at for its sleepiness, Delft is a student town with plenty going on. Its bars and cafés may give the impression to outsiders of being survivors of a bygone era – white-aproned waiters attend to your beck and call in high-ceilinged interiors – but that's the norm in Delft. While other cities offer hot chocolate finished with aerosol cream, cafés here use dollops of real cream in the cocoa and accompany it with a fancier brand of biscuit.

All the sites of interest can be found in the old centre. As soon as you cross over the road from the station towards the city centre, you encounter an introduction to Delft's past: a representation of Vermeer's famous Milkmaid in stone. Delft was traditionally a centre for trade, producing and exporting butter, cloth, beer – at one point in the distant past, 200 breweries could be found alongside its canals – and, later, 'Royal Blue' pottery attracted many admirers from abroad.

The city's subsequent loss in trade has been Rotterdam's gain, but Delft holds on firmly to the artistic heritage of her rich past, which can be observed in the centuries-old gables, hump-backed bridges and shady canals. To appreciate just how little has changed, take a stroll to the end of Oude Delft, the city's oldest canal, cross the busy road to the harbour and compare the view to Vermeer's *View of Delft*, now on display in the Mauritshuis in the Hague (p44).

Sights & museums

De Delftse Pauw
Delftweg 133 (015 212 4920/www. delftsepauw.com). **Open** *Apr-Oct* 9am-4.30pm daily. *Nov-Mar* 9am-4.30pm Mon-Fri; 11am-1pm Sat, Sun. **Admission** free.
Delft is famous for its blue and white tiles and pottery, known as Delft Blue (internationally as Royal Blue). One of the few factories open to visitors.

Het Prinsenhof Municipal Museum
Sint Agathaplein 1 (015 260 2358/ www.prinsenhof-delft.nl). **Open** 10am-5pm Tue-Sat; 1-5pm Sun. **Admission** €6.50; free-€5.50 reductions.
This castle-like structure in the former convent of St Agatha hosts temporary exhibitions, and displays on William of Orange, who was assassinated here in 1584. The bullet holes are visible on the stairs. Admission includes entrance to Museum Lambert van Meerten.

Legermuseum
Korte Geer 1 (015 215 0500/www. legermuseum.nl). **Open** 10am-5pm

Tue-Fri; noon-5pm Sat, Sun. **Admission** €7.50; free-€3 reductions, MK.
The 'Army Museum' houses the country's largest military collection.

Museum Lambert van Meerten
Oude Delft 199 (015 260 2358). **Open** 10am-5pm Tue-Sat; 1-5pm Sun. **Admission** €6.50; free-€5.50 reductions.
This museum offers an overview of the Delft Blue industry and includes a huge range of tiles, with everything from battling warships to randy rabbits. Admission includes entrance to Het Prinsenhof Municipal Museum.

Nieuwe Kerk
Markt 80 (015 212 3025/www.nieuwe kerk-delft.nl). **Open** *Apr-Oct* 9am-5pm Mon-Sat. *Nov-Mar* 11am-4pm Mon-Fri; 10am-5pm Sat. **Admission** €3.30; €1.60-€3 reductions. *Tower* €3; €1.10-€2.80 reductions.
The 'New Church' took almost 15 years to construct and was finished in 1396. It contains the mausoleums of lawyer-philosopher and founder of 'natural law' theory Hugo de Groot and William of Orange (interned alongside his dog, who faithfully followed him into death by refusing food and water), in a black and white marble mausoleum by Hendrick de Keyser. De Keyser also designed the epic 1620 Stadhuis across the Markt.

Oude Kerk
Heilige Geestkerkhof 25 (015 212 3015/www.oudekerk-delft.nl). **Open** *Apr-Oct;* 9am-6pm Mon-Sat. *Nov-Mar* 11am-4pm Mon-Fri; 10am-5pm Sat. **Admission** €3.30; €1.60-€3 reductions.
The town's other splendid house of worship, the Gothic 'Old Church' (c1200), is known as 'Leaning Jan' because its tower stands 2m (over 6ft) off-kilter. Art-lovers should note that it's the final resting place of Vermeer.

De Porceleyne Fles
Rotterdamseweg 196 (015 251 2030/ www.royaldelft.com). **Open** *Apr-Oct*

Day Trips

Schiermonnikoog
Ameland
Terschelling

Hoogebeintum
Dokkum

Vlieland

WADDEN ISLANDS
LEEUWARDEN

GRON-
INGEN

Harlingen
Grouw
Drachten

FRIESLAND

Texel

Sneek
Terherne
Heerenveen

Heeg

DRENTHE

Den Helder
Heeg
Sloten
Lemmer

Steenwijk   Uffelte

Anna
Paulowna
Opperdoes
IJSSELMEER
Emmeloord
Blokzijl   Giethoorn

Schagen   Medemblick
Twisk   Enkhuizen
Urk   Vollenhove
Meppel

Broek-op-
Langedijk
Alkmaar   **Hoorn**
Ketelhaven
Zwartsluis
Kampen

OVER-
IJSSEL

Heiloo
Limmen

NOORD
MARKERMEER

FLEVOLAND
ZWOLLE

Beverwijk
Pumerend
Edam
Lelystad

HOLLAND
Volendam
*Oostvaarders-
plassen*
Flevohof

*Kennemer
Duinen Nat.Pk.*
Zaanstad
Monnickendam
Broek in W.

HAARLEM
AMSTERDAM
Almerestad
Harderwijk

Raalte

Zandvoort
Muiden
Bussum
Deventer

Vogelenzang
Bennebroek
Fort
Loenen
Bunschoten-
Spakenburg

Keukenhof
Hillegom
Naarden
Hilversum
APELDOORN

Ijsse
Aalsmeer
Vreeland
Soestdijk
Zutphen

Noordwijk
Rijnsburg
Oudaen
Breukelen
Slijkstein
*Hoge Veluwe
Nat. Park*

Katwijk
Alphen
Castle
Amersfoort

1. Oud-Loosdrecht
2. Breukeleveen
3. Westbroek
Scheveningen
De Haar
Castle
2 3
Austerlitz
GELDERLAND

LEIDEN
Gouda
UTRECHT
Ede
Oosterbeek

DEN HAAG
Zoetermeer
Wijbijk
Duurstede
ARNHEM

Naaldwijk
DELFT
Oudewater
UTRECHT
Rhenen

Hoek van Holland
ROTTERDAM
Culemborg

Europoort
Schoonhoven
Tiel

Vlaardingen
Gorinchem
NIJMEGEN

Stellendam
Voorne
Putten
Alblasserdam

*Schouwen
Brouwershaven*
DORDRECHT
*De Biesbosch
Nat. Park*
Oss
GERMANY

osterscheldedam
*Goeree-
Overflakkee*
Hoekse-Waard
Geertruidenberg
Drunen
'S-HERTOGENBOSCH

Delta Expo
Zierikzee
Oosterhout
Waalwijk
Uden

iddelburg
Veere
*Noord
Beveland*
Oudenbosch
Kaatsheuvel
Overloon
*De Groote Peel
Nat. Reserve*

issingen
Goes
Yerseke
Roosendaal
BREDA
TILBURG
Helmond

Kapelle
Tholen
NOORD - BRABANT
Nuenen

utelande
Kruiningen
**Bergen op
Zoom**
EINDHOVEN
Venlo

ZEELAND
LIMBURG

*Zeeuws -
Vlaanderen*
Terneuzen
Weert
Thorn

Roermond

**ANTWERPEN
ANVERS**

GERMANY

Sittard   GERMANY

**GENT
GAND**
B E L G I U M
Geleen

Valkenburg
Heerlen

0   50 km
0   30 miles
MAASTRICHT
Schin
AACHEN

© Copyright Time Out Group 2009

9am-5pm daily. *Nov-Mar* 9am-5pm
Mon-Sat. **Admission** €6.50.
Another look behind the scenes of a
Delft Blue pottery factory.

Reptielenzoo Serpo

*Stationsplein 8 (015 212 2184/
www.serpo.nl).* **Open** 10am-6pm
Mon-Sat; 1-6pm Sun. **Admission**
€8.50; free-€7.50 reductions.
Europe's largest collection of poiso-
nous snakes, and other scaly creatures.

Getting there

Delft is 60 kilometres (37 miles)
south-west from Amsterdam along
the A4. Trains from Amsterdam
Centraal Station take just under
an hour (you may need to make
a change at the Hague).

Tourist information

Toeristische Informatie Punt (Tourist Information Point)

*Hippolytusbuurt 4 (0900 515 1555
premium rate/www.delft.nl).* **Open**
Apr-Sept 10am-4pm Mon; 9am-6pm
Tue-Fri; 10am-5pm Sat; 10am-4pm Sun.
Oct-Mar 11am-4pm Mon; 10am-4pm
Tue-Sat; 10am-3pm Sun.

Haarlem

Although Amsterdam is located
in Noord-Holland, Haarlem – 15
minutes away by train – is the
provincial capital. A cycle
ride away from the beaches
of Zandvoort-aan-Zee and
Bloemendaal-aan-Zee, Haarlem is a
smaller, gentler and older version
of Amsterdam. All traces of the
city's origins as a tenth-century
inland sea settlement disappeared
when the Haarlemmermeer was
drained in the 19th century. But it
hasn't lost its appeal: the centre,
with its lively square, canals and
charming almshouses, is beautiful.

Sights & museums

Frans Halsmuseum

*Groot Heiligland 62 (023 511 5775/
www.franshalsmuseum.nl).* **Open**
11am-5pm Tue-Sat; noon-5pm Sun.
Admission €7.50; free-€3.75
reductions, MK.
Housed in what was an elderly men's
almshouse and orphanage (well worth
a visit in themselves), this museum has
a magnificent collection of 16th- and
17th-century portraits, still lifes, genre
paintings and landscapes. The highlight is a group of eight portraits of
militia companies and regents from the
brush of Frans Hals. The museum also
holds vast collections of period furniture, Haarlem silver and an 18th-century
apothecary with Delftware pottery.

De Hallen

*Grotemarkt 16 (023 511 5775/www.
dehallenhaarlem.nl).* **Open** 11am-5pm
Tue-Sat; noon-5pm Sun. **Admission**
€5; free-€2.50 reductions, MK.
De Hallen is a genuinely up-to-the-
minute modern art museum housed in
two interesting old buildings, the
Verweyhal (a 19th-century gentleman's club) and the atmospheric
Vleeshal or 'meat hall', which was originally a 17th-century butcher's market.
Exhibitions focus on cutting-edge
artists, such as Tracey Emin, Sarah
Lucas and Jonathan Meese.

St Bavo

*Grotemarkt (023 553 2040/www.
bavo.nl).* **Open** 10am-4pm Mon-Sat.
Admission €2; free-€1.25 reductions.
This truly enormous church, dominat-
ing Grotemarkt, the main square, provides an excellent point to begin
exploring Haarlem's long history. Built
around 1313, it suffered fire damage in
1328 and reconstruction lasted another
150 years. It's surprisingly bright inside:
cavernous white transepts stand as
high as the nave and make a stunning
sight. The floor is made up of 1,350
gravestones, including one featuring

Haarlem

only the word 'Me' and another long enough to hold a famed local giant.

In the interests of balance, there's also a dedication to a local midget who died of injuries from a game of dwarf-tossing. Ironic really, as it was a sport that he had invented. The centrepiece is the famous Müller organ (1738) – the most photographed organ in the world. An extraordinary gold and red instrument, it boasts an astonishing 5,068 pipes. In its time it has been played by Handel, as well as the ten-year-old Mozart, who squeezed out a few tunes in 1765 while he was on a tour of the Netherlands with his family.

Teylers Museum

Spaarne 16 (023 516 0960/www. teylersmuseum.nl). **Open** 10am-5pm Tue-Sat; noon-5pm Sun. **Admission** €7; free-€2 reductions, MK.

Although it lies somewhat in the shadow of the Frans Halsmuseum, the Teylers is a good example of an Enlightenment museum, with an encyclopedic collection. Founded in 1784, it's the oldest museum in the Netherlands. Fossils and minerals rest besides antique scientific instruments, and there's a superb collection, spanning the 16th to the 19th centuries, of more than 10,000

drawings by Old Masters, including Rembrandt, Michelangelo and Raphael. A new wing hosts temporary art and science exhibitions.

Getting there

By car, Haarlem lies ten kilometres (six miles) west on the A5. Trains from Amsterdam Centraal Station take roughly 15 minutes.

Tourist information

VVV

Verwulft 11 (0900 616 1600 premium rate/www.vvvzk.nl). **Open** *Oct-Mar* 9.30am-5pm Mon-Fri; 10am-5pm Sat. *Apr-Sept* 9.30am-5.30pm Mon-Fri; 10am-5pm Sat; 11am-3pm Sun.

The Hague

Beginning life in the 13th century as a hunting ground for Dutch counts, the Hague's full name, 's Gravenhage, means 'the Count's Hedge'. But the Hague ('Den Haag') is not in fact officially a city. In days of yore, the powers that be did not want to offend its more ancient neighbours, Leiden and Utrecht,

Windmills, tulips and clogs

These perennial Dutch clichés beguile most visitors, no matter how cool they may think they are. And rightly so. They're part of the Netherlands' DNA: you can stroll into a gallery anywhere in the world and see a Van Gogh, but there aren't many places where you can sip beer beside a windmill.

Painted wooden clogs make fantastic wall-decorations and are even seen on some feet: mostly workmen's (they're EU-recognised safety shoes), children's and occasionally those of hicks from the sticks. The improbably fascinating **Klompenmakerij De Zaanse Schans** (Kraaienest 4, Zaandam, 075 617 7121, www.zaanseschans.nl) is a museum detailing the shoe's history and symbolism. It stands in the middle of a 'living' outdoor museum of green painted houses, warehouses and windmills.

Tulips, meanwhile, are ubiquitous, and play a crucial role in sustaining the economy. The most famous place to buy them is Amsterdam's floating flower market **Blomenmarkt** (p145). The place is less dazzling than it sounds, but still looks pretty. For real action, head to Aalsmeer's **flower auction** (Legmeerdijk 313, 0297 392185, www.floraholland.com), which shifts 19 million blooms daily.

Eight windmills still stand in Amsterdam, the most famous of which is **De Gooyer** (Funenkade 5), abutting the award-winning brewery Brouwerij 't IJ (p115). There are also a couple of photogenic examples on Haarlemmerweg: **De 1200 Roe** (No.701) was built in 1632, while **De Bloem** (No.465) is a mere whippersnapper dating from 1878. Both windmills were in use until the 1950s. Seize the opportunity to see the improbably urban **De Otter** (Gillis van Ledenberchstraat 78), from 1638, in Westerpark while you still can. Its future is being wrangled over by the highest court in the land, which is currently deciding whether it should be moved to a place where wind can actually reach the mill.

and so never granted the Hague a status beyond that of a mere town. Nevertheless, it is a hub of power and centre for international justice.

Sights & museums

Binnenhof

Binnenhof 8A (070 364 6144/ www.binnenhofbezoek.nl). **Open** 10am-4pm Mon-Sat. **Admission** €3. The Hague's history begins right here, where, in 1248, William II built a castle. Now parliament buildings occupy the site, and every September Queen Beatrix arrives in a golden coach for the state opening of parliament. Tours are organised daily around the Knights' Hall, where the ceremony takes place.

Escher in Het Paleis

Lange Voorhout 74 (070 427 7730/ www.escherinhetpaleis.nl). **Open** 11am-5pm Tue-Sun. **Admission** €7.50; free-€5 reductions. The Gemeentemuseum's sister museum, Escher in het Paleis, is filled with further examples of Escher's wonderfully expressive art.

Gemeentemuseum Den Haag

Stadhouderslaan 41 (070 338 1111/ www.gemeentemuseum.nl). **Open** 11am-5pm Tue-Sun. **Admission** €9; free-€7 reductions, MK. The star of this gallery is Piet Mondrian's *Victory Boogie Woogie*, bought for €36 million in 1998. The museum also holds the world's largest collection of Mondrians, plus several pieces by MC Escher – not to mention one of the ever best fashion collections. **Event highlights** Cézanne – Picasso – Mondriaan (until 24 Jan 2010).

Madurodam

George Maduroplein 1 (070 416 2400/ www.madurodam.nl). **Open** *Sept-Mar* 9am-6pm. *April-June* 9am-8pm daily. *July, Aug* 9am-11pm daily. **Admission** €14.50; free-€13.50 reductions.

An incredibly detailed miniature city that serves up every Dutch cliché in the book: windmills turn, ships sail and trains speed around the world's largest model railway. If you visit the Madurodam on a long summer's evening, when the models are illuminated from within by 50,000 miniature lamps, you should be prepared for your sceptical appreciation to evaporate completely and to be replaced by unalloyed, child-like wonder.

Mauritshuis

Korte Vijverberg 8 (070 302 3456/ www.mauritshuis.nl). **Open** *Sept-Mar* 10am-5pm Tue-Sat; 11am-5pm Sun. *April-Aug* 10am-5pm Mon-Sat; 11am-5pm Sun. **Admission** €10.50 incl audio tour, free reductions, MK. Once a home for local counts, like much of the Hague, the Mauritshuis now opens its doors to the public. It houses one of the most famous art collections in the world, displaying works by Rubens, Rembrandt and Vermeer. **Event highlights** Vermeer (until late 2010), Philips Wouwerman (Nov 2009-Feb 2010).

Panorama Mesdag

Zeestraat 65 (070 364 4544/www. mesdag.nl). **Open** 10am-5pm Mon-Sat; noon-5pm Sun. **Admission** €6; free-€5 reductions. This building houses the largest painting in the Netherlands, measuring 120m (400ft) in circumference, from which the museum takes its name. Painted by Hendrik Willem Mesdag (and with the assistance of the great Amsterdam painter George Hendrik Breitner, then still a student), it presents a depiction of the landscape of Scheveningen, which visitors can examine from an observation platform. The Panorama Mesdag also displays works by artists belonging to the Barbizon School and the Hague School; and its collection features seascapes by Roelofs and Mauve, as well as genre paintings by Alma-Tadema.

AMSTERDAM BY AREA

Getting there

By car, the Hague is situated 50 kilometres (31 miles) south-west of Amsterdam on the A4, then the A44. Trains from Amsterdam Centraal Station to Den Haag station take 50 minutes; you may need to change at Leiden.

Tourist information

VVV

Hofweg 1 (0900 340 3505 premium rate/www.denhaag.com). **Open** 10am-6pm Mon-Fri; 10am-5pm Sat; noon-5pm Sun.

Leiden

Canal-laced Leiden derives a good deal of its picturesque charm from the fact that it's home to the Netherlands' oldest university. It was founded here in 1575 and was the place of study of such notable alumni as the French philosopher René Descartes, sixth president of the United States John Quincy Adams and many members of the Dutch royal family. The old town teems with students, bikes and bars, and features the highest concentration of historic monuments anywhere in the country, so it's the perfect destination for a charming weekend of sightseeing.

Sights & museums

Hortus Botanicus Leiden

Rapenburg 73 (071 527 7249/www. hortusleiden.nl). **Open** *Apr-Oct* 10am-6pm daily. *Nov-Mar* 10am-4pm Tue-Sun. Mar 10am-4pm daily. **Admission** €5; free-€3 reductions.
More than 6,000 species of flora are represented at one of the world's oldest botanical gardens, including descendants of the country's first tulips. First, you have to walk down an alley to discover this peaceful oasis.

Molenmuseum de Valk

2e Binnenvestgracht 1 (071 516 5353/www.molenmuseumdevalk.nl). **Open** 10am-5pm Tue-Sat; 1-5pm Sun. **Admission** €3; free-€1.70 reductions, MK.
If Dutch clichés are what you came here to see, head straight to the 'Falcon Windmill Museum', an erstwhile mill where you can see the old living quarters, machinery and a picturesque view over Leiden. For an even better panorama, travel to the top of the Burcht, a 12th-century fort situated on an ancient mound in the centre.

Naturalis

Darwinweg 2 (071 568 7600/www. naturalis.nl). **Open** 10am-5pm Tue-Fri; 10am-6pm Sat, Sun. **Admission** €11; free-€9 reductions, MK.
At Holland's main natural history museum, you'll find a staggering ten million fossils, minerals and assorted stuffed animals.

Rijksmuseum van Oudheden

Rapenburg 28 (071 516 3163/www. rmo.nl). **Open** 10am-5pm Tue-Sun. **Admission** €8.50; free-€7.50 reductions, MK.
Perhaps Leiden's most noteworthy museum, this houses the largest collection of archaeological artefacts in the Netherlands. Of particular interest is the display of Egyptian mummies and an exhibition of bog finds.

Rijksmuseum voor Volkenkunde

Steenstraat 1 (071 516 8800/www. rmv.nl). **Open** 10am-5pm Tue-Sun. **Admission** €8.50; €4 reductions, MK.
The National Museum of Ethnology showcases cultures of Africa, Oceania, Asia, the Americas and the Arctic.

Stedelijk Museum de Lakenhal

Oude Singel 28-32 (071 516 5360/ www.lakenhal.nl). **Open** 10am-5pm

Euromast p158

Tue-Fri; noon-5pm Sat, Sun. **Admission** €4; free-€2.50 reductions. MK.

In the Golden Age of the late 16th and 17th centuries, Leiden grew fat on textiles and spawned three great painters: Rembrandt van Rijn, Jan van Goyen and Jan Steen. Although few works by these masters remain in Leiden today, this museum does have a Rembrandt, plus works by other Old Masters and fascinating collections of pewter, tiles, silver and glass.

Getting there

By car, Leiden is 40 kilometres (24 miles) south-west of Amsterdam on the A4. Trains from Amsterdam Centraal Station take 35 minutes.

Tourist information

VVV

Stationsweg 2D (0900 222 2333 premium/www.vvvleiden.nl). **Open** *Jan-Mar, Sept-Dec* 11am-5.30pm Mon; 9.30am-5.30pm Tue-Fri; 10am-4.30pm Sat. *Apr-Aug* 11am-5.30pm Mon; 9.30am-5.30pm Tue-Fri; 10am-4.30pm Sat; 11am-3pm Sun.

Rotterdam

The antithesis of Amsterdam, this port city – its nickname is the Havenstad or 'harbour city' – brings a touch of urban grit to the Dutch landscape. Almost entirely flattened during World War II, the city has blossomed into a concrete-and-glass jungle, and what it lacks in charm it makes up for with creativity and innovation. In fact, the city remains in an almost continuous state of regeneration: a fine example of this is Rotterdam Centraal Station, which is currently being rebuilt. Such construction may mean that your entry point into the city is a building site, but the developments promise to be breathtaking – and should be well worth the long wait – when the station finally opens in 2010.

Euromast

*Parkhaven 20 (010 436 4811/www.
euromast.nl).* **Open** *Apr-Sept* 9.30am-
11pm daily. *Oct-Mar* 10am-11pm daily.
Admission €8.70; free-€5.60
reductions.

A bird's-eye view of the whole city and
its dockyards – and way beyond – can
be had from this tower, if you can han-
dle the precipitous height of 185m
(607ft). Some 100m (330ft) up, there's a
café-restaurant and even two hotel
suites. There are also three rather ver-
tiginous thrills: Euroscoop is a rotating
lift, and the foolhardy can abseil or take
a death slide from 100m.

Historical Museum Rotterdam

*Korte Hoogstraat 31 (010 217 6767/
www.historischmuseumrotterdam.nl).*
Open 11am-5pm Tue-Sun.
Admission €3; free reductions.

This child-friendly museum includes
the Dubbelde Palmboom ('Double
Palm Tree'), housed in an old granary
in Delfshaven and exploring life in the
Meuse Delta from 8000 BC to the present day, and Het Schielandshuis, a
17th-century mansion, another of the
few buildings spared by the bombing.

Kijk-Kubus

*Overblaak 70 (010 414 2285/www.
kubuswoning.nl).* **Open** 11am-5pm
daily. **Admission** €2.50; free-€2
reductions.

Rotterdam's Oude Haven (Old Harbour)
is a work of imaginative modernism,
the pinnacle of which lies in the form
of Piet Blom's yellow cubic houses.
Constructed during the 1970s, Kijk-
Kubus remains a modernist monument. Some are private residences;
others are being converted into a hostel, due to open in summer 2009.

Kunsthal

*Westzeedijk 341 (010 440 0301/
www.kunsthal.nl).* **Open** 10am-5pm
Tue-Sat; 11am-5pm Sun. **Admission**
€7.50; free-€4.50 reductions.

Designed by Rem Koolhaas's locally
based OMA bureau, the Kunsthal offers
over 3,000 sq m (32,000 sq ft) worth of
art, design and photography displays,
and features regular travelling shows.

Museum Boijmans van Beuningen

*Museumpark 18-20 (010 441 9400/
www.boijmans.nl).* **Open** 11am-5pm
Tue-Sun. **Admission** €9; free-€4.50
reductions, free Wed. MK.

The city's principal art museum is
home to a magnificent collection of traditional and contemporary art, including works by such masters as Bruegel,
Van Eyck and Rembrandt.

Netherlands Architecture Institute

*Museumpark 25 (010 440 1200/
www.nai.nl).* **Open** 10am-5pm Tue-
Sat; 11am-5pm Sun. **Admission** €8;
free-€5 reductions, MK.

Favourite city son and starchitect Rem
Koolhaas designed Rotterdam's cultural
heart, the Museumpark, where you'll
find outdoor sculptures and five museums. This one, which opened in 1993,
gives an overview of the history and
development of architecture, with particular emphasis on the city of Rotterdam
itself. It also hosts regular temporary
exhibitions on architecture-related subjects and has an extensive archive that
will be of interest to experts.

Getting there

By car, Rotterdam is 73 kilometres
(45 miles) south of Amsterdam on
firstly the A4, and then the A13.
Direct trains from Centraal Station
in Amsterdam take about one hour.

Tourist information

Use-it

*Schaatsbaan 41-45 (010 240 9158/
www. use-it.nl).* **Open** *Sept-April*

Utrecht

9am-5pm Tue-Sat. *May, June* 9am-6pm
Tue-Sun; *July, Aug* 9am-6pm Tue-Sun;
1pm-5pm Mon.
A kind of 'young person's VVV', this
place offers loads of tips for trips to the
city, plus some free lockers in which to
ditch your backpack.

VVV

*Coolsingel 5 (0900 403 4065 premium
rate/www.rotterdam.info).* **Open**
9am-5.30pm Mon-Thur, Sat; 9am-9pm
Fri; 10am-5pm Sun.

Utrecht

Utrecht is one of the oldest cities in
the Netherlands, and during the
Middle Ages, it was the biggest.
A religious and political centre for
hundreds of years, the city was
once home to 40 places of worship,
all with a skyline of towers and
spires. From a distance, it must
have looked like a holy pincushion.
However, there's more to Utrecht
than just history: its university is
one of the largest in the country
– still expanding and employing
architects such as Rem Koolhaas
(who designed the Educatorium) –
and the centre bustles with trendy
shops and cafés. Happily, too, the
Hoog Catharijne, the country's
biggest shopping mall, will soon
be knocked down. But until then,
you'll have to negotiate its
labyrinthine layout, following
the signs to 'Centrum' to exit
Centraal Station.

As for the surrounding
countryside, Utrecht lies in an area
that is rich in castles, forests and
arboretums. Slot Zuylen (Zuylen
Castle, Tournooiveld 1, Oud Zuilen,
030 244 0255, www.slotzuylen.com)
overlooks exquisite waterfalls
and gardens. Check out the concerts
and shows in Kasteel Groeneveld's
gorgeous gardens (Groeneveld
Castle, Groeneveld 2, Baarn, 035
542 0446, www.kasteelgroeneveld.nl),
to the north-east of Utrecht. Take a
stroll in the Arboretum von Gimborn

(Velperengh 13, 030 253 5455/
www.bio.uu.nl/bottuinen)
in Doorne, then pop over to the
Kasteel Huis Doorn (Doorn Castle,
Langbroekerweg 10, 034 342 1020,
www.huisdoorn.nl). This will
answer a question that's probably
been puzzling you for ages: what
happened to the Kaiser after World
War I? In fact, Wilhelm II lived
here in exile for 20 years before
eventually passing away in 1941.

Sights & museums

Centraal Museum

*Nicolaaskerkhof 10 (030 236 2362/
www.centraalmuseum.nl).* **Open**
11am-5pm Tue-Sun. **Admission** €8;
€2-€6 reductions. MK.
A varied collection, ranging from Van
Gogh artworks to modern art and fashion. A house opposite the museum is
dedicated to Miffy creator Dick Bruna,
who was born and lives in the town.

Domtoren

*Domplein (030 236 0010/www.
domtoren.nl).* **Open** noon-6pm Mon;
10am-6pm Tue-Fri; 10am-5pm Sat;
noon-5pm Sun. **Admission** €7.50;
free-€6.50 reductions.
Reaching more than 112m (367ft), the
cathedral tower is the highest in the
country. The panorama is worth climbing 465 steps to reach: spectacular
vistas stretch 40km (25 miles) to
Amsterdam. The neighbouring space
was once occupied by a huge church,
which was destroyed by a tornado in
1674. Inside the Domkerk, you'll see
before and after sketches.

Museum Catharijneconvent

*Lange Nieuwstraat 38 (030 231 3835/
www.catharijneconvent.nl).* **Open**
10am-5pm Tue-Fri; 11am-5pm Sat,
Sun. **Admission** €8.50; free-€7.50
reductions.
The St Catharine Convent Museum is
located in a beautiful late-medieval

building. Mainly dedicated to Dutch
religious history, it also has a great collection of paintings by Old Masters,
including Rembrandt.

Nationaal Museum van Speelklok tot Pierement

*Steenweg 6 (030 231 2789/www.
museumspeelklok.nl).* **Open** 10am-5pm
Tue-Sun. **Admission** €8; free-€7
reductions.
Although it sounds as though it's only
for hurdy-gurdy fanciers and organ
grinders, this museum – which houses
the world's biggest collection of automated musical instruments, is great
fun, especially the regular guided tours
that bring the street organs, cuckoo
clocks and rabbits in hats to life for visitors of all ages.

Rietveld-Schröderhuis

*Prins Hendriklaan 50/Ticket office at
Erasmuslaan 5 (030 236 2310/www.
rietveldschroderhuis.nl). Tour bus from
Centraal Museum, leaving hourly
between 11am and 2pm, Thur-Sun.*
Open 11am-5pm Thur-Sun. MK.
Admission €15; €7-€13 reductions.
Another Utrecht-born celebrity in the
Centraal Museum's collection is De Stijl
architect and designer Gerrit Rietveld,
who is best known for his rectangular
chairs and houses. The Rietveld-
Schröderhuis, on the outskirts of the
city centre, can be reached on the
Centraal Museum's tour bus.

Getting there

Utrecht is 40 kilometres (25 miles)
south-east of Amsterdam. Direct
trains from Amsterdam Centraal
Station take half an hour.

Tourist information

VVV

*Domplein 9 (0900 128 8732 premium
rate/www.utrechtyourway.nl).* **Open**
noon-6pm Mon; 10am-6pm Tue-Fri;
10am-5pm Sat; noon-5pm Sun.

Essentials

Lloyd Hotel p175

Hotels

Amsterdam has always had a shortage of accommodation – in fact, a recent industry study suggested that the region could use another 100 hotels by 2015. The question is, where to put them in this densely packed town? Well, the local folks behind **CitizenM** (see box p167), came up with their own unique solution: just stack up some shipping containers and rent them out as 'budget luxury' accommodation. With global ambitions, they've already got two locations in Amsterdam. Meanwhile, just east of Centraal Station, over on Oosterdokseiland, construction is underway on what will be the biggest (550 rooms) hotel in the country, at a cost of €150 million. Operated by the UK's City Inn chain, it plans to open in 2010.

Nearby are two of the city's more successful newcomers, **Lloyd Hotel** (p175), which occupies a former prison, and the luxurious **Grand Hotel Amrâth Amsterdam** (p121),

located in a former shipping office. A pattern seems to be emerging whereby existing buildings are revamped in favour of construction from scratch. Even the hostel **Stayokay Amsterdam Zeeburg** (p175) has been renovated to combine reasonable prices with the pretensions of a designer hotel.

The best way to experience the local version of Dutch hospitality is to stay in a B&B. Far from the dowdy seaside associations that the term conjures up, B&Bs are often designed to their stylish owners' high specifications. However, be warned: if you're on a budget, then bed-and-breakfasting is seldom the most economical option.

Hotels cluster around particular districts of Amsterdam: the Museum Quarter and the Canals district have plenty, whereas the Pijp and Jordaan, alas, contain only a few hotels. A general rule of thumb is to avoid those near the station or Red Light District.

Money matters

Credit card payment isn't always accepted in this quaint old city, particularly in smaller places, so check first. A rate may or may not include the city tax of five per cent, which could be added on to your final bill. Before booking, it's always worth checking for special deals on hotels' own websites, or on more commercial hotel websites – www.bookings.nl (also in English) is a good place to start.

The Old Centre

Barbizon Palace
Prins Hendrikkade 59-72 (556 4564/ www.nh-hotels.com). Tram 1, 2, 4, 5, 9, 13, 16, 17, 24, 25, 26. €€€
This flash branch of the reliable home-grown NH chain is opposite Centraal Station, and so it's ideal if you're making an early start. Public areas are decked out in sleek monochrome, making the rooms themselves (in bland hotel beige) a little disappointing. That said, facilities include conference rooms in a 15th-century chapel and a Michelin-starred restaurant.

Flying Pig Downtown
Nieuwendijk 100 (420 6822/group bookings 428 4934/www.flyingpig.nl). Tram 1, 2, 5, 13, 17. €
A stalwart of the Inter-railing scene. Young (it doesn't accept guests over 40 or under 18) backpackers flock here from around the world: they organise walking tours and in-line skating for free. There are also branches near to the Vondelpark and on the beach at Noordwijk-aan-Zee; the latter comes into its own in the summer, with watersports, beach activities and barbecues.

Grand Hotel Amrâth Amsterdam
NEW *Prins Hendrikkade 108-114 (552 0000/ www.amrathamsterdam.nl). Tram 1, 2, 5, 9, 13, 17, 24.* €€€€

SHORTLIST

Best newcomers
- CitizenM (p167)
- Grand Hotel Amrâth Amsterdam (p163)

Contemporary design
- Bilderberg Jan Luyken (p176)
- Kamer01 (p173)

Local flavour
- Greenhouse Effect (p165)
- Le Maroxidien (p165)
- Van Ostade Bicycle Hotel (p177)
- Xaviera Hollander Bed & Breakfast (p177)

Best nests for culture vultures
- Ambassade Hotel (p169)
- Hotel 717 (p171)
- Lloyd Hotel (p175)

Rooms with a view
- Dikker & Thijs Fenice Hotel (p171)
- Hotel Okura Amsterdam (p177)
- Mövenpick Hotel Amsterdam City Centre (p175)

Cheap and cheerful
- Hotel Leydsche Hof (p171)
- Hotel Prinsenhof (p173)
- Stayokay Amsterdam Zeeburg (p175)

Sophisticated style
- Dylan (p169)
- Grand Hotel Amrâth Amsterdam (p163)
- InterContinental Amstel Amsterdam (p173)
- Sofitel the Grand Amsterdam (p166)

Central location
- RHO Hotel (p166)
- Victoria (p166)

Quirky interiors
- Lloyd Hotel (p175)
- Winston Hotel (p169)

ESSENTIALS

Make the most of London life

The Amrâth nods handsomely to Dutch seafaring supremacy and the birth of an architectural movement. Considered to be the first exemplar of the Amsterdam School, this century-old shipping office bursts with creative brickwork and sculpture. It sports 137 rooms, 26 suites and a pool. A deluxe classic.

Grand Hotel Krasnapolsky
Dam 9 (554 9111/www.nh-hotels.com). Tram 1, 2, 4, 5, 9, 13, 14, 16, 17, 24, 25, 26. €€€€
Bang in the centre of Amsterdam, right opposite the Royal Palace, facilities here are really excellent: restaurants, bars, a ballroom, masseur and a winter garden for a relaxing weekend brunch. Options range from suites to compact rooms at the back.

Greenhouse Effect
Warmoesstraat 53-55 (624 4974/www. greenhouse-effect.nl). Tram 4, 9, 24, 25. €
If you're planning to disappear in a cloud of cannabis smoke, this place above a coffee shop (p73) is where to rest your addled head. Some rooms feature shared facilities, several are kitted out in trippy styles and others have good canal views. Breakfast is served until midday and there's also a bar.

Hotel des Arts
Rokin 154-156 (620 1558/www.hoteldesarts.nl). Tram 4, 9, 14, 16, 24, 25. €€
A snug hotel exuding a touch of faded glamour, rooms are decorated with clunky, polished period furniture and ornate chandeliers – although some of them are also a little dark. Most are very spacious, however, and are geared towards groups and families. Near the main shopping street, with most sights within easy walking distance.

Hotel de l'Europe
Nieuwe Doelenstraat 2-14 (531 1777/ www.leurope.nl). Tram 4, 9, 14. €€€€
Another landmark hotel with views across the Amstel, this is the place for indulgent splurges or honeymoon hide-

Flying Pig Downtown p163

aways: think marble bathrooms and Bulgari toiletries. The bridal suite has a four-poster bed and a two-person jacuzzi in the room; it's also one of the few hotels in Amsterdam to boast a swimming pool, and there's a highly rated restaurant, Excelsior.

Ibis Amsterdam Centre
Stationsplein 49 (638 9999/www.ibishotel.com). Tram 1, 2, 4, 5, 9, 13, 17, 24, 25. 26. €€
If you're arriving late or leaving early, this place is ideal. Right next to Centraal Station, there's 24-hour takeaway food (sandwiches and juices) and breakfast is served from 6am-noon. It's nothing fancy, just the reliable Ibis formula of comfort and reasonable facilities.

Le Maroxidien
NEW *Prins Hendrikkade 534 (400 4006/www.lemaroxidien.com). Tram 1, 2, 5, 9, 13, 17, 24.* €€€
This floating B&B in a historical houseboat has a charming hostess, three guest rooms (themed Morocco, India and Mexico) two common bathrooms and a living room. Great organic breakfast.

ESSENTIALS

Nova

*Nieuwezijds Voorburgwal 276 (623 0066/
www.novahotel.nl). Tram 1, 2, 5.* €€
The five charming townhouses that
make up Nova are comfortable, plain-
ly furnished (yet good-looking in an
IKEA sort of way), and smell fresh as
daisies since the place went totally no-
smoking in February 2007. The hotel
is also handily located for the
Nieuwezijds nightlife as well as the
main cultural sights.

Renaissance Amsterdam

*Kattengat 1 (621 2223/www.marriott.com).
Tram 1, 2, 4, 5, 13, 17.* €€€
An upmarket option for exploring the
bohemian charms of the Jordaan and
Harlemmerstraat, this 400-roomed
place compensates for its flowery decor
with luxuries like in-house movies,
interactive videos and DVDs, making
it a good bet for flush families with
recalcitrant kids. There's also a
babysitting service. In 2008, the rooms
and restaurant were renovated, an
executive lobby was added and the
hotel was generally spruced up.

Residence Le Coin

*Nieuwe Doelenstraat 5 (524 6800/www.
lecoin.nl). Tram 4, 9, 14, 16, 24, 25.* €€
On a quiet, café-lined street between
the Old Centre and the central shopping district, this medium-sized hotel
arranged across seven buildings has
spacious, very stylish rooms in muted
colours. Drenched in light thanks to big
windows, furnishings are a classy mix
of old and new, with designer chairs
and lots of shiny wood. The attic rooms
are particularly full of character, and
many rooms come with kitchenettes,
making this a good bet for families.

RHO Hotel

*Nes 5-23 (620 7371/www.rhohotel.nl).
Tram 1, 2, 4, 5, 9, 13, 16, 17, 24, 25.* €€
If your budget doesn't stretch as far as
the swankier and more expensive
hotels on and around Dam square, this
hotel matches on location, if not on

interior design or style. On a backstreet
bustling with bars, restaurants and
theatres, the art deco lobby harks back
to the days when it was a gold mer-
chant's, although the rooms themselves are surprisingly plain.

Sofitel the Grand Amsterdam

*Oudezijds Voorburgwal 197 (555 3111/
www.thegrand.nl). Tram 4, 9, 16, 24, 25.*
€€€€
Centuries of history in a luxurious courtyard hotel. Rooms are spacious and airy
thanks to big windows; bathrooms are
embellished with Roger & Gallet
smellies; and the suites range from
junior to royal. Not exactly a bargain,
there are nevertheless deals like the
appropriately named Dream Package,
which includes champagne, dinner and
use of the spa. An indulgent high tea in
the Council Chamber is open to non-
guests everyday from 30-52.

Swissotel

*Damrak 96 (522 3000/www.amsterdam.
swissotel.com). Tram 1, 2, 4, 5, 9, 13, 14,
16, 17, 24, 25.* €€€
One of the best-looking of the big international chains, this place is geared
towards the business market, but it's
still a good destination for pleasure
seekers. It's next to Dam square and
near department store De Bijenkorf,
and all rooms have big beds and on-
demand films and music. Pricier rooms
come with espresso machines and
suites overlook Dam Square.

Victoria

*Damrak 1-5 (6234255/www.parkplaza.com/
amsterdamnl_victoria). Tram 1, 2, 4, 5,
9, 13, 16, 17, 24, 25, 26.* €€
A stalwart of the hotel scene, the public areas of this 300-roomed hotel opposite Centraal Station decked out in
browns, creams and reds look dapper.
Rooms are a good size, and come with
all the trappings. The excellent health
club and pool are open to guests and
non-guests alike – fees vary.

Budget luxury in a box

Welcome to the future of hotels: the shipping container at **CitizenM**. Due to the housing shortage in Amsterdam, local students have long been living in these humble units, but it's safe to say that CitizenM is the first initiative to utilise them as the basis for a 'budget luxury' designer hotel.

CitizenM's initiator is Rattan Chadha, who left his role as founder and CEO of Amsterdam-based clothing chain Mexx to cover the globe with shipping container hotels. The first opened at Schiphol Airport in 2008 and was the result of a partnership with advertisers KesselsKramer, who commissioned local design gurus Concrete to style it, and Philips to do the technology.

The idea was to strip things down to the bare essentials: 14 square-metre (150-square-foot) rooms are created and assembled off-site, and have wall-to-wall windows, a shower pod, a toilet pod, a king-size bed with luxury linens, flatscreen TV, and a 'mood pad', which controls all of the above plus the lights and temperature.

The resulting accommodation is surprisingly comfortable. While the branding is aimed at the new young, global jet-set class, so far it seems that traditional business travellers are keen to make use of CitizenM in the name of taking advantage of a (relative) bargain – prices slide according to demand, but rarely exceed €70 a night.

Meanwhile, if the lobby feels like a Vitra furniture showroom (albeit one with self-service check-in), that's because it is. And for those arriving late or making an early start, there are refreshments available 24/7 from the 'canteen'.

At press time, a second, more central location is scheduled to open: CitizenM Amsterdam City (Prinses Irenestraat 30/www. citizenmamsterdamcity.com). There are plans to open another 20 hotels over the next five years, on prime sites in major European cities – a third is due to open in Glasgow before the end of 2009.

CitizenM
Schiphol Airport (www.citizenm.com). NS train station Schiphol. **€€**.

www.treesforcities.org

Trees for Cities
Charity registration number 1032154

Travelling creates so many
lasting memories.

Make your trip mean something for
years to come - not just for you but
for the environment and for people
living in deprived urban areas.

Anyone can offset their flights,
but when you plant trees with
Trees for Cities, you'll help create
a green space for an urban
community that really needs it.

To find out more visit
www.treesforcities.org

Leave
Your
Mark

Create a green future for cities.

Winston Hotel

*Warmoestraat 129-131 (623 1380/www.
winston.nl). Tram 4, 9, 16, 24, 25.* €
The legendary Winston has a youthful,
party-loving atmosphere and rooms
decorated in eccentric, eclectic style,
ranging from monochrome to kinky
S&M den decor. Cheaper dormbeds are
available, but are much less fun.
There's also a bar and club (p78).

Western Canal Belt

Ambassade Hotel

*Herengracht 341 (555 0222/www.
ambassade-hotel.nl). Tram 1, 2, 5.* €€€
Staff in this literary hotel are discreet
and attentive, and rooms – from single
to suite to apartment – are decorated in
Louis Quatorze style. There's also a
library, the many shelves of which are
loaded with signed tomes by illustrious
former guests, which residents are free
to peruse at their leisure.

Amsterdam Wiechmann

*Prinsengracht 328-332 (626 3321/www.
hotelwiechmann.nl). Tram 1, 2, 5, 7, 10,
17.* €€
From a suit of armour in reception to
teapots and toasters in the breakfast
room, retro touches adorn this long-
established Jordaan hotel. Decor errs on
the chintzy, but it's cosy nevertheless,
and costlier rooms look on to the canal.

Dylan

*Keizersgracht 384 (530 2010/www.dylan
amsterdam.com). Tram 1, 2, 5.* €€€€
Outrageous elegance is the key in the
Dylan's raspberry, turmeric or coal
rooms, detail-obsessed bar and restaurant boasting chef Dennis Kuipers's
French-inspired menu. Everything,
from the alignment of the cushions to
the service, is well thought out.

Estherea

*Singel 303-309 (624 5146/www.estherea.
nl). Tram 1, 2, 5.* €€€
Spread over several elegant houses at
the spectacular epicentre of the canals,

Amsterdam Wiechmann

this hotel has been run by the same
family for decades. The emphasis is on
understated luxury: rooms are swathed
in Fortuny-style fabrics and have DVD
players (on request) and marble bathrooms. For those hot summer days
(and nights), air-conditioning has
recently been installed.

't Hotel

*Leliegracht 18 (422 2741/www.thotel.nl).
Tram 1, 2, 5, 13, 14, 17.* €€
A stylish bolthole on a beautiful canal
in the Jordaan, this prosaically named
place is fitted throughout in 1920s-
inspired style. Bauhaus prints adorn
the walls, the colour scheme is muted
and the armchairs are design classics.
All rooms have great views on to the
canal or the rear garden and all are spacious. Split-level room eight, tucked
away up in the eaves of the building, is
especially full of character.

Hotel Brouwer

*Singel 83 (624 6358/ www.hotelbrouwer.nl).
Tram 1, 2, 5. 13, 17.* €
These eight neat, en suite rooms all
look on to the Singel canal, but it's not
the place for extras. However, if you're

after well-priced accommodation in a longstanding family hotel, you're in for a treat. Unusually for budget class, there's a lift, plus TVs in the doubles.

Hotel Pulitzer

Prinsengracht 315-331 (523 5235/www. starwoodhotels.com). Tram 13, 14, 17. €€€€
Sprawling across 25 canal houses, rooms are big and stylish in this glamorous hotel. There's a lovely garden and, in August, the classical music Grachtenfestival takes place in and around the grounds, making it an excellent choice for music fans.

Singel Hotel

Singel 13-17 (626 3108/www.singelhotel. nl). Tram 1, 2, 5. 13, 17. €
This medium-sized, 32-roomed hotel is ideally located for canal and Jordaan hikes, and for arrival and departure by train (it's a five-minute walk from Centraal Station). Inside its solid 17th-century walls, rooms are plain and furnished in a modern, basic style; they are generally clean and tidy, and all ensuite. But be warned that the street-facing rooms can be noisy.

Toren

Keizersgracht 164 (622 6352/www. thetoren.nl). Tram 13, 14, 17. €€€
This building has been a Golden Age mansion, a prime minister's home, a university and even a hiding place for persecuted Jews during World War II. Now it's a family-run hotel and comes with all the usual trappings: opulent fabrics, grand public rooms and attentive staff. Standards are a bit of a cramp, but deluxe rooms have jacuzzis, and the bridal suites even come with elegant double whirlpool baths.

Southern Canal Belt

American Hotel

Leidsekade 97 (556 3000/www. amsterdamamerican.com). Tram 1, 2, 5. €€€€

This dazzling art nouveau monument looks extra spruce now that a fountain has been added to its terrace, and its public areas – like the buttressed in-house Café Americain – are all eye-pleasing. Rooms (not including suites) are pretty cramped, although they do enjoy views of the canal or square below. The decor is smart-but-bland hotel standard.

Amsterdam Marriott Hotel

Stadhouderskade 12 (607 5555/www. marriott.com). Tram 1, 2, 5. €€€€
Set right next to the lovely Vondelpark, the Marriott was given a thorough overhaul in 2007, so it's goodbye to the dowdy green and brown gentleman's club styling of yesteryear, and hello to soothing yellows and modern greys offset with contemporary furnishings. All 392 rooms now come equipped with high-thread-count linen and luxury duvets. Bathrooms have gone similarly upmarket, with cherry wood and granite surfaces and cascade showerheads. The restaurant, Quoy, is something of a well-kept secret.

Banks Mansion

Herengracht 519-525 (420 0055/www. banksmansion.nl). Tram 4, 9, 14, 16, 24, 25. €€€
Once you check into this grand hotel in a former bank building, everything is for free – yep, drinks in the lounge, movies in your room, and even the minibar. This classy form of an all-inclusive holiday also involves a pillow menu, cascade showerheads, plasma TVs and DVD players. Needless to say it's hardly bargain basement stuff, but look out for deals on the website.

Bridge Hotel

Amstel 107-111 (623 7068/www.the bridgehotel.nl). Tram 4, 9, 14. €€
Gloriously isolated on the eastern bank of the Amstel, this private hotel in a former stonemason's workshop is just a few minutes from the bright lights of Rembrandtplein, and well situated for

Mövenpick Hotel Amsterdam
City Centre p175

the Plantage and Jodenbuurt. Rooms are simple and bright; river views cost more. There are apartments and a studio for stays longer than three days.

Dikker & Thijs Fenice Hotel

Prinsengracht 444 (620 1212/www.dtfh. nl). Tram 1, 2, 5. €€€

This well-established place is owned by a publisher, so authors often drop in. Set in an 18th-century warehouse near Leidseplein, rooms are plain but smart, while the glamorous penthouse has glass walls for unsurpassed views over the rooftops. At breakfast, guests are bathed in jewel-coloured light from the stained-glass windows.

Hotel 717

Prinsengracht 717 (427 0717/www.717 hotel.nl). Tram 1, 2, 5. €€€€

The epitome of understated glamour, this small, flower-filled place emphasises searching the globe for the best accoutrements: linens from the USA, bespoke blankets from Wales, spring mattresses from London. There is

afternoon tea daily and a garden. Guests are the type who shed euros on antiques in the Spiegelkwartier.

Hotel Agora

Singel 462 (627 2200/www.hotelagora.nl). Tram 1, 2, 5. €€

Ideal for botanists stocking up on bulbs, this homely little place is in an 18th-century house on a canal near the floating flower market. What Agora lacks in extras, it more than makes up for with nice touches like conservatory breakfasts and a garden. Rooms are plain but neat and comfortable and all enjoy lovely canal or garden views.

Hotel Leydsche Hof

Leidsegracht 14 (623 2148/www.freewebs. com/leydschehof). Tram 1, 2, 5. €

A hidden gem on a genteel canal just minutes from Leidseplein; the Piller family lovingly cares for the seven bright, simply decorated rooms in their charming 17th-century house. All are are done out in dark wood, and the high-ceilinged breakfast chamber boasts a striking marble fireplace.

ESSENTIALS

Wanted.
Jumpers, coats
and people with
their knickers
in a twist.

From the people who feel moved to bring us their old books and CDs, to the people fed up to the back teeth with our politicians' track record on climate change, Oxfam supporters have one thing in common. They're passionate. If you've got a little fire in your belly, we'd love to hear from you. Visit us at **oxfam.org.uk**

Be Humankind (X) Oxfam

Hotel de Munck

Achtergracht 3 (623 6283/www.hotel demunck.com). Tram 4, 7, 10. €€
This higgledy-piggledy place in an old Dutch East India Company captain's house is perched on a secluded little canal near the river. Rooms here are plain and basic (and some are looking rather tired), though they are clean and neat. The breakfast room is a delight, though, with a 1950s jukebox and walls plastered with old album covers.

Hotel Prinsenhof

Prinsengracht 810 (623 1772/ www.hotel-prinsenhof.com). Tram 4. €
This dinky, ten-room hotel is near the nightlife and foodie Utrechtsestraat and has helpful staff. Rooms them-selves (some have canal views) are sim-ple, some share facilities, and they're all clean and tidy. Those physically less able should note that the stairs are very steep.

InterContinental Amstel Amsterdam

Professor Tulpplein 1 (622 6060/www. intercontinental.com/ams-amstel). Tram 7, 10. €€€€
They don't come much posher than this: if movie stars or royalty are in town, they almost always lay their heads in one of the huge, soundproofed rooms or luxury suites here. Staff are liveried, the restaurant is Michelin-starred (now with chef Roger Rassen), and every service imaginable is pre-sent, pool included. If money is no object or it's a once-in-a-lifetime splurge, this is the place for you.

Kamer01

NEW *Singel 416 (06 5477 6151/www. kamer01.nl). Tram 1, 2, 5.* €€€
A very stylish, gay-friendly B&B that recently moved to this location in sum-mer 2009. Expect more of the same warm hospitality, plus huge showers, circular beds, iMacs, flatscreen TVs and DVD players. There's a minimum two-night stay.

Marcel van Woerkom

Leidsestraat 87 (622 9834/www.marcel amsterdam.com). Tram 1, 2, 5. €€
Artist Marcel has been letting rooms in his stylish 'creative exchange' since 1970: chances are you'll run into artists or designers admiring the artworks. Despite calling itself a B&B, you only get the bed, but nearby there are plenty of breakfast options. Book well in advance.

Mercure Hotel Arthur Frommer

Noorderstraat 46 (622 0328/www. mercure.com). Tram 4, 16, 24, 25. €€€
On a residential street within walking distance of the sights and the local nightlife, this courtyard hotel is in one of the nicest locations in town by far, near Amstelveld and with restaurant-lined Utrechtsestraat also very close at hand. Rooms are spacious and smart, though not overburdened with fancy extras. There's also a bar that's popu-lar with guests and non-guests.

Nicolaas Witsen

Nicolaas Witsenstraat 4 (623 6143/www. hotelnicolaaswitsen.nl). Tram 4, 7, 10, 25. €€
One of the few hotels to fill the gap between museums and the Pijp, this place, though plain, functional (and a tad overpriced), is well placed for both serious culture vultures and fun-seek-ers. Ground-floor rooms can get noisy but plusses include free Wi-Fi and a lift. The excellent deli on the corner encourages in-room midnight feasting.

Seven Bridges

Reguliersgracht 31 (623 1329/www.seven-bridgeshotel.nl). Tram 4, 16, 24, 25. €€
The ideal destination for hermits who want a luxury hidey-hole far from the madding crowd, this hotel is also con-venient for the museums and trips into the city centre. There are no public spaces, just eight antique-packed rooms. Breakfast is served in bed on Villeroy and Boch crockery. One of Amsterdam's best-kept secrets.

WHEREVER CRIMES AGAINST HUMANITY ARE PERPETRATED.

Across borders and above politics.
Against the most heinous abuses
and the most dangerous oppressors.
From conduct in wartime
to economic, social, and cultural rights.
Everywhere we go,
we build an unimpeachable case
for change and advocate action
at the highest levels.

HUMAN RIGHTS WATCH TYRANNY HAS A WITNESS

WWW.HRW.ORG

HUMA
RIGHT
WATC

Jodenbuurt, the Plantage & the Oost

Eden Lancaster

Plantage Middelaan 48 (535 6888/www. edenhotelgroup.com). Tram 9, 14. €€
If you're planning on taking the kids to the excellent Artis zoo, this hotel is just across the road, and its triple and quad rooms are very much aimed at families. Although it is a little way from the more central sights, the main railway station is a short tram ride or 20-minute walk away, and there are several good cafés in the immediate vicinity.

Hotel Adolesce

Nieuwe Keizersgracht 26 (626 3959/ www.adolesce.nl). Trams 9, 14/Metro Waterlooplein. €
You won't get any breakfast at this unfussy place near the Skinny Bridge, but guests can help themselves to drinks, fruit and chocolate in the lounge. Rooms are pretty plain – the attic room is nicest – but it's close to both the Hermitage Amsterdam (p113) and Waterlooplein flea market (p118).

Hotel Arena

's Gravesandestraat 51 (850 2400/www. hotelarena.nl). Tram 3, 7, 10. €€
A hotel, restaurant and club in an old orphanage, a ten-minute tram ride from town, it's the one-stop-shop of food, booze and boogie. Standard and larger rooms are a bit boring, but pricier, extra large ones and suites are kitted out by leading local designers.

Stayokay Amsterdam Zeeburg

Timorplein 21 (551 3190/www.stayokay. com). Trams 3, 7, 10, 14. €
This new branch of the reliable hostel chain in a grand old school building is aimed at families and discerning hostellers. Rooms sleep two to six. Designed in warm reds with mosaic floors and sleek furniture, hostelling never looked so good.

The Waterfront & North

Amstel Botel

NDSM Werf Pier 3 (626 4247/www. amstelbotel.nl). Ferry. €
Housed in a large boat, Amstel Botel has recently changed locations from near Centraal Station. Now it's a 15-minute free ferry ride from behind the station. This is good, clean accommodation with a few frills like in-house movies. The bar (9am-1am) has pool, pinball and a jukebox.

Ideaal II

Opposite Levantkade 51 (419 7255/www. houseboats.nl). Tram 10. €€
An inspired and indulgent option, this converted cargo boat near the up-and-coming cultural quarter sleeps up to five, and comes with two bathrooms, jacuzzi, stainless steel kitchen and decks dedicated to sunbathing and swimming. At night, you'll sleep on (what else?) a waterbed. Overnight stays are possible, but longer ones make more economic sense. Check the website for excellent last-minute deals.

Lloyd Hotel

NEW *Oostelijke Handelskade 34 (561 36 04/ www.lloydhotel.com), Tram 10, 26.* €
This former youth prison has been reinvented as one- to five-star accommodation complete with a new 'cultural embasssy'. Fitting in nicely in this harbour neighbourhood which has always been famed for its modern residential architecture, Lloyd features the work of hotshot Dutch designers, Atelier van Lieshout and Marcel Wanders.

Mövenpick Hotel Amsterdam City Centre

Piet Heinkade 11 (519 1200/www.moeven pick-hotels.com). Tram 25, 26. €€€
A glamorous multi-storey branch of the Swiss chain recently opened on the banks of the IJ. Rooms are decorated in muted modern greys and woods. The

Truelove Antiek & Guesthouse

more expensive ones include access to the 'executive lounge' and have great views over the water and the city.

The Jordaan

Frederic Rentabike
Brouwersgracht 78 (624 5509/www. frederic.nl). Bus 18, 21, 22, 348, 353. No credit cards. €€
This bike shop also does a nice sideline in renting out six houseboats, located all around town, from sleek vessels to more homely numbers. Houseboat no.3, on the Prinsengracht, is big, stylish, central and has internet access.

Truelove Antiek & Guesthouse
Prinsenstraat 4 (320 2500/06 248 056 72 mobile after 6pm/www.truelove.be). Tram 1, 2, 5. €€
Above an antiques shop (now the hotel reception), this dinky place is decorated with the odd quirky piece from the selection downstairs. The attic room is best, but all come with CD player, TV and kettle. There's also an apartment located on Langestraat.

Between Art and Kitsch
Ruysdaelkade 75 (679 0485/www. between-art-and-kitsch.com). Tram 16, 24. €
Actually, technically speaking it's located between the museums and the Pijp. This B&B has just two rooms: one is decorated in mock art deco with authentic period knick-knacks; the other is faux Baroque. Both rooms certainly live up to the name's promise, making it the quirky accommodation option. On a nice canal, it's great for culture vultures keen to get out there and explore.

Bilderberg Jan Luyken
Jan Luykenstraat 58 (573 0730/ www.bilderberg.nl). Tram 2, 3, 5, 12. €€
One of the city's most stylish secrets, this place – complete with spa and a wine bar – is just a skip from the upmarket shops along PC Hooftstraat. Rooms feature designer touches and wall-mounted CD players, and are something of a bargain for a place with these looks and facilities. Check for special packages: the Amsterdam Beauty Arrangement, for example, gets you a cocktail, B&B, and a spa session for under €110 per person.

College Hotel
Roelof Hartstraat 1 (571 1511/www. thecollegehotel.com). Tram 3, 5, 12, 24. €€€
Part of the city's hotel and catering college and thus staffed by students. Boutique styling and some glam touches ensure that prices are far from pocket-money. Some rooms, though lovely, are small; pay top dollar to get oodles of space, though most of the suites have now converted into two or three separate spaces, ideal for families. There's a bar and an ambitious modern Dutch restaurant. Perhaps because of the hotel's educational function, service can be unpredictable.

Hotel V

Victorieplein 42 (662 3233/www.hotelv. nl). Tram 4, 12, 25. €€
Hotel V is a bit of a hike from the sights, but tram no.4 stops right outside and the Pijp is only a 15-minute walk away. This boutique B&B-style hotel is ideal for business travellers sick of sterility; it's near the business district of Zuid. There's sleek decor in all rooms, but you won't find much in the way of extras. That said, the lounge, with its pebbly fireplace and furry pouffes, looks lovely. A second location opened in 2009 at Weteringschans 136.

Hotel Vondel

Vondelstraat 28-30 (612 0120/www. hotelvondel.nl). Tram 1, 2, 3, 5, 7, 10, 12. €€€
Another well-hidden gem near the museums and Amsterdam's more upmarket shopping district, this chic little place is covered with art and boasts a lovely decked garden. Rooms, including junior and family suites, are designer driven, with Burberry-check blankets, chandeliers and nice swanky bathrooms. Unusually for such a trendy hotel, families are welcome.

Xaviera Hollander Bed & Breakfast

Stadionweg 17 (673 3934/www.xaviera hollander.com). Tram 5, 24. €€
Prudes avert your eyes, since you won't want to stay in the home of the original Happy Hooker. Rooms, upstairs in Xaviera's own banker-belt villa or in a hut at the bottom of her garden, are nice, but guests come here mainly for a truly outrageous anecdote – or several – from the lady herself.

The Pijp

Hotel Okura Amsterdam

Ferdinand Bolstraat 333 (678 7111/www. okura.nl). Tram 12, 25. €€€€
This multi-storey, multi-tasking, very smart business-class stopover has everything captains of industry need:

Between Art and Kitsch

a top-floor cocktail bar, top of the range French restaurant, Le Ciel Bleu; a full-size pool and health club; and sushi bars. Rooms are done up in suitably masculine style and range from small standards to the huge (and hugely expensive) presidential suite on the 21st floor.

Hotel Savoy

Ferdinand Bolstraat 194 (644 7445/www. savoyhotel.nl). Tram 3, 12, 25. €€€
One of a limited number of accommodation options in the area, housed in an imposing red-brick Amsterdam School building, it has been restyled as a swanky concept hotel, which suits the Pijp right down to the ground.

Van Ostade Bicycle Hotel

Van Ostadestraat 123 (679 3452/ www.bicyclehotel.com). Tram 3, 12, 16, 24, 25. €
This staging post for pedal-pushers was one of the first places to stay in the Pijp. Staff can suggest trips and rent out bikes. Rooms are comfy and there are loads of excellent places nearby to refuel for the day ahead or wind down after a long, hard ride around town.

ESSENTIALS

Getting Around

Arriving & leaving

By air

Schiphol Airport

0900 0141 premium rate/
www.schiphol.nl
Amsterdam's airport lies 18
kilometres (11 miles) south-west of
the city. There's only one terminal
building, but within that there are
four departure and arrival halls.

Connexxion Airport
Hotel Shuttle

Connexxion counter, Section A7,
Arrivals, Schiphol Airport (038 339
4741/www.airporthotelshuttle.nl).
This bus from Schiphol to
Amsterdam departs at least every
30 minutes between 6am and 9pm.
Anyone who buys a ticket (€14.50
single/(€22.50 return) can use it, not
just hotel guests. Drop-off points
are the 100-odd allied hotels; see the
website for schedules, destination
hotels and their booking services.

Airport trains

Trains leave approximately every
ten minutes between 5am and
midnight (after which they depart
hourly). The journey to Centraal
Station takes about 20 minutes.
Buy your ticket (€3.90 single)
before you board, or you're highly
likely to incur a €35 fine. You are
also charged an extra €0.50 if you
buy your ticket from a counter;
instead use the machines which
also have English instructions.

By taxi

A fixed fare from the airport to the
south and west of the city costs
around €30, and to the city centre
about €40. Bear in mind that there

are always plenty of licensed taxis
beside the main exit. You can also
book your taxi ahead on the
Schiphol website (www.schiphol.nl).

By bus

Long-distance international
Eurolines coaches (560 8788/
www.eurolines.nl) stop at Amstel
station, Julianaplein 5, in the south-
east of the city, connected to
Centraal Station by Metro and train.

By train

A range of national trains operated
by **NS** (www.ns.nl), where e-tickets
can be bought, as well as
international services, stop at
Centraal Station in the city centre
or in some cases Schiphol airport.

In town

Getting around Amsterdam is very
easy: there are efficient, cheap and
integrated trams, metros and buses,
and in the centre most places can
be got to on foot. Locals tend to get
around by bike, and there are also
boats and water taxis. Public
transport provision for those with
disabilities, however, is dire.

The best way to travel is by
tram, with a network of routes
through the centre (buses and the
Metro are more for outlying suburbs).

GVB

Stationsplein CS, Old Centre: New Side
(0900 8011 premium rate/ www.gvb.nl/
english). Tram 1, 2, 4, 5, 9, 13, 16, 17,
24, 25, 26. **Open** *Phone enquiries* 8am-
10pm daily. *In person* 7am-9pm Mon-
Fri; 10am-6pm Sat, Sun.
The GVB runs Amsterdam's Metro,
bus and tram services, and can also

provide detailed information and departure and arrival times on all of them, as well as sell tickets.

Fares & tickets

An OV-Kaart chip card is to be phased in during 2009 for all public transport, but meanwhile a *strippenkaart* (strip ticket) system operates across trams, buses and metros: prices begin at €1.60 for a strip of two units (one journey in one zone) bought on the tram/bus, or purchased from machines for the Metro. Cheaper are 15-unit (€7.30) or 45-unit (€21.60) cards, bought from GVB offices, post offices, train stations and many supermarkets and tobacconists. Kids under three travel free; older children (four to 18) and seniors (65+) pay reduced fares. *Strippenkaarten* must be stamped on boarding trams/buses or entering Metro stations. For the sake of convenience, Amsterdam is divided up roughly into five separate zones: Noord (north), West, Centrum, Oost (east) and Zuid (south).

Journeys work on the principle of one unit for the journey, plus one unit for each zone, so for a single zone, stamp two units; for two zones stamp three and so on.

If the tram is conductorless, stamp the *strippenkaart* in the yellow box near the doors: fold it so the unit you need to stamp is at the end. On conductored trams and buses, the *strippenkaart* is stamped for you. On the Metro, stamping machines are located near the entrance. More than one person can travel on one strip ticket, but the correct number of units must be stamped per person.

Stamped cards are valid for an hour and allow transfer to other buses/trams/metros, or across all three. *Strippenkaarten* are valid for a year from the date of the first stamping. Unlimited 24-hour tickets

costing €7 (€11.50 for 48 hours, €15 for 72 hours and €18 for 96 hours), and the Iamsterdam Pass that's valid for one day at €33 (including canalbus ticket) can also be purchased from either the GVB or Amsterdam Tourist Board.

Don't even think about travelling without a ticket: inspectors make regular checks, and passengers without tickets are hit with €35 on-the-spot fines.

Trams & buses

Trams run from 6am Mon-Fri, 6.30am Sat and 7.30am Sun. Night buses (numbered 348 to 392) take over later (12.30am-7.30am daily), and all go to Centraal Station. Night bus stops are indicated by a black square with the bus number printed on it. During off-peak hours and at quiet stops, stick out your arm to let the driver know you want to get on. Signs at tram and bus stops show the name of the stop and line number, and boards indicate the full route.

Other road users must remember that a tram will only stop if absolutely necessary. Cyclists should listen for tram warning bells and cross tramlines at an angle that avoids the front wheel getting stuck. Motorists should avoid blocking tramlines: cars are allowed to venture on to them only if turning right.

Metro

The Metro uses the same ticket system as trams and buses (see above) and serves suburbs to the south and east. Three separate lines, 51, 52 and 53, terminate at Centraal Station (sometimes abbreviated to CS). Trains on the city Metro run from 6am Mon-Fri (6.30am Sat, 7.30am Sun) to around 12.15am on a daily basis.

Taxis

Most taxis are operated by the central office **TCA**. They're hard to hail on the street, but ranks are found around the city; most central are the ones at Centraal Station, by the bus station at the junction of Kinkerstraat and Marnixstraat, on Rembrandtplein and Leidseplein. Cabs can be ordered on 777 7777. Wheelchairs will only be carried in taxis if folded, but there is a service for wheelchair users (633 3943, 7am-5pm daily); be sure to book journeys at least a day in advance.

Getting a taxi in Amsterdam is relatively straightforward, but check that the meter starts at the minimum charge (€7.50, with first two kilometres included) and ask the rough cost of the journey before setting out. Even short journeys are expensive: on top of the minimum charge, it costs €2.20 per kilometre for the first 25 kilometres, €1.75 per kilometre for the next 25 kilometres, and €1.45 thereafter.

If you feel as though you have been ripped off (cases are relatively rare), ask for a receipt and contact the TCA (650 6506, 9am-5pm Mon-Fri) or the police.

Driving

If you absolutely must bring a car to the Netherlands, join a national motoring organisation beforehand. This should then issue you with booklets that explain what to do in the event of a breakdown in Europe. To drive a car within the Netherlands, you need a valid national driving licence, although **ANWB** (see below) and many car hire firms favour photocard licences (Brits need the paper version as well for this to be legal; the photocard takes a couple of weeks to come through if you're applying from scratch). You'll need proof that the vehicle has passed a road safety test in its country of origin, as well as an international identification disk, a registration certificate and relevant insurance documents.

Car hire

Local car hire (*autoverhuur*) firms generally expect drivers to be over 21 with at least a year's experience, and a valid national driving licence (with photo) and passport. All require a credit card deposit.

Dik's Autoverhuur
662 3366/www.diks.net

Hertz
612 2441/www.hertz.nl

Parking

Parking is a nightmare: the centre is metered from 9am until at least 7pm (midnight in many places), setting you back up to €5 an hour; ticketing is very common. Parking passes for daytime (9am-7pm, €30; 24 hours, €45) and weekly passes (9am-7pm, €180; 24 hours, €270) can be bought from **Stadstoezicht** (www.stadstoezicht.amsterdam.nl). Bear in mind that after controlled hours, parking at meters across the city is completely free, and prices can vary between neighbourhoods.

Car parks

Car parks are indicated by a white 'P' on a blue square sign. **ANWB Parking Amsterdam Centraal** (Prins Hendrikkade 20A in the Old Centre: New Side, 638 5330) is open 24 hours daily and charges €4 per hour, or €55 per day. Many nearby hotels offer a 10% discount on parking here. Europarking (Marnixstraat 250, 0900 446 6880 premium rate) in Oud West is slightly cheaper, charging €3.60

per hour, or €36 per day, but is only open 7am-1am Mon; 6.30am-1am Tues, Wed; 6.30am-midnight Thur; 24 hours Fri-Sun. Both accept payment by credit card. You can also consider Park and Rides (see www.bereikbaaramsterdam.nl for the locations) which are €6/day. When leaving your car, empty it of valuables: cars with foreign number plates are particularly vulnerable to break-ins.

Fines

The year 2009 saw the abolition of the wheel clamp (though it can still be applied to people who owe more that five traffic tickets).

Fines are €49.60 plus the price of one hour of parking in that section of town and can be paid within 48 hours at one of two service points: Daniel Goedkoopstraat 7-9 (open 7am-11pm daily, also acts as car pound) and DeClercqstraat 42-44 (open 8am-4.30pm Mon-Sat). If you suspect your car has been towed away, call 251 2121.

Petrol

There are 24-hour petrol stations (*tankstations*) at Gooiseweg 10, Sarphatistraat 225, Marnixstraat 250 and Spaarndammerdijk 218.

Water transport

Amsterdam is best seen from the water. Sure, there are canal cruises, but they don't offer the freedom to do your own exploring. You can try to bond with a local boat owner; otherwise your options are limited to the pedal-powered canal bike or pedalo. Upon rental, don't ignore the introductory rundown of the rules of the water (put at its most basic: stick to the right and be very wary of canal cruisers, who always assume that size makes right).

Pedaloes

Canal Bike

Weteringschans 24, Southern Canal Belt (626 5574/www.canal.nl). **Open** *Summer* 10am-10pm daily. *Winter* 10am-6pm daily at Rijksmuseum; also weekends at Westerkerk and Leidseplein.

Canal buses

Canal Bus

Weteringschans 26, Southern Canal Belt (623 9886/www.canal.nl). Tram 7, 10, 16, 24, 25. **Open** 10am-7pm daily.

Water taxis

Water Taxi Centrale

Stationsplein 8, Old Centre: New Side (535 6363/www.water-taxi.nl). Tram 1, 2, 4, 5, 9, 13, 14, 17, 24, 25, 26. **Open** 8am-midnight daily.

Cycling

There are bike lanes on most roads, marked by white lines and bike symbols. Never leave a bike unlocked, and use two locks. Most bikes have pedal-backwards brakes (as opposed to handlebar-mounted), which take some getting used to. There are plenty of places to rent bikes, for about €10 a day, but the following two places are friendly. Note that a passport and/or credit card is required.

Rental

Frederic Rentabike

Brouwersgracht 78, Jordaan (www.frederic.nl / 624 5509). Bus 18, 22. **Open** 9am-7pm daily.

StarBikes Rental

De Ruyterkade 127, The Waterfront (www.starbikesrental.com/ 620 3215). A 5-minute walk east of Centraal Station. **Open** 9am-7pm daily.

Resources A-Z

Accident & emergency

In the case of minor accidents, you can just turn up at the outpatient departments of the following city hospitals (*ziekenhuis*). All are open 24 hours a day, seven days a week.

Academisch Medisch Centrum

Meibergdreef 9, Zuid (566 9111/first aid 566 3333). Metro Holendrecht.

Boven IJ Ziekenhuis

Statenjachtstraat 1, Noord (634 6346/first aid 634 6200). Bus 34, 37, 92, 93, 94, 173.

Onze Lieve Vrouwe Gasthuis

's Gravesandeplein 16, Oost (599 9111/ first aid 599 3016). Tram 3, 7/bus 37/ Metro Weesperplein or Wibautstraat.

St Lucas Andreas Ziekenhuis

Jan Tooropstraat 164, West (510 8911/ irst aid 510 8412). Tram 13/ bus 19, 47, 80, 82, 97/Metro Jan van Galenstraat.

VU Ziekenhuis

De Boelelaan 1117, Zuid (444 4444/first aid 444 3636). Tram 16, 24/Metro Amstelveenseweg/bus 62, 142, 166, 170, 171, 172, 176, 310.

Banks

There's little difference between the rates of exchange that are offered by banks and bureaux de change, but banks do tend to charge less commission than other places. Dutch banks buy and sell foreign currency and exchange travellers' cheques, but few give cash advances against credit cards.

ATMs

Cash machines are found at banks, supermarkets and larger shops such as HEMA. If your switch card carries the Maestro or Cirrus symbols, you should be able to withdraw cash from ATMs, although it's worth checking with your bank that it's possible to do so, and what the charges are.

Customs

EU nationals who are over 17 years of age may import goods into the Netherlands for their personal use. Other EU countries may still have limits on the quantity of goods permitted on entry. For citizens of non-EU countries, however, the following limits apply:

- 200 cigarettes or 50 cigars or 250 grams tobacco;
- two litres of non-sparkling wine or one litre of spirits (over 22 per cent alcohol), or two litres of fortified wine (under 22 per cent alcohol);
- 60cc/ml of perfume;
- 500g coffee or 200g coffee extracts or coffee essence;
- 100g tea or 40g tea extracts or tea essence;
- other goods to the value of €430.

Dentists

To find a dentist (*tandarts*), call 0900 821 2230. Operators can put you in touch with your nearest dentist, and telephone lines are open 24 hours for those with more urgent dental emergencies. Otherwise, you'll need to make yourself an appointment at one of the following.

AOC Tandartsenpraktijk
Wilhelmina Gasthuisplein 167, Oud West (616 1234). Tram 1, 2, 3, 5, 12. Open 9am-noon, 1-4pm Mon-Fri.
AOC offers emergency dental treatment and a recorded service : if you call 686 1109, they will inform you where a walk-in clinic in your area will be open at 11.30am and 9.30pm that day.

TBB
570 9595/0900 821 2230.
A 24-hour service that can refer callers to a dentist. Bear in mind that calls are charged at a premium rate.

Disabled

Winding, cobbled streets, poorly maintained pavements and steep canal house steps can present real difficulties to the physically less able, but the pragmatic Dutch can generally solve problems quickly. Most large museums, cinemas and theatres have decent disabled facilities. The Metro is accessible to wheelchair users with normal arm function, but most trams are inaccessible to wheelchair users, due to their high steps. The AUB and Amsterdam Tourist Board produce brochures listing hotels, restaurants and attractions, which cater well for the physically less able.

Electricity

The Netherlands uses standard European 220V, 50-cycle AC voltage via two-pin continental plugs. Visitors from Britain will need an adaptor; American visitors may need a transformer.

Embassies

American Consulate General
Museumplein 19 (575 5309/http:// amsterdam.usconsulate.gov). Tram 2, 3, 5, 12, 16, 24/bus 170.

Australian Embassy
Carnegielaan 4, the Hague (070 310 8200/0800 0224 794 Australian citizen emergency phone/ www.australian-embassy.nl).

British Consulate General
Koningslaan 44 (676 4343/ www.britain.nl). Tram 2.

British Embassy
Lange Voorhout 10, the Hague (070 427 0427/www.britain.nl).

Canadian Embassy
Sophialaan 7, the Hague (070 311 1600/www.canada.nl).

Irish Embassy
Dr Kuyperstraat 9, the Hague (070 363 0993/www.irishembassy.nl).

New Zealand Embassy
Eisenhowerlaan 77N, the Hague (070 346 9324/visas 070 365 8037/ www.nzembassy.com).

Gay & lesbian information

COC Amsterdam
Rozenstraat 14, (626 3087/www. cocamsterdam.nl). Tram 10, 13, 14, 17. **Open** Telephone enquiries 10am-4pm Mon-Fri.
The Amsterdam branch of COC deals with the campaigning side of gay life.

Gay & Lesbian Switchboard
Postbus 11573 (623 6565/www. switchboard.nl). **Open** noon-10pm Mon-Fri; 4-8pm Sat, Sun.
General information and advice on safe sex, from friendly English-speakers.

Helplines

Alcoholics Anonymous
625 6057 (24hr manned service)/ www.aa-netherlands.org.

A lengthy but informative message in English and Dutch gives the times and dates of meetings, and contact numbers for counsellors. The website is in English, and you can locate meetings by day or by town.

Narcotics Anonymous
662 6307/www.na-holland.nl.
Offers a 24-hour answerphone service in English and Dutch, with counsellors' phone numbers.

SOS Telephone Helpline
675 7575. **Open** 24hrs daily.
A counselling service – comparable to the Samaritans in the UK and Lifeline in the US – for anyone who is suffering emotional problems. English isn't always understood at first, but keep trying and someone will be able to help.

Internet

All global ISPs have a presence here (check websites for numbers). Most hotels are well equipped, with dataports in the rooms, terminals in the lobby, or Wi-Fi throughout.

Freeworld
Nieuwendijk 30, Old Centre: New Side (620 0902). Tram 1, 2, 5, 13, 17, 20. **Open** 9am-1am daily. **Rates** €1/30mins. No credit cards.
This is also a coffeeshop.

Internet Café
Martelaarsgracht 11, Old Centre: New Side (no phone/www.internet cafe.nl). Tram 4, 9, 16, 20, 24, 25. Open 9am-1am Mon-Thur, Sun; 9am-3am Fri, Sat. **Rates** from €1/30mins. No credit cards.

Left luggage

There's a staffed left-luggage counter at Schiphol Airport (601 2443/www.schiphol.nl), where you can store luggage for up to one month, open daily from 6am to 10.45pm (€6 per item for 24 hours and €4.50 per item for each day thereafter). It also has automated lockers, accessible 24 hours daily (from €6 per 24hrs). There are more lockers in the arrival and departure halls, and central Amsterdam has plenty of lockers at Centraal Station, with 24-hour access (they charge from €4 for 24hrs).

Lost property

Centraal Station
Stationsplein 15, Old Centre: Old Side (0900 321 2100 premium rate/ www.ns.nl). Tram 1, 2, 4, 5, 9, 13, 16, 17, 24, 25, 26. **Open** 8am-6pm Mon-Fri; 7am-5pm Sat.
Items found on trains are kept for three days at the office on the east side of the station, after which they are forwarded to Centraal Bureau Gevonden Voorwerpen (Central Lost Property Office), 2e Daalsedijk 4, 3551 EJ Utrecht (030 235 3923, 8am-5pm Mon-Fri), where they are stored for three months. If you pick up belongings personally, the collection will cost €10, whereas having them posted costs €15 and upwards.

GVB Lost Property
Arlandaweg 100 (0900 8011 premium rate/460 6060). Tram 12. **Open** 8am-11pm Mon-Fri.
Wait at least a day or two before you call, describe what you lost on the bus, metro or tram and leave a contact telephone number. GVB will call you back if your property is found. Alternatively, there's an online form (in Dutch) for lost property at www.gvb.nl that you can fill in, although it takes up to three days to receive a response.

Police Lost Property
Korte Leidsedwarsstraat 52 (14 020). Tram 1, 2, 5, 7, 10. **Open** *In person* 9am-4pm Mon-Fri. *By phone* noon-3.30pm Mon-Fri.
Before trying to collect your property here, check the local police station.

Opening hours

Banks are open 9am-5pm, Mon-Fri. **Bars** are open at various times throughout the day and close at about 1am Mon-Thur, Sun; 2am or 3am Fri, Sat. **Shops** are open 1-6pm Mon (although many stay closed on this day); 10am-6pm Tue-Fri (some until 9pm Thur); 9am-5pm Sat. Many central shops are open on Sunday.

Pharmacies

Dam Apotheek

Damstraat 2, Old Centre: Old Side (624 4331). Tram 4, 9, 14, 16, 24, 25. **Open** 8.30am-5.30pm Mon-Fri; 10am-5pm Sat. This pharmacy has extended opening hours. Outside these times, call Afdeling Inlichtingen Apotheken (694 8709) for a 24-hour service that will direct you to your nearest late-opening chemist.

Police stations

For details and contact information regarding local police stations, look under 'Politie' in the Gouden Gids.

Amsterdam Tourist Assistance Service (ATAS)

Nieuwezijds Voorburgwal 104-108 (625 3246). Tram 1, 2, 5, 6, 13, 17. **Open** 10am-10pm daily.

Hoofdbureau van Politie (Police Headquarters)

Lijnbaansgracht 219 (0900 8844 premium rate). Tram 1, 2, 5, 7, 10. **Open** 24hrs daily.

Post offices

Post offices are usually open 9am-5pm Mon-Fri; 9.30am-1pm Sat. The postal information line is available on 058 233 3333. The main post office stands at Singel 250, Old Centre: New Side (0900 767 8526 premium rate). It's open 9am-6pm Mon-Fri; 10am-1.30pm Sat.

Safety

Amsterdam is a relatively safe city, but do take care. The Red Light District is rife with undesirable characters who, though not violent, are expert pickpockets; be vigilant, especially on bridges; and don't ever make eye contact with anyone who looks as though they are up to no good, drug dealers especially.

Be extra careful to watch out for thieves on the Schiphol train; if you cycle, lock your bike up well (two locks are advisable). Keep valuables in your hotel safe, don't leave bags unattended, and ensure your cash and cards are tucked away, and preferably zipped up in your bag.

Smoking

As of summer 2008, the Netherlands imposed a smoking ban in all public indoor spaces. As for cannabis, locals have a relaxed attitude, but smoking it isn't acceptable everywhere in the city: use your discretion, and if in doubt, ask before you spark up.

Telephones

Amsterdam's dialling code is 020; to call within the city, you don't need to use the code. If dialling from outside the Netherlands, use the country code 31, followed by the number. Drop the first '0' of the area code; for Amsterdam, use 20 rather than 020. US mobile phone users should make sure they call their phone provider in advance of departure, to check their mobile's compatibility with GSM bands.

Public phones

Public phones take cards not coins, available from the Tourist Board, tobacconists, stations and post offices. Many also take credit cards.

ESSENTIALS

Time

Amsterdam is one hour ahead of Greenwich Mean Time (GMT). All clocks on Central European Time (CET) now go back and forward on the same dates as GMT.

Tipping

Service charges are included in hotel, taxi, bar, café and restaurant bills. However, it's polite to round up to the closest euro for small bills or the nearest five for larger sums, although tipping 10% is becoming more common (leave the extra in change rather than filling in the credit card slip). In taxis, most people tip 10%.

Tourist information

Amsterdam Tourist Board (VVV)

Stationsplein 10, Old Centre: New Side (0900 400 4040/ www.iamsterdam.com). Tram 1, 2, 4, 5, 9, 13, 16, 17, 24, 25, 26. **Open** 9am-6pm daily.

The main tourist office stands right outside Centraal Station. English-speaking staff change money and provide up-to-date information on transport, entertainment and day-trips. They can also arrange hotel bookings (for a fee), and excursions or car hire for free. Brochures detail walks and cycling tours, plus you'll find cassette and digital tours, maps and a monthly listings magazine, Day by Day. The information line has an English-language service (€0.40/min). There's a plan to rebrand all offices IAMSTER-DAM, but at press time no dates were available, so look out for signs.

Other locations: Leidseplein 1 (10am-5.30pm daily); Centraal Station, platform 2B 15 (11am-7pm Tue-Sat); Schiphol Airport, arrivals hall 2 (7am-10pm daily).

Translators & interpreters

Amstelveens Vertaalburo

Ouderkerkerlaan 50, Amstelveen (645 6610/www.avb.nl). Bus 142, 149, 165, 166, 170, 171, 172, 175, 186, 187, 199, 215, 216, 300. **Open** 9am-5pm Mon-Fri. No credit cards.

Mac Bay Consultants

PC Hooftstraat 15, Museum Quarter (24hr phoneline 662 0501/fax 662 6299/www.macbay.nl). Tram 2, 5. **Open** 9am-7pm Mon-Fri.

Visas

EU citizens do not require a visa; citizens of the US, Canada, Australia and New Zealand need a valid passport for stays of up to three months. Otherwise, apply for a tourist visa. EU nationals with a resident's permit can work here; for non-EU citizens, it's hard to get a visa without a job in place.

When to go

Climate

Amsterdam's climate is changeable. January and February are the coldest months, and summers tend to be humid. If you have a grasp of Dutch, call the weather line on 0900 8003 (€0.60/min), otherwise search for the weather forecast via Google.

Public holidays

Known as 'Nationale Feestdagen' in Dutch, these include New Year's Day, Good Friday, Easter Sunday and Monday, Koninginnedag (Queen's Day, 30 April), Remembrance Day (4 May), Liberation Day (5 May), Ascension Day, Whit (Pentecost) Sunday and Monday, Christmas Day and Boxing Day.

Vocabulary

Almost every person you'll come across in Amsterdam will speak good English, and you'll be able to get by without a word of Dutch during your stay. However, a bit of effort goes a long way, and locals are appreciative of those visitors polite enough to take five minutes to learn some basic phrases. Here are a few that might help.

Useful expressions

Hello hallo/dag; **goodbye** tot ziens/dag; **yes** ja; **yes please** ja, graag; **no** nee; **no thanks** nee, dank je; **please** alstublieft; **thank you** dank u; **excuse me** pardon; **do you speak English?** spreekt u Engels?; **sorry, I don't speak Dutch** het spijt me, ik spreek geen Nederlands; **I don't understand** ik begrijp het niet; **I am ill** ik ben ziek; **good** goed; **bad** slecht; **big** groot; **small** klein; **nice** mooi; **tasty** lekker; **open** open; **closed** gesloten/dicht; **entrance** ingang; **exit** uitgang; **the bill** de rekening; **hotel room** hotelkamer; **single/ twin/ double bedroom** eenpersoonskamer/ tweepersoonskamer met aparte bedden/ tweepersoonskamer; **I want** ik wil graag; **how much is** wat kost

Getting around

Bus bus; **car** auto; **tram** tram; **train** trein; **ticket/s** kaart/kaarten; **street** straat; **square** plein; **canal** gracht; **left** links; **right** rechts; **straight on** rechtdoor; **far** ver; **near** dichtbij; **here** hier; **there** daar; **where is** waar is

Places

Shop winkel; **bank** bank; **post office** postkantoor; **pharmacy** apotheek; **hotel** hotel; **bar** bar; **restaurant** restaurant; **hospital** ziekenhuis; **bus stop** bushalte; **station** station

Time

Now nu; **later** straks; **morning** ochtend; **afternoon** middag; **evening** avond; **night** nacht; **today** vandaag; **yesterday** gisteren; **tomorrow** morgen; **what time is** hoe laat is; **what's the time?** hoe laat is het?; **noon** middag; **midnight** middernacht; **at eight o'clock** om acht uur; **quarter past eight** kwaart over acht; **20 past eight** tien voor half negen; **25 past eight** vijf half negen; **half past eight** half negen; **25 to nine** vijf over half negen; **quarter to nine** kwaart voor negen

Numbers

0 nul; **1** een; **2** twee; **3** drie; **4** vier; **5** vijf; **6** zes; **7** zeven; **8** acht; **9** negen; **10** tien; **11** elf; **12** twaalf; **13** dertien; **14** veertien; **15** vijftien; **16** zestien; **17** zeventien; **18** achttien; **19** negen-tien; **20** twintig; **21** eenentwintig; **22** twee'ntwintig; **30** dertig; **40** veertig; **50** vijftig; **60** zestig; **70** zeventig; **80** tachtig; **90** negentig; **100** honderd; **101** honderd een; **200** tweehonderd; **1,000** duizend; **1,000,000** een miljoen

Days & months

Monday maandag; **Tuesday** dinsdag; **Wednesday** woensdag; **Thursday** donderdag; **Friday** vrijdag; **Saturday** zaterdag; **Sunday** zondag; **January** januari; **February** februari; **March** maart; **April** april; **May** mei; **June** juni; **July** juli; **August** augustus; **September** september; **October** oktober; **November** november; **December** december

Menu Glossary

Basics

Bestek cutlery; **brood** bread; **broodje** bread roll; **glas** glass; **lepel** spoon; **menukaart** menu; **mes** knife; **peper** pepper; **de rekening** the bill; **vork** fork; **wijnkaart** wine list; **zout** salt

Snacks

Bitterballen mini croquettes filled with meat and potato; **borrel/bittergarnituur** platter of snacks to accompany drinks (usually sausage, salami, cheese and *bitterballen*); **borrelnoten** crispy coated nuts; **frikadel** a popular, deep-fried skinless sausage with mysterious ingredients; **kaassouffle** cheese fritter, only tasty when it is served very hot; **kroket** croquette filled with meat and potato; **oliebollen** deep-fried dough balls that are traditionally served around New Year, either plain or supplemented with raisins, currants and/or diced apples; **pannekoek** pancake; **patat** French fries/chips, also called *frites*; **patat met** French fries/chips with mayonnaise; **pindas** peanuts; **saucijzenbroodje** hot sausage roll made with puff pastry; **snert** a thick pea soup, also called *erwtensoep*; **tostis** grilled ham and/or cheese sandwiches; **uitsmijter** cheese and/or ham on bread topped with three fried eggs

Meat

Bal/gehaktbal meatball; **biefstuk** steak; **bio** organic; **eend** duck; **kalf** veal; **kalkoen** turkey; **kip** chicken; **lam** lamb; **rund** beef; **scharrel** free-range; **spek** bacon; **struisvogel** ostrich; **varkensvlees** pork; **vlees** meat; **worst** sausage

Fish

Ansjovis anchovies; **gambas** prawns; **garnalen** shrimps; **gerookte** smoked; **haring** herring; **maatjesharing** first herring of the season; **makreel** mackerel; **mosselen** mussels; **oesters** oysters; **paling** eel; **tong** sole; **tonijn** tuna; **venusschelpen** clams; **vis** fish; **zalm** salmon; **zeeduivel** monkfish; **zeevruchten/zeebanket** seafood

Fruit & vegetables

Aardappel potato; **aardbei** strawberry; **appel** apple; **bosbes** blueberry; **champignons** mushrooms; **citroen** lemon; **druiven** grapes; **framboos** raspberry; **fruit/vruchten** fruit; **groenten** vegetables; **kersen** cherries; **knoflook** garlic; **kruiden** herbs; **limoen** lime; **rauwkost** coleslaw; **rijst** rice; **sinasappel** orange; **zuurkool** sauerkraut

Puddings & cakes

Flensje crêpe; **gember** ginger; **griesmeel** semolina; **hangop** strained thick yoghurt; **honing** honey; **koek** cake; **koekje** biscuit; **roomijs/ijs** ice-cream; **slagroom** whipped cream; **stroop** syrup; **suiker** sugar; **toetje** dessert; **vla** custard

Dairy

Blauwe kaas blue cheese; **boter** butter; **geitenkaas** goat's cheese; **kaas** cheese; **magere/halfvolle/volle melk** skimmed/semi-skimmed/full milk; **oud/extra belegen** mature; **roomkaas** cream cheese; **schapenkaas** cheese made from sheep's milk

Index

Sights & Areas

ESSENTIALS

ESSENTIALS

Discover the city from your back pocket

Essential for your weekend break, 25 top cities available.

lght Centuurbaad
Dusartstraat

Cornelis Troostraat

van Ospade Straat
Dusartstraat

**TIME OUT GUIDES
WRITTEN BY
LOCAL EXPERTS**
visit timeout.com/shop